TRANSLATING ORIENTS:
BETWEEN IDEOLOGY AND UTOPIA

Translating Orients
Between Ideology and Utopia

Timothy Weiss

UNIVERSITY OF TORONTO PRESS
Toronto Buffalo London

© University of Toronto Press Incorporated 2004
Toronto Buffalo London
Printed in Canada

ISBN 0-8020-8958-5

Printed on acid-free paper

National Library of Canada Cataloguing in Publication

Weiss, Timothy, 1949–
  Translating Orients : between ideology and Utopia / Timothy
Weiss.

  Includes bibliographical references and index.
  ISBN 0-8020-8958-5

  1. Orient – In literature.   2. Literature, Modern – 20th century –
History and criticism.   3. Oriental literature – 20th century – History
and criticism.   I. Title.

  PR129.O75W43 2004   809′.93325′0904   C2003-905493-4

University of Toronto Press acknowledges the financial assistance to its publishing program of the Canada Council for the Arts and the Ontario Arts Council.

University of Toronto Press acknowledges the financial support for its publishing activities of the Government of Canada through the Book Publishing Industry Development Program (BPIDP).

To Charlotte and the happy years at 23C, Block 7, Royal Ascot

Contents

PREFACE ix

Introduction 3

1 Borges's Search, or the Bibliophilic Orient 19

2 'Without Stopping': The Orient as Liminal Space in Paul Bowles 43

3 The Living Labyrinth: Hong Kong and David T.K. Wong's *Hong Kong Stories* 79

4 Where Is Place? Locale and Identity in Kazua Ishiguro's *When We Were Orphans* and Ricardo Piglia's *La ciudad ausente* 109

5 At the End of East/West: Myth in Salman Rushdie's *The Moor's Last Sigh* 145

6 Identity and Citizenship in a World of Shame 176

Neither Subjects nor Objects: In the Middle Way 203

NOTES 217

BIBLIOGRAPHY 227

INDEX 243

Preface

One of the great pleasures of living in Hong Kong is that one can hear in the same musical concert Stravinsky's 'The Song of the Nightingale,' Vittorio Monti's 'Csárdás' arranged by Xu Ke, Yang Yong's 'River Songs for Erhu and Orchestra,' the world première of Chen Yi's 'Fiddle Suite for Huqin and Orchestra,' and Maurice Ravel's 'Ma Mère L'oye,' with the oriental overtones of 'Empress of the Pagodas' and 'The Magic Garden.' Hong Kong has been and still remains a place of cultural interactions and translations. There is never a moment here when the wheels of culture and society stop turning and the exchanges cease; everyone and everything is in continual movement and transformation. Leave for a few weeks or a few months and the city will not be the same when you return. The transformative spirit of Hong Kong stands everywhere in the background of this book, just as it is part of the inspiration with which one is filled at a concert where cultures and melodies interact, separate discordantly, and harmonize. At the concert hall I enter a utopian space apart from the pressing crowds on the sidewalks, the homeless persons in the underpass, and the general rigour and crush of daily life for the majority of the city's seven million people. On the other side of the wall that encloses the quiet garden of the concert hall, the traffic hurtles past and the rush-hour pollution lingers. Still, this evening's concert and all the people associated with it – from composers to performing artists, organizers, and audience – testify to a reality and anticipate a possibility: the invitation of cultures and their mutual exchange and enrichment of one another. Listening to music, whether the Hong Kong Philharmonic Orchestra at City Hall or an erhu player on a street corner, has taught me that these exchanges and transformations are always taking place – somewhere.

I thank Hong Kong for seven years of inspiration and challenges, but since I began thinking about the topics and issues that this book addresses a long time ago, I also want to return to other places and people and thank them as well. In 1988–9, while working on a different book, *On the Margins: The Art of Exile in V.S. Naipaul* (University of Massachusetts Press, 1992), I spent one year in Tunis, Tunisia, as a Senior Fulbright scholar, and certainly the people I met and my experiences there are very much a part of this book. The same is true of Algeria and Morocco, where in 1993–4 I had the good fortune to spend a second Fulbright year; even during a period of political tensions and violence in Algeria, I was welcomed and treated with hospitality. I have great respect for the intelligence, courage, open-mindedness, and generosity of the people I knew in Algiers and during my two-year sojourn in these three Maghrebine countries; the diversity and richness of North African cultures made a lasting impression on me.

Although this book takes a view that differs from that of his seminal study *Orientalism*, I wish to honour here Edward Said, who died afer a ten-year struggle with leukemia in New York on 14 September 2003. Of those persons and organizations that have helped me bring this book project to completion, I wish to thank the Department of English at the Chinese University of Hong Kong for their financial support. I thank my colleagues, especially the former chair, Kwok-kan Tam, who gave me the opportunity to teach in Hong Kong, and the current departmental chair, David Parker, for their encouragement while working on this project. I thank the readers of the manuscript, who made many helpful suggestions without which the book could not have taken its present form. I thank Jill McConkey, Editor of English Literature and Modern Languages at the University of Toronto Press, for her comments, support, and encouragement, Barbara Porter, of the Managing Editorial Department, and John St James, for his careful copy-editing. Finally, I thank my wife, Charlotte, for her research, comments, editing, and proofreading – among a thousand and one other things.

TRANSLATING ORIENTS:
BETWEEN IDEOLOGY AND UTOPIA

Introduction

As its title suggests, this book will be about a process as well as a subject matter. Of the four terms or concepts embedded in the title, the first term, 'translating,' indicates the *how* of the study, which treats interpretation as a transformative process in which new meaning emerges by way of a shift from one medium or register to another. This transformative process may apply to experiences or texts, to the author's shaping of materials and translation of it across media (e.g., Rimsky-Korsakov's adaptation of *The Thousand and One Nights* to a musical medium in *Shéhérazade*), or the reader's role in the interpretation of a poem, a painting, travel in a foreign country, and so forth. The second term, 'Orient' – here used as a singular noun – points to the *what* of the study; its subject matters are texts that reference Asian, North African, or Middle Eastern societies and their traditions, as well as contemporary questions of individual and communal identity that issue from the transformative encounters with those texts. The third and fourth terms, 'ideology' and 'utopia,' stand for the two poles between which interpretation as a form of translatability moves: that is, the fixity of a closed viewpoint as opposed to the openness of possibility. Putting these four terms together, then, translating is an act that orients – here, a verb – because the process is cognitive and heuristic; it maps the world not in the sense of delineating a pre-given form, location, and organization, but rather in the sense of charting its emergence and possibilities. We could say that the word 'orients' denotes not only this process, but also what the process generates: 'Orients,' new mappings of the world, or what I will call emergent realities. In seeking to chart and represent, any interpretation runs the risk of becoming fixed or frozen in its descriptions (i.e., ideological); yet in its recursive and endless movement (for it is always 'in the middle,' so to speak), interpretation as translation seeks the possible, the not-as-yet conceived or articulated (i.e., the utopian). During the course of the remainder of this Introduction, and in the following chapters, I shall elucidate and elaborate these basic ideas and explain the ways in which the *how* (the approach) and the *what* (the subject matter) of this study differ from other literary studies that treat the broad topic of the Orient and East–West interactions and confluences.

Any book refers to and depends on other books; that is certainly true of this study. In terms of its subject matter, the principal work that it references and on which it depends is Edward Said's influential *Orientalism* (1978), and the numerous articles and books that it inspired, whether positively or negatively; so influential has it been, one could argue, that almost every article or book written in the field of postcolonial studies directly or indirectly references *Orientalism* and its successor, *Culture and Imperialism* (1993).[1] As Said himself has pointed out, his approach derives from discourse analysis as developed by Michel Foucault in *L'Archéologie du savoir* and *Surveiller et punir: Naissance de la prison*.[2] According to this analysis, knowledge is constructed through discourse formations that regulate what can be thought and said during a particular historical moment or epoch; consequently, 'claims of knowledge and the exercise of power' become 'indissociable' (Gare, 'Understanding Oriental Cultures,' 310). In his analysis of the politics of Western ethnocentricism, Said distinguishes between a latent Orientalism, a kind of deep structure defined by unity and synchronicity, and a manifest Orientalism, a sort of surface structure that shows heterogeneity and change (Prakash, 'Orientalism Now'). How the latent and manifest structures relate to and interact with one another is never convincingly explained, however, and Orientalism as discourse formation remains enclosed and reproductive. 'The fundamental problem with Foucault's approach to history, and correspondingly with Said's attack on Orientalism, is that ... this approach precludes even the possibility of understanding other cultures,' Arran E. Gare contends:

> [I]f all statements are generated by some framing episteme or discursive formation, then how is it possible to defend any particular episteme or discursive formation, or make statements that bring to consciousness the history of previous epistemes or discursive formations?. ... Said, taking over Foucault's archaeology and genealogy, is in the awkward position of condemning not only most, but all Orientalists because he has virtually presupposed that there is no such thing as the understanding of cultures, that statements or

representations can be nothing but exercises of power as parts of discursive formations. And at the same time he has undermined any basis to justify his own critique. ('Understanding Oriental Cultures,' 315)

To simplify and to state this in other words, Said's approach maximizes – to the point of determinism – the reproductive capacity of the discourse formation and the role that prejudgments or prejudices play in knowledge and power, while it minimizes or ignores the role of interpretation and innovation. His critique of Western ethnocentrism turns into a blanket condemnation (as well as a blanket dispensation, for who can be held to blame, after all? the discourse formation? the historical moment?), as illustrated in this well-known passage:

> Beneath the idioms there was a layer of doctrine about the Orient; this doctrine was fashioned out of the experiences of many Europeans, all of them converging upon such essential aspects of the Orient as the Oriental character, Oriental despotism, Oriental sensuality, and the like. For any European during the nineteenth century – and I think one can say this almost without qualification – Orientalism was such a system of truths ... It is therefore correct that every European, in what he could say about the Orient, was consequently a racist, an imperialist, and almost totally ethnocentric. Some of the immediate sting will be taken out of these labels if we recall additionally that human societies, at least the more advanced cultures, have rarely offered the individual anything but imperialism, racism, and ethnocentrism for dealing with 'other' cultures. (*Orientalism* 203–4)

The metaphor 'beneath' indicates that Saidian discourse analysis is primarily vertical, consists of a digging or a stripping away or an unmasking of something to reveal its (false) essence. It is also, of course, genealogical in its sketching of the ancestry of Orientalism. In *Culture and Imperialism* Said further developed the basic ideas of the first book and addressed some of its shortcomings; his stance toward individual identity and historical, cultural embodiment opens considerably. In the 'Introduction' he writes: 'I do not believe that authors are mechanically determined by ideology, class, or economic history, but authors are ... shaped by that history and their social experience in different measure' (xxii). On the book's final page he concludes: 'No one today is purely *one* thing. Labels like Indian, or woman, or Muslim, or American are no more than starting-points, which if followed into actual experience for only a moment are quickly left behind' (336). From our own lives we know this to be true; however, one still wonders how the archaeological-genealogical methodology can account for it. The methodology of Said's two influential studies does not differ significantly, although in *Culture and Imperialism* he does pay heed to 'the creative and interpretive imagination' (xxii).

In contrast to that methodology, this study takes primarily a phenomenological-hermeneutic approach (or translational approach). The process of translating Orients – as a horizontal movement within a labyrinth of intertextual and experiential relations – differs from the verticality of Saidian analysis of Orientalism, which involves an archaeological excavation and genealogical tracing that reveals finally a recurrent idea. Approaching interpretation as a form of translatability can overcome limitations inherent in the archaeological-genealogical approach. First, the comprehension of texts and experiences, although viewed as embodied in culture and society, does not occur within the closed systems of discourse formations; the 'place' of interpretation is neither the discourse (subject matter) nor the viewpoint (register) but an emergent space. Furthermore, interpretation as translation operates recursively and continually adjusts its own register and output to new information. It changes all the time. Second, *like* the archaeological-genealogical approach, the translational approach eschews subjectivities, for it has the capacity to treat reader and author as non-autonomous (i.e., *not* intrinsically independent). Third, it can account for repatternings of cultures and the possibility of understanding between them, which occur during the recursive give-and-take of translation as an open system of exchanges among interrelated networks. Fourth, it can address non-fixed entities and groundlessness (i.e., the lack of metaphysical, epistemological foundations), for it does not depend on a transcendent regulator or something outside of itself as an ultimate reference point and rule. Fifth, it can address incommensurabilites that exceed the grasp of human limitations such as the idea of the universe or God; it approaches these from within and attempts to know them experientially, recursively processing information in discrete steps and continually reaching toward what newly emerges in each discrete processing. In sum, the translational approach does not treat texts as enclosed within a controlling discourse formation; it accepts the notion of cultural, historical embodiment – the strength of Said's approach – yet its processing of texts as open systems can accommodate and account for change and transformation. Furthermore, the translational approach can process a larger range of texts and experiences than can the archaeological-genealogical approach. I will elaborate on all of these points later in the Introduction and in subsequent chapters, but for the moment I want to establish some assumptions and traits that distinguish the phenomenological-hermeneutic approach that I will take in this study and that differentiate it from the discourse analysis of Foucault and Said. These are (1) the mutual implication of subject and object; (2) the active, constructive role of the reader; (3) knowledge as dependent on interpretation; (4) reality as emergent; and (5) interpretation as translatability.

Mutual implication. In Husserlian terms, phenomenology insists that 'the primordial *meaning of the objective world* is its mode of engaging human consciousness'; all meaning, therefore, is located 'neither in the mind alone, nor in the world alone, but in the intentional relationship between the two' (Kearney 15). Although the concept of mutual implication, or interdependence, has radically challenged fields of knowledge in the twentieth century, this idea, it could be argued, has been around a long time; it is at least as old as Buddhism – thousands of years old, in other words. In *L'Infini dans la paume de la main* (*Infinity in the Palm of the Hand*) Matthieu Ricard, drawing upon Buddhist scripts and sayings, likens human consciousness to a crystal that takes on the colour of whatever place it is put (26). Buddhism and phenomenology have many points of intersection, but Buddhism does differ from Husserlian phenomenology in its emphasis. Whereas the latter tends toward subjectivism, the former seeks a 'middle way' in which there are neither subjects nor objects. There are only interdependencies; the mind is embodied in relations.[3] I will discuss this middle way in conjunction with interpretation as translatability.

Active, constructive role of the reader. Mutual implication, or interdependence, implies a bond between the text and the reader, or between the world of the text and the world of the reader. '[P]henomenology has its starting-point in the incomplete aspect of the literary text,' Paul Ricoeur explains ('Between the Text and Its Readers' 399). The text is incomplete, first, in that it has blanks or 'places of indeterminacy,' to use Roman Ingarden's phrase, that the reader fills in;[4] and second, the 'intentional correlate' of the text's sequence of signs depends upon the reader to bring it to life – to actualize or reconfigure it. Any reader-oriented, as opposed to strictly structuralist, approach to literature has an aspect of phenomenology, and this is the primary sense in which I use the term.

Knowledge as dependent on interpretation. Hermeneutics emphasizes that all knowing involves interpretation. In counterposing his archaeological-genealogical approach to hermeneutics, Foucault attacked methodologies 'related to the synthetic activity of the subject' (quoted in Gare, 'Understanding Oriental Cultures,' 313). It seems to have been an older version of hermeneutics that Foucault had as his target, however. During the past decades, hermeneutics as presented by Hans-Georg Gadamer, Paul Ricoeur, and Wolfgang Iser, among others, has extended its range; it would be much too limiting to define hermeneutics today as primarily an operation that privileges ancient documents and seeks to get in touch with or restore the intention of the author of the text, a direction dominant in romantic hermeneutics. Rather, post-Heideggerian hermeneutics, Ricoeur explains, more properly focuses on something *in front of* the text rather than *behind* or before it: 'What is interpreted in a text is a proposed world in which I could live and could project my particular possibilities as appropriate to that world' (*Temps et récit* 1: 122). Contemporary hermeneutics considers the literary text's looking toward or fore-casting of 'possible worlds,' which concomitantly depend on the reader's constructions or reconfigurations of a text that was itself a configuration of life experience.[5]

Reality as emergent. For contemporary hermeneutics, reality is emergent. That is to say, interpretation does more than reveal hidden meaning in a traditional hermeneutical sense; it also produces it through revisioning and reconfiguring, which may be thought of as the contextualizing that a reader brings to and the highlighting that he/she gives a particular textual reading. To read is to put a text in a new context, but there is also something more that occurs in a heuristic reading: reality emerges. As Nelson Goodman contends in *Languages of Art*, authors and readers 'make' the world, as do all people who bring their imagination to bear on whatever kind of intellectual work they carry out, whether it be '[w]riting a poem; telling a story; construing a hypothesis, a plan, or a strategy' (Ricoeur, 'The Function of Fiction' 122–3).[6] In Ricoeur's words, 'imagination is "productive" not only of unreal objects, but also of an expanded vision of reality' (ibid.). In *Hermeneutics of Poetic Sense* literary scholar Mario J. Valdés draws out the consequences of this basic idea in terms of shifts of aesthetic theory: 'We are today witnesses to a major shift in aesthetic theories ... I am speaking of the possibilizing aesthetics that proposes that the work of art always awaits completion in the imagination of the perceiver or reader' (24). It is the reader and the world of the text that are the focus of phenomenological-hermeneutic approaches, and this particular textual world is related to others, hence the concepts of intertextuality and cultural imaginary: the 'world' in the largest sense refers to 'the ensemble of references opened up by all kinds of texts, whether practical or poetic' that the individual reader has read, encountered, and remembered in one form or another.[7] In their interactions, these encounters enlarge one's experiences; they add to reality, expanding it: 'It is in fact to fiction' – a shorthand in this case for 'literature' in general – Ricoeur asserts, 'that we owe to a large extent the broadening of our horizon of existence' (*Temps et récit* 1: 121). The diverse Orients of this study constitute constructed worlds in the phenomenological, hermeneutical sense of realities emerging from the reader's encounter with a text; however, I wish to take a step beyond this position and the hermeneutics of Gadamer, Ricoeur, and Valdés, and propose an approach that more clearly steers a middle course between subjects and objects.

Interpretation as translatability. All interpretation is a form of translation, Wolfgang Iser contends in *The Range of Interpretation*. This is neither a tautology nor a recasting of old terminology, for as will become clear, a key concept that interpretation as translatability adds to hermeneutics is that of 'liminal space,' a threshold from which new understanding and transformations of reality emerge. I will later compare this liminal space – which Iser refers to as a 'blank' – to the Buddhist notion of the 'middle way,' which refuses the autonomy of subjects (or subjectivities) on the one hand and of objects on the other. Emergence is the 'hallmark of interpretation' in a double sense: 'it indicates the ever-widening ramifications of our attempts to bring things about,' and the 'charting of the reality we live in' (*Range of Interpretation* 183). Simply stated, to understand something involves taking a subject matter and transposing it into a register. We do this when we read a text, bringing our own contextualized understanding and conceptual framework (in a broad sense, the register) to bear on the alien world of the text (the subject matter). Interpretation is necessary because as readers we confront certain blanks that must be filled in order for the material to become comprehensible; these are never filled in completely, though, because the register into which we seek to translate the material is not identical to it and undergoes change with our life experience and with the different conceptual frameworks that we bring to texts. The dynamic of translation, then, is two-directional: what gets translated is not only an object into a subject but also a subject into an object. Translation is often a recursive process, modifying and adjusting its framework and output according to varying input and new feedback. The residue of the untranslatable in every translation refuels the cycle, which itself intends to transform the foreign into the familiar, the new into the comprehensible, and does so to varying degrees; the blanks or liminal space constitutes the barrier as well as the fuel in this – in theory – unending process. Every interpretation depends, therefore, on the subject matter to be translated and the manner of negotiating the liminal space; the mode of translation will vary accordingly (ibid. 241).

Iser discusses four modes or procedures of translation (although these should be thought of as categories within which there is variation): 'authority,' the 'hermeneutic circle,' the 'recursive loop,' and the 'travelling differential.' The first of these, authority, stabilizes a text; for a given author or literary work, it translates the text into a historically conditioned situation, or makes the text available by bringing to bear on it the cultural code of contemporary readers (33, 36). Odd as it may sound, *Orientalism* as an interpretive work shows certain characteristics of this category, for what Said has done is to bring a postcolonial sensibility (a cultural code from the perspective of the formerly colonized) to bear on a large body of texts. Iser is certainly astute in pointing out that today the literary canon has less to do with 'authority' than with 'cultural capital'; it has become both a marketplace and a political battleground (46). The hermeneutic circle, a mode attributed to Friedrich Schleiermacher, entails a procedure wherein 'each part can be understood only out of the whole to which it belongs, and vice versa' (quoted in Iser 62). Normally the subject matter of hermeneutics is written texts of various sorts, from sacred to legal to literary, but it may also treat other sorts of 'texts,' such as historical monuments or other traces of the past. When the subject matter to be translated exceeds the boundaries of written texts – for example, self or culture – then another strategy or mode of translation becomes indispensable. The third of these modes, the recursive loop, dominates when the subject matter to be translated remains open and changing and is marked by the accidental and unexpected. 'The recursive loop bec[omes] prominent,' Iser elaborates, 'when entropy ha[s] to be controlled ... or encounters between cultures or levels of culture ma[k]e it necessary to negotiate between the familiar and the alien, not least [of all because] ... what is initially beyond reach will respond to an intervention from a standpoint outside itself' (173–4).

But why, we might ask, does subjectivity or culture require an act of translation in order to be understood? I have already suggested the answer in my comparison of the liminal space (which translation initiates or opens up) to the Buddhist notion of the middle way, that is, a way that affirms neither subjects nor objects. Understanding subjects and cultures requires translation because neither subjects nor cultures exist intrinsically as autonomous or independent entities; they exist interdependently, in relation. They have neither beginning nor end, and change continuously. Such an explanation has a Buddhist slant, but Iser himself approaches such a position when he contends that it is the groundlessness of cultures that makes translation a *sine qua non*:

> [M]utual translatability might be conceived as the hallmark of culture, not least because the latter, since the advent of the modern age, can no longer be grounded in an etiological myth. If an impenetrable groundlessness replaces the etiological myth as the mainspring of culture, the necessary stability can only be provided by a network of translatabilities ... The life of culture realizes itself in such recursive loops, and it begins to dry up when the loop is discontinued by elevating one of the achievements of its interchange into an all-encompassing form of representation. Representation runs counter to translatability, whose ongoing transformations are brought to a standstill by equating culture with one of its conspicuous features. The recursive loop, however, is able to process groundlessness ... This paradigm has a dual code: it makes tangible what analytically remains ungraspable, and as a mode of translatability it provides access to what is beyond the terms of empiricism. (208)

In Iser's commentary it becomes clear that representation and translation counterpoise different tendencies, with the former aiming toward a stabilizing of the unfamiliar and foreign, while the latter tends toward an ongoing process of more refined differentiations. Viewing cultures as interdependent and therefore groundless as autonomous entities, and as capable of being understood only through a recursive loop of ongoing interpretations, offers a way out of the *cul-de-sac* of the archaeological-genealogical methods of Foucault and Said. Understanding emerges through interactions that need never end, because one never arrives at either a fixed self or a fixed collectivity such as culture. Rather than the closure of essence, interdependence makes for transformation and the openness of possibility. I will skip over the fourth mode of translation, the travelling differential – one of considerable interest but not for my purposes here – by simply noting that it attempts to translate incommensurabilites such as the concept of God and other absolutes that no register of translation can encompass. I will touch on this fourth mode in chapter 1, which attempts to translate the experience of mystery in Jorge Luis Borges's Oriental fiction.

To sum up, interpretation as translation focuses more on heuristic cognition than representation. It seeks a new understanding, but given that it works with self-generated terms and perspectives, this understanding has necessarily an exploratory and heuristic quality. Since it operates horizontally within interrelationships, interpretation can process within-ness and groundlessness. It does not seek to generate a hierarchy of values, but rather to find a way, to adjust to an emergent reality, to seek a possibility and/or to experience (and therefore know partially) an aspect of an incommensurable. 'Whenever we translate something into something else,' Iser explains, 'the register is nothing but the bootstraps by which we pull ourselves up toward comprehension' (*Range of Interpretation* 7). As approach, translation acknowledges its own limitations and the groundlessness of self and world without surrendering deterministically and hopelessly to them; in the mixed landscape of fundamentalism (i.e., rigid, fixed identities) and nihilism (i.e., groundlessness) that is the contemporary predicament, translation takes a positive approach, for it addresses an emergent reality (the liminal space between subject matter and register) and in that way opens up possible, anticipatory worlds.

To illustrate a bit more specifically how the translational approach differs from the archaeological-genealogical approach, I want to briefly consider three works: Luis Vaz de Camões's *Os Lusíadas* (*The Lusiads*, (1572), Giuseppe Verdi's opera *Nabucco* (1842), and Katherine Mansfield's short story 'The Daughters of the Late Colonel' (1922).

In December 1999, after more than five hundred years of Portuguese rule, the territory of Macau reverted to Chinese sovereignty, becoming, as its Cantonese sister city Hong Kong did two years prior, an autonomous administrative region. Although Portuguese navigators in the sixteenth century would sail farther north beyond Macau to mainland China and what is today Taiwan, this tiny colony marked the farthest reach of the Portuguese Eastern empire, which included eastern Africa, the Malabar Coast of southern India, and parts of Malaysia and Indonesia. The literary work that commemorated the exploits of Vasco da Gama and other navigators who founded that empire, Camões's *The Lusiads*, became the Portuguese national epic; more than any book that preceded it, such as *The Travels of Marco Polo* (1271), it fashioned for the first time in European literature a global imaginary, bringing Europe, Africa, Asia, and the Americas into the framework of a world picture. *The Lusiads* commemorates history – a European, specifically Portuguese, exploration and discovery that extends from Africa to East Asia;

the Orient of this epic poem is, at least to a degree, metaphoric and mythic, part of a larger classical and medieval imaginary of the universe based on a Ptolemaic system of centres and harmonies. The poem views the new lands that it charts and celebrates from the tinted perspective of these old centrisms and hierarchies; furthermore, it views da Gama and the Portuguese through the lens of classical myths and legends, with their binaries of rivalries and their tendency to designate an enemy who must be fought and overcome. Camões's poem would seem, then, a perfect candidate for the archaeological-genealogical approach. A nascent Orientalism in *The Lusiads* emerges from various aspects of this identity formation, with its links to the rivalries between Christian Europe and the Muslim world during the Crusades, in the Iberian Peninsula and beyond, and to the centrisms and hierarchies of the Ptolemaic system and the medieval world view. The Moors – the designated enemy – are systematically devalued. Their beliefs are reduced to the level of 'superstitions'; their character is blackened, and their identity is linked with the devil, either through reference to Bacchus, who sometimes aids them, or more directly to the 'Demo, verdadeiro' (Canto VIII, st. 46).

A translational approach to this poem would take as its subject matter not only the text but also perhaps the notion of Camões the traveller, and explore how the poem shows aspects of a processing of a traveller's confrontation with the stange and the new; as its registers of translation it might take concepts such as national identity, geographic space, and civilization. The liminal space of this interpretation would be the emerging reality of Orients as multicultural worlds; this space is neither subject nor object but an interrelationship that begins to take shape in the process of the translation, or the reaching toward a new understanding. This approach can address the ideological and representational aspects on which Said might focus, but in addition it reaches beyond them to something equally relevant to the contemporary moment.

It goes almost without saying that the Orient is a multifaceted symbol in the poem: as a symbol *for* something (i.e., 'a template for charting something new'), Camões infuses the Orient with a utopian sentiment, most famously in the 'the Isle of Love' stanzas where Tethys unveils to da Gama the farthest reaches of the Eastern world. As symbol the Orient has both an ideological and a utopian content; through the poem's intertwining of fact and fable emerges a nascent Orientalism, on the one hand, and an anticipatory vision of a multicultural world on the other.

We find intimations of the latter in the poem's foregrounding of Asia's vastness and multiplicity and in the diverse customs of the people da Gama encounters or learns about. '[W]hat other epic contains so many different nationalities?' inquires Landeg White rhetorically in the introduction to a new English translation of the poem (xi). A list of the different peoples and places – legendary as well as historic – mentioned in the poem, would total in the hundreds. 'Strange things' and 'different customs,' such as the caste system of India, ethnic dress, and vegetarianism, constitute sources for comment and wonder (Canto VII, st. 41). Given these elements, to reduce the epic to issues of ethnocentrism and power relationships would be to miss a significant imaginative element: with this epic poem, the world becomes a larger, more varied space than it had ever been in a previous Western literary work. The wonder and utopian possibility are captured in the Portuguese imperative verb 'olha' ('look'), which Tethys repeats several times as she shows da Gama the reaches of the Eastern world: 'In this vast land are a thousand nations / Of which even the names are unknown' (Canto X, st. 126, ll. 1–2). A translational approach would not ignore the embodiment of the poem in society and history (i.e., what is *behind* the text), but it would also consider what is *in front of* the text: how it anticipates a multicultural awareness and complex world with which, more than four hundred years after the poem's publication, we are still trying to come to grips.

Giuseppe Verdi's opera *Nabucco* (1842) would seem another perfect candidate for a discourse analysis of Western ethnocentrism and power. In the opera's libretto we have some of the raw stuff of Orientalism: the Babylonians (or Assyrians) versus the Hebrews, Baal versus Jehovah, the imperial conquerors versus the enslaved, and dramatic conversions (like the thunderbolt that strikes Nabucco) from one camp to the other. The time frame of the story is the sixth century (587 BC), during the period of Nebuchadnezzar's conquest of the eastern Mediterranean; the setting ranges from the Temple of Solomon in Jerusalem to the Hanging Gardens and royal court of Babylon. The two points that I wish to emphasize in regard to this opera are that interpretation depends on the viewer/reader and that texts are polysemous, effectively resisting the meanings that they might seem to convey or that we assign to them. This opera, whose libretto, written by the Italian Temistocle Solera, Verdi initially refused, was a colossal success, with some fifty-seven performances alone at La Scala in Milan in 1842. The opera's spectacle and its spirited music, including the famous chorus of the Hebrew slaves – 'Va, pensiero, sull'ali dorate' ('Fly, thought, on golden wings') – were doubtlessly responsible for that success, but so, it would seem, was the cultural encoding of the opera, interpreted by Italians as expressing their own national aspirations. Verdi transforms the chorus into the voice of the nation, with the remarkable, unexpected result that the chorus of the Hebrew slaves became the unofficial national anthem of Italy, sung throughout the country in 1842 after the opera's phenomenal success. The public of Verdi's day translated/transformed the opera's Oriental elements into a yearning for its own (Italian) national identity: 'The audience was quick to detect in *Nabucco* something closer to home than just an exotic story.'[8] How do we respond to this opera today? To each his or her own view, but I approach it through the registers of identity, solidarity, love, and conversion; the Oriental element is preposterous – even more so than a Hollywood biblical-film extravaganza of the 1950s – but the emergent reality of a world in which liberation of the enslaved would triumph inspires the audience and fills them with hope. How would this opera be interpreted by contemporary viewers in Palestine or Iraq, for example? Who can say – and who can say how it will be interpreted a hundred years from now? In the process of contemporary interpretations the opera continues its transformation, different today from what it was in Verdi's Italy and likely to be different still again in the future. Interpretation is, simply, this unending metamorphosis, for any representation depends on the viewers' perception and cognition of cultural codes that are themselves in constant transformation: nothing means anything in and of itself.

The third example, Mansfield's 'The Daughters of the Late Colonel,' takes us into the early decades of the twentieth century. Although a discourse can always be analysed as a manifestation of its underlying episteme, Said would have little or nothing to say about this story, since any Orient to which it might be related falls outside the purview of *Orientalism*. I want to make two points here: first, the Orient of this story is primarily utopian rather than ideological, expressing a desire for a prospective identity, and second, this Orient suggests an atypical response to power and the tyranny of the everyday, that is, the response of 'mindfulness' and, ultimately, compassion.[9] The final scene's key, transformative image is a smiling Buddha, and the entire story can be interpreted from the registers of gender and Buddhism, so as to shed light on the daughters' predicament as well as the inspirations and disappointments of Katherine Mansfield's own life. A story about women in domestic confinement, on the periphery of the active world, stunted in their growth by the patriarchal order to which they have acquiesced, 'The Daughters of the Late Colonel' pays tribute to Mansfield's closest friend – in the words of biographer Claire Tomalin, to her 'faithful wife,' Ida

Constance Baker. In the climactic scene, the smile of the Buddha releases the daughter's (Constantia's) repressed desires: 'She walked over to the mantelpiece to her favourite Buddha. And the stone and gilt image, whose smile always gave her such a queer feeling, almost a pain and yet a pleasant pain, seemed to-day to be more than smiling. He knew something; he had a secret' (*The Garden Party* 116). What the Buddha knows is that all those things that seem so urgent and important – just those things that Josephine and Constantia have troubled themselves over in attending to the colonel's beck and call – have suddenly vanished, because these things have been non-permanent (or 'illusions,' in the Buddhist logic of existence). The patriarchal colonel embodies the ideological and the anti-utopian; his death releases the daughters from a subtle tyranny and gives them a new chance at living and at understanding their lives. The double perspective of Buddhism (i.e., all things are empty and interdependent, and for this reason in continual transformation) as a register of interpretation enables readers to perceive the daughter's liberation as a movement that passes by way of groundlessness (here, death) in its insight into the transformative nature of self and world. In treating this short fiction, the translational approach might take different registers, with gender and Buddhism as two possibilities for highlighting the material and discovering an emergent reality in the interaction of reader's and text's worlds. For Mansfield, the Orient was a transformer and a hope, a heuristic vehicle that she employed to carry her beyond the limitations of Western perspectives toward an anticipatory identity.[10]

In subtitling this study 'Between Ideology and Utopia' I have sought to demarcate a spectrum within which translations of Orients move, ranging from the rigidity and fixity of closed viewpoints and static identities to the openness of possibility. In its pejorative sense Orientalism is an ideology, yet as neither subjects nor objects Orients are an emergent reality and may have an anticipatory and utopian quality. Literary texts that pertain circumstantially to Asia, North Africa, and the Middle East are the subject matter of this study, but we could also say that Orients are the liminal space or the emerging reality that the translations of this subject matter bring about. These translations move between the poles of ideology and utopia, which Ricoeur contends exemplify different aspects of identity and the imagination. The former preserves with pictures, whereas the latter projects fictions or redescriptions of life. The picture can become frozen and take on an obsessive or pathological quality; conversely, the fiction can cease to be responsive to contemporary predicaments and challenges and become escapist (*Lectures on Ideology and Utopia* 310–11). Ideology and utopia might also be thought of, then, as different sides of the same coin; where there is ideology, there is also probably utopia – and vice versa. This may sound confusing, but it helps to think of representation and translation as complementary yet opposing tendencies. Representation fixes something in place, and therefore helps clarify the world, yet no sooner has it been clarified than this representation begins to harden into the ideological; to break up the ideological, a redescription must emerge or be brought across a liminal space, the threshold between what is graspable and what eludes our reach. Interpretation as translation is a heuristic operation that seeks to bring about these transformations of texts and experiences – to keep them alive.

The chapters of this book treat the Orient as subject matter and Orients as emergent reality. The first part, chapters 1 and 2, considers the Orient as texts and then as experiences. The second part, chapters 3 to 6, considers reorientations, or translations, of Orients by way of several contemporary writers and thinkers in terms of four focal topics: postcolonial (Hong Kong) identity, the concept of place and the relationship of place and identity, the revisioning of cultural imaginaries (e.g., the end of East/West?), and the question of transcultural values and/or new universals in the twenty-first century.

Chapter 1, 'Borges's Search, or the Bibliophilic Orient' adopts the translational registers of Islam, the baroque, Gnosticism, and Buddhism to elaborate the South American writer Jorge Luis Borges's conception of the Orient as a library or immense textual network encompassing the world; it focuses in particular on the process of mystery in *Historia universal de la infamia*. Chapter 2, '"Without Stopping": The Orient as Liminal Space' interprets voyages in the works of Paul Bowles, an American sojourner in North Africa whose writings constitute a critique of the West and an exploration of transformative identities. The principal exposé of the chapter treats travel and travel writing in *Their Heads Are Green and Their Hands Are Blue*. Chapter 3, 'The Living Labyrinth,' analyses the predicament of culture and identity in post-1997 Hong Kong, specifically in terms of one Hong Kong / London writer, David T.K. Wong and his short-story collection, *Hong Kong Stories* (1996), an attempt to describe a passing identity and to project a future one by way of a fictional anthology of the city and its inhabitants. Chapter 4, 'Where Is Place? Locale and Identity in Kazua Ishiguro's *When We Were Orphans* and Ricardo Piglia's *La ciudad ausente*,' examines the interdependence of place and identity, beginning from a premise of Italo Calvino – 'all cities are invisible cities' – and extending this to an exploration of displacement and interrelatedness within literary, cultural imaginaries. Chapter 5, 'At the End of East/West: Myth in Salman Rushdie's *The Moor's Last Sigh*' explores the critical, reorienting capacity of legend, myth, and story, focusing on the author's critique of fundamentalist ideologies and the utopian capacity of fiction to redescribe reality and project new identities and worlds. Chapter 6, 'Identity and Citizenship in a World of Shame,' looks for new ideas about individual and group identity, affiliation and responsibility – all of which, the chapter contends, demand reorientation. It draws principally on literary and critical works of Édouard Glissant, Amin Maalouf, Tzvetan Todorov, and V.S. Naipaul – and secondarily on a disparate group of philosophers, sociologists, scientists, literary scholars, and intellectuals, including Paul Ricoeur, George Steiner, Ernst Bloch, Emmanuel Lévinas, Gianni Vattimo, Jean-Baptiste de Foucauld, Matthieu Ricard, and Trinh Xuan Thuan. Along with chapter 5, this chapter seeks to reorient notions of national and ethnic identity. Finally, 'Neither Subjects nor Objects: In the Middle Way' recapitulates and extends key concepts of this book: interpretation as translation, Orients, place, and identity.

1. Borges's Search, or the Bibliophilic Orient

In Manoel de Oliveira's film *Palavra e Utopia* (2000), a fictional dramatization based on letters, sermons, and other historical documents, the seventeenth-century Jesuit priest Father Antonio Vieira dedicates his life to fighting slavery and the mistreatment of Africans and Amerindians in the New World. As a missionary, Father Vieira is also a traveller, voyaging between Portugal and Brazil as well as to European capitals such as Rome, where he seeks support from the pope, among other powerful church figures, in his struggle against Inquisitional authorities who seek to silence him and block the transmission of his ideas. The film is very much about authority and ideologies, but it is also about the power of the word to redescribe the world and put forward utopias, one of which Father Vieira elaborates in an inspiring sermon: to spread the word of Christ, the Portuguese (and Europeans) can no longer content themselves to speak a single language; everyone, now, must learn to speak all the languages of all the peoples of the world, and there is nothing more noble than to embark on this humanistic journey.

When I think of Father Vieira's utopian vision, I cannot help but think of the fantastic stories of Borges, who often applied his imagination to such impossible possibilities. 'La biblioteca del Babel' might be read as an attempt to conceive of the dark side of a world like the one that Father Vieira announces. There is no end to the manner in which the world may be perceived and transformed linguistically and metaphorically. For the Portuguese writer Joaquim Maria Machado de Assis, 'A vida é uma opera' ('Life is an opera'); for the Danish composer Carl Nielsen, 'Music is life, and like it, inextinguishable';[1] for the Chilean poet and filmmaker Alexandro Jodorowsky, reality is a dance; for the Argentinean Jorge Luis Borges, life is a library. 'Reading books, writing books, talking about books. In a profound manner, [Borges] was conscious of continuing a dialogue begun thousands of years ago and which, he believed, would never end,' biographer Alberto Manguel explains (quoted in Le Naire, 'Eternel Borges' 37).

All the above metaphors translate something from experience into a particular register of signs and symbols, and all of them are true. In this chapter I will explore translations, especially of Oriental materials, in Borges's fiction, for Borges is perhaps the first (modern) Western writer to treat the Orient as neither subject nor object, but as emergent reality. When we read this fiction, we know instinctively that it is different from other fantasy literature, even that with an Oriental slant. At the edge of the fantasy are a swarm of philosophical and religious ideas; there is an intellectual depth to the world-making. Borges, it has been said, is mystery itself. And yet in reading his stories, which I will interpret from the registers of Islam, Gnosticism, and Buddhism, we often encounter an emptiness finally within the mystery. It is this experience of groundlessness that makes the foray into his stories challenging today – and most 'Oriental.'

Borges's Orients

For Borges, the Oriental derives from texts and books; it constitutes an imaginative space, a feeling, a collection of philosophical ideas. This is an important characteristic that marks the difference between Borges and other twentieth-century Western writers for whom notions of the Oriental derive from a lived experience. For a writer such as Paul Bowles, who sojourned more than a half a century in Tangier, Morocco, and who often treats North African subject matter in his fiction, the Orient constituted an alternative manner of being, a borderline, a liminal space.[2] Borges never lived in the East; he travelled to Asia on one occasion only, briefly visiting Japan. So his fascination with things Eastern grows out of his love for books, and is linked with an aesthetic passion for things exotic (i.e., beyond normal boundaries) and enigmatic. 'When he was very young,' Borges's mother recalls in an interview with the French publication *L'Herne*, 'he became enthusiastic about Egyptian things, and he read about them – read with no end in sight – until he threw himself into Chinese literature; he has a lot of books on the subject. In short, he loves everything mysterious' (quoted in Monegal, *Jorge Luis Borges* 38). Although the East and the Orient do have geographic referents, vague though they might be, for Borges these denotations pale before the evocative power of words and concepts. In the essay 'The Thousand and One Nights,' Borges speaks poetically of the connotative meanings of the Orient; he translates the word/metaphor into a gamut of existential correlatives. The word has a singular, magical quality, he notes, not least because, in Spanish, contained within the word 'Orient' by 'happy chance' is the word 'oro' (gold), a colour he associates with sunrise and sunshine. The Orient is the place of wealth and beginnings, he says. It belongs to a certain poetics of space. In 'Metáforas de Las Mil y Una Noches' ('Metaphors of the Thousand and One Nights'), Borges identifies four groups of metaphors within the idea of the Orient, or specifically the Orient of *The Thousand and One Nights*.[3] The first group, the 'river,' contains transformations and metamorphoses of various sorts. Its central notion is that of life's fluidity. The second group, the 'weave and weft of the carpet,' contains a seeming chaos of colours and lines that, at the proper distance, shows a secret order. Its patterns of dizzying complexity include numbers and bizarre geometries of fate. The third group, dreams, features labyrinthine landscapes where there are twists and turns and stories within stories. The fourth group, the 'map of time,' covers an indefinite region without beginning or end. Borges's Orient, then, combines magic with fate, pattern with fluidity, dreams and paradox. He conceives of the Orient as an impressionistic, poetic, imaginative landscape, rather than as something principally geographic: 'There is something that we feel as the Orient, something I have not felt in Israel but have felt in Granada and in Córdoba. I have felt the presence of the East, and I don't know how I can define it; perhaps it's not worth it to define something that we feel instinctively' (*Seven Nights* 48). Elaborating further, he inquires:

> How does one define the Orient (not the real Orient, which does not exist)? I would say that the notions of East and West are generalizations, but that no individual can feel himself to be Oriental. I suppose that a man feels himself to be Persian or Hindu or Malaysian, but not Oriental ...
>
> What is the Orient, then? It is above all a world of extremes in which people are very unhappy or very happy, very rich or very poor. A world of kings, or kings who do not explain what they do. Of kings who are, we might say, as irresponsible as gods. (Ibid. 51)

To push the idea a bit further, one could say that the Orient for Borges exists primarily as an intertextuality. In this sense the tales of *The Thousand and One Nights* are at once individual and segmented yet circular and unending because they are linked in a chain that is the story of the world as a web of interconnected causes and effects, or fates: 'In [its] title ... there is something very important: the suggestion of an infinite book. The Arabs say that no one can read *The Thousand and One Nights* to the end. Not for reasons of boredom: one feels the book is infinite' (*Seven Nights* 50). To sum up these ideas, we could say that for Borges the Orient has the shape of a story; in this story-within-stories one eventually finds, he surmises, one's own tale and destiny. There is, then, a pervasive intertextuality encompassing not only all stories but also all lives. This resembles the Arabo-Islamic notion of *mektoub* (i.e., everything has already been written in Allah's book); the idea of all relatedness equally recalls Buddhist ideas. The Buddhist term for this is 'interdependence' (*shunyata*), which also translates as 'empty' or 'devoid of inherent existence' (Hayward and Varela 26).

Borges's treatment of other Eastern traditions, such as Indian and Chinese, parallel those of his interpretation of Arabo-Islamic texts. So, for example, the themes and concepts of magic, the world as illusion, fate, multiplicity, and infinity are common to his commentary on all of these traditions. In addition to the essay 'Buddhism,' which like 'Metaphors of the Thousand and One Nights' appears in the collection *Siete noches*, Borges co-authored with Alicia Jurado a monograph entitled *Qué es el Budismo* (*What Is Buddhism*) (1976). This long essay gives an overview of Buddhist legend, history, antecedents, doctrines, and various sects. The most interesting aspect of the book is Borges's commentary on things Eastern that indirectly touches on his own art and fiction. In the chapter on Tantric Buddhism, Borges notes that a belief in magic is common to various Indian sects, although this 'magic' may take the form of a trick or a hallucination: 'In this country magicians abound: the current traveler believes that he sees a man toss a rope into the air and then climb it, but the photograph shows that this is actually an hallucination concocted by the magician' (127). The larger idea here is that, in the Eastern view of things, the visible world is only part of the totality of being, which also comprises the invisible and the imaginary (55). A belief in magic implies a belief in the paradoxical nature of the world. In the chapter on Zen Buddhism, Borges discusses the famous concept of *koan*, 'a question whose response does not correspond to laws of logic' (136). Certainly in his own fiction, Borges creates dizzying effects through paradoxes and puzzles. The difference between the koan and Borgesian paradox would seem to be that the latter does not abandon logic for intuition, but rather depends on it to achieve its full force. A certain verbal slight-of-hand and radical change of perspective play a part in the workings of both techniques.

Closely related to magic and dizzying paradox is the notion of the world as spectacle or illusion. In *Qué es el Budismo*, Borges discusses the philosophy of Sankhyam, according to which '[t]he immaterial soul is a spectator, a witness, not an agent' (40). We find a literary correlative of this concept in the detachment of Borges's narrators as well as in the game-like quality of stories such as 'La Lotería de Babilonia' ('The Lottery of Babylon') and 'El Jardín de los senderos que se bifurcan' ('The Garden of Forking Paths'). The universe transforms into one immense game, whether *ajedrez* for the Muslim or chance for a believer of another persuasion; quoting the German mystic Angelus Silesius, Borges writes: 'Everything is a game executed by the divinity' (44). Buddhists (and Hindus) hold that the world is an illusion: 'Brahman destroys and creates the universe in cycles: both operations are magical or hallucinatory in nature. Already in the Vedas, God is cast as the Maker of Spells who creates the world of appearances by means of the magic force of Maya, illusion' (43). Whether Shahrazad or God spins the illusions would seem to matter little; the important idea is that the notion of illusion and world as spectacle belong more to Eastern traditions than to Western. One of Borges's favourite anecdotes – mentioned in at least three pieces – is that of the Chinese philosopher Chuang Tzu, who dreamed that he was a butterfly; upon waking he ponders whether he Chuang Tzu has dreamed that he is a butterfly or a butterfly has dreamed that he is Chuang Tzu ('Sueño de la mariposa').[4] Borges transforms the idea behind this anecdote into the story 'Las ruinas circulares' ('The Circular Ruins') and varies it further in 'El otro' ('The Other'). Not only is the world an illusion, but so is the individual 'ego.' According to Buddhism 'each person is an illusion, dizzyingly produced by a series of momentary and isolated persons' (*Qué es el Budismo* 72).[5] Borges treats a variation of this idea in 'El Inmortal' ('The Immortal') and 'The Garden of Forking Paths,' among other stories.

Certainly one reason that Borges was drawn to things Oriental is the eclecticism of certain Eastern perspectives, which suited the protean nature of his imagination. Buddhism and other Eastern teachings show adaptability and flexibility, he points out: 'When Ashoka, emperor of India, became a Buddhist, he did not try to impose his new religion on anyone. A good Buddhist can be a Lutheran or Methodist or Presbyterian or Calvinist or Shintoist or Taoist or Catholic' (*Seven Nights* 59). In *Qué es el Budismo* this idea of protean compatibility is broadened further:

'In the Orient, one religion is not incompatible with others; some sects ... incorporate elements of Taoism and of Confucianism. The Chinese mind is hospitable; temples are constructed that house all three religions impartially' (121). Certainly we find the colouring and transformation of these ideas in Borges's stories, which often mix different philosophical and religious perspectives.

The concept of fate, so important in Islam, has its counterpart in the Buddhist concept of reincarnation and transmigration of souls. *Karma* is the law of the universe, Borges explains, distinguishing between Western and Buddhist concepts of divinity and justice: In Buddhism 'there is no equivalent to a juridical divinity who parcels out rewards and punishments; each act carries within itself the germ of a reward or a punishment that may not occur immediately but may be fatal' (*Qué es el Budismo* 70). The process of judgment may be long – indeed, endless. Whether by way of *The Thousand and One Nights* or in Buddhism and Hinduism, Borges finds in the Orient the concept of infinity, with all its fantastic possibilities. 'Buddhism, like Hinduism, from which it originates, postulates an infinite number of worlds, all of identical structure. To affirm that the universe is limited is a heresy; to affirm that it is without limit, is likewise heretical; to affirm that it is neither one nor the other is also a heresy' (ibid. 53). In 'El budismo' in *Siete noches*, Borges explains that the ideas of transmigration of souls and the infinite find their way into Western philosophy through the Stoics and Pythagoreans. The Buddhist notion of karma expresses the idea that one's life has been preordained by a previous life. 'Karma is a cruel law,' he remarks, 'but it has a curious mathematical consequence: if my present life is determined by my previous life, that previous life was determined by another, and so on forever. That is to say: the letter z is determined by y, y by x, x by w, w by v, except that this alphabet has an end but no beginning. The Buddhists and the Hindus, in general, believe in a living infinity' ('Buddhism' 70). It goes almost without saying that many of Borges's stories translate this notion of infinity into one form or another: 'The Book of Sand,' for example, with its infinite book; 'The Garden of Forking Paths,' with its infinite bifurcation of futures; and 'The Zahir,' with its notion of limitless transformation of limited, quotidian objects, like a coin. In sum, in Buddhism, Chinese philosophy and literature, and Arabo-Islamic works like *The Thousand and One Nights* Borges found philosophical, imaginative, and ludic elements to nurture his protean spirit. His notion of the Orient was composed of all of them. At the same time, it is important to insist that because Borges does not allow himself to be limited by binaries, he finds East in West and West in East. It is not a question of geography or politics, but rather of literary and philosophical traditions, with all their cross-currents and exchanges. It is, more importantly, a question of how Borges translates or transforms the material and how the reader responds to it and seeks to comprehend it.

Mystery in *Historia universal de la infamia*

Borges's Orient was varied and idiosyncratic, drawing on and improvising on aspects of Persian, Arabic, Indian, Chinese, and Japanese cultural heritages – as well as the Anglicized and Europeanized translations of those cultures and literatures as he encountered them through his readings in Spanish, English, German, and French. One of Borges's earliest works, *Historia universal de la infamia* (1935) shows a specifically *Arabian Nights* influence in many of its segments and a broader, Oriental intertextuality (Persian, Chinese, Japanese) in others. In the 'Postface du Traducteur' in *Histoire universelle de l'infamie*, a French translation of this collection, Roger Caillois examines Borges's use of sources, noting that his translations or adaptations read very much like his own original work. In 'El Tintorero en mascarado, Hákim de Merv' ('The Masked Dyer, Hakim of Merv'), for example, Borges retains only the bare sketch of the history; none of the sources upon which he drew indicates that Hakim is a leper, a key element in the denouement of Borges's tale. The Hakims of other texts, including Thomas Moore's *Lalla Rookh*, meet their end in diverse ways. Borges follows none of these intrigues, concocting his own dramatic finale. Caillois concludes that Borges's tale is quite original. In fact, he transforms the materials, giving them new emphases and highlights. He applies his own creative registers of translation to the histories and legends that serve as the base of many of the stories in this collection.

In this section of the chapter I would like to look in detail at Orients that emerge in Borges's translation/transformation of this material. The register with which I will interpret these stories is mystery, specifically asking the question, Does mystery have a cultural aspect? The word 'mystery' derives from the Greek verb *myein* ('to close') – to close, that is, the lips and eyes of the person being initiated (the *mystēs*) into a cult. As Walter Burkert explains, the Latin translation of *mysteria*, *myein*, and *myesis* as *initia*, *initiare*, and *initatio* reveals that mysteries are 'initiation ceremonies, cults in which admission and participation depend upon some personal ritual to be performed on the initiand. Secrecy and in most cases a nocturnal setting are concomitants of this exclusiveness' (*Ancient Mystery Cults* 7–8). In mystery cults, whose origins probably lie in the prehistoric Near East, various kinds of initiatory activities were involved, such as meals, dances, and other rituals.[6] The mystery cults thrived in ancient Greco-Roman times and developed in parallel with Christianity, with which some of the cults share certain features. To demarcate itself from these cults, the Church hierarchy strategically fixed the dates of its most significant celebrations: thus, Christmas was set on 25 December so as to push into the background the festival of the sun god; the Epiphany on 6 January in order to supplant an Egyptian festival; and Easter in the spring to overshadow pagan fertility festivals.[7] In time, the denotations of the word 'mystery' became generalized and secularized, taking on the contemporary meaning with its distinct ontological and epistemological accents: 'A hidden or secret thing; a matter unexplained or inexplicable; something beyond human knowledge or comprehension; a riddle or enigma' (*Oxford English Dictionary*). Within the secular, non-theological meaning of mystery lie traces of non-Western, Gnostic ways of thinking about and being in the world. The notions of game and artifice are also present. Fundamentally, mystery would seem to mediate experiences of limitation and opposition, encompassing an interplay between the visible and the hidden, the known and the unknown.

In *Historia universal de la infamia* the section entitled 'Etcétera' features five vignettes that draw on the *Arabian Nights* and/or the Persian Arabo-Islamic tradition of story; into these and other stories in the collection Borges infuses elements of the baroque, Gnosticism, opera bouffa, and postmodernism, which is the slant that my interpretation of them will take. The first two tales, 'La cámara de las estatuas' and 'Historia de los dos que soñaron,' are drawn directly from *The Thousand and One Nights*. Distinguished by its skilful use of repetition and variation, 'The Chamber of Statues' – like a baroque fugue – mixes magic, morality, and history. The tale provides a poetic explanation of the eighth-century Spanish loss of Andalusia: that is, a king who will not leave well enough alone insists on opening a castle door, with its twenty-four locks that twenty-four kings before him have put firmly in place and have refused to tamper with. Upon forcing his way into the castle's locked chambers, he finds marvel upon marvel, including sculptured statues of Arabic horsemen, with their scimitars and lances at ready. In the seventh and final chamber, at the end of a long corridor the king finds an inscription that reads: 'If any hand dare open the door of this castle, living warriors after the likeness of the figures here depicted will conquer the kingdom' (*Universal History* 111). And so it comes to pass, with the Moors crossing the narrow straits from North Africa and installing themselves in central and southern Spain for the next seven hundred years.

The sense of mystery in this story derives from the interplay between the reader's curiosity about what lies behind the locked castle doors and a careful progression of effects. Each detail serves the story's end, either introducing a new element of mystery or reinforcing it; in the conclusion, the magical, spectacular aspect of the tale resolves into the quotidian and the historical. In terms of mystery, the tale has a tripartite structure corresponding to the following process or journey: (1) a barring of the way, (2) entry into a hermetic space, and (3) revelation. All three stages of the process pose problems of interpretation to the reader, and to struggle to understand or interpret is precisely to take the journey of mystery that the tale proposes. With the opening of each lock and entrance into each new chamber, the tale creates suspense and a sense of marvels. In addition to wondering what lies within the final chamber, the reader also wonders how the contents of each chamber are related one to another: for example, how do figurines of Arabs seated on camels relate to a map of the world and to a circular mirror? Thus, the tale can also be thought of as a puzzle, or a series of related puzzles that demand interpretation. The locked door that the king is warned not to open is a prevalent motif in *The Thousand and One Nights*; this metaphor is polysemous, but one of its significances would seem to be a universal division between what is known (the present) and what is unknown (the future), and between what is permitted and what is forbidden or what is beyond human limitations. The door is an apt metaphor for the phenomenological quality of mystery itself: a barring of the way, an opening and closing, a concealing and a revealing. Mystery has a structure, but this structure depends in part on the reader.

In this tale, mystery has both a universal and a culturally specific component. I have already mentioned the locked door as a story motif that one encounters again and again in *The Thousand and One Nights*; the use of numbers and the twisted path toward the story's resolution constitute two other culturally specific elements. But there is also something even more fundamental, conveying a metaphysical attitude: the sense of mystery in the tale illustrates the Islamic belief of *mektoub* (i.e., 'it was written'), which holds that Allah knows all and that all has already been determined. It illustrates the moral lesson that human beings have a limited vision and knowledge and therefore should submit to the omniscience and omnipotence of God. The images of the story embellish this basic lesson. Mystery has an aspect of *cache-cache* (hide-and-seek), yet from an Islamic perspective mystery always finds its clarification in Allah's intentions. So it is tempting to conjecture that a culturally specific element of this tale and of Oriental tales in the style of *The Thousand and One Nights* is that the meaning of the mystery is implicit at the very beginning of the story. In Western stories, we must wait until the end for the solution; in these orientalized stories we must also wait until the end for the particularized solution, yet the message revealed by the mystery is always the same and knowable even at the beginning: *mektoub*, God is all-powerful and all-knowing; we are not. The next story is perhaps an even better illustration of this.

'Tale of the Two Dreamers' treats familiar themes of dreams, belief, and fate, all drawn together in the form of a Borgesian paradox. The plot is simple: a man from Cairo has a dream in which another man pulls a gold coin out of his mouth and tells him to go to Isfahan, a city in Persia, where he will find his fortune. The Cairoan leaves the next day; upon arrival in Isfahan, he encounters numerous misfortunes; he is beaten, mistaken for a thief, sent to jail, and then expelled from the country by a local magistrate. Before expelling him the magistrate chides the Cairoan for his gullibility: 'O man of little wit,' he says insultingly, 'thrice have I dreamed of a house in Cairo in whose yard is a garden, at the lower end of which is a sundial and beyond the sundial a fig tree and beyond the fig tree a fountain and beneath the fountain a great sum of money. Yet I have not paid the least heed to this lie; but you, offspring of a mule and devil, have journeyed from place to place on the faith of a dream. Don't show your face again in Isfahan. Take these coins and leave' (*Universal History* 116). The Cairoan returns home, digs beneath the fountain of his garden and uncovers the treasure.

In addition to its value as a simple, entertaining tale, the story also serves as an allegory, which may be approached differently depending on the highlighting that the reader gives to various elements. If, for example, we highlight the cultural element – that is, if we attempt to translate or situate ourselves within the cultural framework of the tale – then the meaning and moral clarify accordingly. In this tale mystery concerns the nature of dreams and the divine; the intentionality of Allah, who seems to employ suffering and misdirection as part of the intrigue, seems inscrutable. It would appear that Allah, like hermeneuticists such as Paul Ricoeur, prefers 'la voie longue,' or the long road to meaning (*Le conflit des interprétations* 20); that is to say, the Cairoan can understand his dream (or his subjectivity) only by way of the journey he takes and his interpretation of another man's dream. As Ricoeur puts it, the comprehension of self passes by the detour of the comprehension of the other; or in slightly different words, 'comprendre le monde des signes, c'est le moyen de se comprendre' ('understanding the world of signs is the means to self-understanding') (*Le conflit des interprétations* 260). The tale concerns this path to self-knowledge as well as a corollary idea, the interrelatedness of all things in the world: the man from Cairo's dream and life intermesh with the life and dream of the *capitán* in Isfahan. Dreams can be mysterious; coincidence can be mysterious. These things are universally true. However, the story especially emphasizes that the ways of fate are crooked and unfathomable.[8] Culturally speaking, the mystery hinges on a question, Why would Allah send to a poor, insignificant man a dream that leads him to further suffering and humiliation? In the end, Allah's plan becomes clear and all is revealed, as the final sentences of the story underscore: 'In this way God blessed him, rewarded him, and raised him up. God is generosity itself, God is that which is hidden' (my translation) (*Historia universal* 120). The tale, then, is an allegory of life for the devout Muslim: follow the dictates of Allah, and you will be rewarded in the end is its message. Here, then, the cultural context seems to play an important part in guiding our interpretation of this tale, establishing the particular emphases of the moral. This particular cultural context, if the reader has the capacity to enter it imaginatively, orients the hermeneutic of mystery.

Be that as it may, the tale as allegory is not exhausted by an interpretation that highlights its specifically cultural component. Other interpretations remain not only possibilities, but have in fact passed into the texts of other authors. Readers who know Paulo Coelho's popular contemporary novel *O alquimista* (*The Alchemist*) (1988) will perhaps recognize that Coelho, like Borges, has dipped into and transformed the same magical tale from *The Thousand and One Nights*. In *The Alchemist* the interpretation takes the form of an individual's quest for something unknown, purportedly a treasure buried in the pyramids; Coelho's interpretation of the allegory secularizes and psychologizes the Islamic element of the tale and directs the focus on the process of individuation and realization of selfhood. Coelho's rewriting touches on still another aspect of the tale that itself could be highlighted and elaborated in an interpretation slightly different in emphasis from the two already mentioned. This third interpretation would be a commentary on an idea central to hermeneutics that authenticity of self depends on a continuing interpretation and reinterpretation. So from this perspective, the hidden treasure of the tale stands as a symbol of the authentic self, and the journey that the man from Cairo undertakes stands for the continual process of interpretation that authenticity of self demands. In this context, an essay of Ricoeur entitled 'Heidegger et la question du sujet' may prove illuminating; here Ricoeur explicates the phrase, in our everyday lives 'chacun est l'autre et personne n'est soi-même' (*Le conflit des interprétations* 229). The basic idea would seem to be that we are often alienated from authenticity and must engage in a continual interpretation of ourselves vis-à-vis others and life experiences. Ricoeur writes: '[T]he recovery of self proceeds not only from a phenomenology, in the sense of an intuitive description, but also from an interpretation precisely because the [authentic] self is forgotten; it must be recovered by an interpretation that brings it out of the shadows' (ibid.). Given a certain highlighting, that could also be an allegorical interpretation of Borges's tale and Coelho's *O alquimista*: there is something hidden; the quest to find what is hidden is long and labyrinthine, with the treasure buried where one least expects it and with information about how to find it mixed up with the lives of others and the confusion of the world. The tale is, after all, not about one person who dreams, but about *two* persons and *two* dreams that are related; an intricate chain of events brings them together. Given this highlighting, the tale can be read as a thematizing of authenticity via intersubjectivity.

'El Espejo de tinta' ('The Mirror of Ink'), like other tales in 'Etcétera,' treats magic, fate, and the crooked, winding road to justice; Borges's translation and recomposition of the material draws out its baroque and spectacular possibilities. He attributes the tale to Sir Richard Burton, but scholars have been unable to track it down (*Histoire universelle de l'infamie* 237). Borges may have mistaken the source, or he may have changed the germ of the source beyond recognition; in any case, it is the register of the translation/recomposition more than the subject that matters. Within Eastern traditions, whether Islamic or Buddhist, the individual is accountable for his/her actions; fate does not alter this accountability, but rather incorporates it and figures it into the calculations. Those who torment and inflict sufferings on others shall themselves be repaid in kind, either in this life or the next, such is the law of Allah and of karma. 'The Mirror of Ink' illustrates this principle. In the tale a wizard, Abd-er-Rahman al-Masmudi, is held captive by the 'cruellest' of Sudanese rulers, Yaqub the Ailing, who forces him to demonstrate his magical powers. The wizard conjures images from a pool of ink poured in the palm of Yaqub's right hand, and phantasmagoric scenes pass before the king's eyes as he gazes into his cupped palm (*Universal History* 126–7). The passage is worth quoting, for it shows the baroque style of Borges's translation of the subject matter:

> the cities, the climates, the kingdoms into which the earth is divided; the treasures hidden in its bowels; the ships that ply its seas; the many instruments of war, of music, of surgery; fair women; the fixed stars and the planets; the colors used by the ungodly to paint their odious pictures; minerals and plants, with the secrets and properties they hold locked up in them; the silvery angels, whose only food is the praise and worship of the Lord; the awarding of prizes at schools; the idols of birds and kings buried in the heart of pyramids; the shadow cast by the bull that holds up the world and by the fish that lies under the bull; the sandy wastes of Allah the All-Merciful. He saw things impossible to tell, like gaslit streets and the whale that dies on hearing the cry of a man.[9]

One of these arabesque images is the Man with the Mask, who becomes part of the background of a kaleidoscope of events, increasingly violent, that Yaqub and the wizard Abd-er-Rahman witness. When the king demands to be shown an execution, it is the Man with the Mask who steps forward to the beheading; the mask is lifted, and the face behind the veil is Yaqub's. The king collapses at the moment of the phantasmagoric execution, taken into the spectacle of images and the emerging reality of justice. In the West, we have lost touch with the primordial power of the image/symbol to reach out and shape life, but this power still holds sway in Oriental cultures (e.g., the image of the eye painted on doors of North African homes).

'The Mirror of Ink' teaches that everything in the world is related. If one is cruel to others, one will be dealt cruelty in return; this constitutes a salient message in Oriental tales, but also in folk tales and Greek tragedy, and so one could not argue that this trait in itself is culturally specific. There is something more here, though. The tale particularly illustrates the all-powerfulness of Allah, the final arbiter, and concludes with this culturally specific recitation: 'Glory to Him, who endureth forever, and in whose hand are the keys of unlimited Pardon and everlasting Punishment' (*Universal history* 129). The essential predicament in this and other tales in 'Etcétera' is the barrier, door, or veil separating human power and comprehension from the divine. Fate travels a crooked, labyrinthine path; truth is often obscure or concealed, and emerges only at the end of the path. Mystery is a veil placed before the reader's eyes; to follow the path of the story, to interpret it correctly, is to begin to remove the veil. The manner in which the unveiling occurs constitutes a culturally specific element. In these tales, with their origin in Oriental materials pervaded by the spirit of Islam, the culturally specific element often concerns how the will of Allah will be shown or revealed. Yaqub is cruel; God does not allow such cruelty to go unpunished, so when will the punishment come and how will it come? If we highlight the Islamic element of the tales as we read them, then mystery takes on a certain colouring and significance. The tales' intentionality, manifest even in atmospherics and seeming banalities, encourages the reader not only to enter the mystery but also to experience it from a particular cultural slant, as much as that might be possible.

Borges's Oriental tales generally operate according to two basic principles: things are never what they seem, and there is no eluding things as they are. The essentially empty spectacle of *Arabian Nights* metamorphoses is counterpointed by an underlying sombre strain of unchangeable finality. Borges treats the latter with a mixture of opera bouffa, the baroque, or black humour; a new sense of reality emerges in his transformation of the material, as in the opening paragraph of 'El Espantoso redentor Lazarus Morrell' ('The Dread Redeemer Lazarus Morrell'). So much has come, Borges muses, from the Spanish missionary Bartolomé de las Casas's innocent suggestion to Charles the Fifth that Africans be brought to the Caribbean to relieve the suffering American Indians; de las Casas acts out of faith and humanitarian concern, yet his counsel ironically leads to much horror, the infamy of African slavery in the Americas and many other things:

> To this odd philanthropic twist [de las Casas's suggestion] we owe, all up and down the Americas, endless things – W.C. Handy's blues; the Parisian success of the Uruguayan lawyer and painter of Negro genre, don Pedro Figari; the solid native prose of another Uruguayan, don Vicente Rossi, who traced the origin of the tango to Negroes; the mythological dimensions of Abraham Lincoln; the five hundred thousand dead of the Civil War and its three thousand three hundred millions spent in military pensions; the entrance of the verb 'to lynch' into the thirteenth edition of the dictionary of the Spanish Academy ... (*Universal History* 19)[10]

This list could go on infinitely; its emergent reality takes us to the threshold of a comprehension, combining as it does incompatibilities of all sorts, ranging from the horrible to the felicitous, the trivial to the incommensurable. To the question 'What is fate?' Borges responds: it is that 'name we give [to] the infinite, ceaseless chain of thousands of intertwined causes' (*Historia universal* 37). 'Our destiny,' he writes, 'is not frightful because it is unreal; it is frightful because it is irreversible and iron clad' (*Labyrinths* 234). These remarks offer a clue to the author's preference for Oriental subject matter, in which fate plays a major role, and suggest an aspect of the essential quality of mystery. What makes something mysterious is not necessarily its obscurity or vagueness, but rather its clear finality and irreversible closure. Detective stories and other popular fiction that depend on mystery play with this tension between the open and the closed, or between obscurity and finality: in the detective-fiction formula, the murder is set before the readers' eyes; the resolution of the murder then occupies the rest of the story. Within the imaginative world of the *Arabian Nights*, fate takes the place of murder in the detective-fiction formula, and this fate is always Allah's will; the particular working out of an individual's fate, like the solving of a mystery in a whodunit, has lots of twists and turns, and this is where magic in stories of the *Arabian Nights* genre enters. Magic, a sudden, unexpected opening, counterpoints fate, with its definitive closing. Whereas the resolution in a whodunit is secular, in the world of *The Thousand and One Nights* and Borges's tales the sacred is an unfathomable and irreversible closure. Again, it would seem that mystery can be given at least some distinctive cultural highlighting.

'The Masked Dyer, Hakim of Merv' is perhaps the most deftly written piece in *Historia universal de la infamia*; it is organized imagistically and dramatically into six brief segments: 'La purpura escarlata' ('The Scarlet Dye'), 'El toro' ('The Bull'), 'El leopardo' ('The Leopard'), 'El profeta velado' ('The Veiled Prophet'), 'Los espejos abominables' ('The Abominable Mirrors'), and 'El rostro' ('The Face'). Just as the narrative proceeds according to a series of images, so too each section introduces one or more mysteries about the masked prophet's life and career. The first section concerns Hakim's birth, apprenticeship as a dyer, and mysterious disappearance, before which he destroys the cauldrons and cubes used for immersing textiles as well as a scimitar and a bronze mirror. As a clue to this mysterious disappearance, the narrator suggests that Hakim, torn between the conflicting appeals of an Angel and Satan, begins to view all colour as a falsification of the world. Only whiteness, the absence of colour, is truth. Mystery in this tale has a Gnostic highlighting, which I shall say more about shortly.[11] The second section introduces the mystery of Hakim's visage: he appears to have the head of a bull, which he covers with a mask; the reader later discovers that leprosy has disfigured him. Section three retrospectively recounts the legend of how Hakim lost his human head and gained his supernatural powers; his mask protects ordinary mortals from a view that would blind them, for Hakim purportedly utters words so ancient that they ignite a fire in his mouth and a glorious splendour in his face. In sections four and five the mysteries surrounding Hakim take a further Gnostic turn: at the core of his beliefs is a speculation that the world is a projection of images, or parodies, and that acts and objects of this world, such as procreation and mirrors, are to be shunned because they increase and perpetuate that illusion: 'At the root of Hakim's cosmogony is a spectral god. This godhead is as majestically devoid of origin as of name or face ... The lord of th[e] lowermost heaven is he who rules us – shadow of shadows of still other shadows – and his fraction of divinity approaches zero.' The conclusion follows: 'The world we live in is a mistake, a clumsy parody. Mirrors and fatherhood, because they multiply the parody, are abominations (*Universal History* 84). Section six solves the tale's primary mystery, but because the solution is itself ambiguous, remnants of the mysterious persist. Hakim is a leper, and his veil is designed to hide the leprosy and turn the personal misfortune into a political and religious power. A second explanation is Hakim's own: the state of sin in which human beings live prevents them from seeing his real splendours.

Throughout the tale's six sections, Borges incorporates cultural elements within the composition of the mystery, which could be categorized and analysed in terms of atmospherics, symbols, and intertextual referencing to Gnostic traditions. In the first category we find elements such as the Arabian desert as well as references to *The Thousand and One Nights* and historical figures and texts from Arabo-Islamic traditions. All the dates in the story use the Islamic rather than Gregorian calendar, thus marking off the story's referential space as outside the ken of Western time. Similarly, images and symbols such as the dyer and the veil are given an Oriental accentuation. Although we might think of these elements as the clothing surrounding the body of mystery itself, or as creating a mood in which the reader enters the imaginative space of the author's text, there may be something more fundamental at play, to which the Gnostic highlighting in the tale points. Mystery is an incertitude that can never be completely resolved, and this incertitude – and capacity of illusion – concerns the nature of the self and the world.

That the world itself may be a parody, a cruel and inverted game, is a possibility that Gnosticism embraces, for its core doctrines hold that the inner spirit must be liberated from a world that is basically deceptive, oppressive, and evil. Here the notion of mystery takes a sombre turn; we are no longer talking about mystery as a revelation, but as an unmasking of the parody and the falsehood of words and the world. To take this line of thought in a slightly different (postmodern) direction, Hakim doubles for the author; his parodies of the Prophet parallel the author's rewritings of the sources from which he draws the tale. Just as Hakim misleads others to believe in his supernatural powers, so too the author leads the readers into the game of mystery, whose endpoint may in fact be a deception or an emptiness. What is behind the veil? In this case, only an anticlimax. If we compare 'Hakim of Merv' to another well-known short story whose mystery derives from the veil as central symbol, Nathaniel Hawthorne's 'The Minister's Black Veil' (1836), we see that both demonstrate that mystery depends on interpretation, but only Borges takes the additional step of translating mystery into a cipher. Behind the veil, behind the mystery, there is finally an emptiness; could we say that this is fundamentally an Eastern message?

A few words about two other pieces, 'Un doble de Mahoma' ('A Double for Mohammed') and 'La viuda Ching, pirata' ('The Widow Ching, Lady Pirate'). The former returns indirectly to the tale of Hakim, the leprous dyer who pretends to be a prophet, by extending the logic of the tale's Gnostic references and overtones. Beginning with characteristic Borgesian wit and humour, this bagatelle toys with an idea whose source the author lists as the mystic Emanuel Swedenborg: the Almighty, as a concession to the beliefs of Muslims, appoints a delegate to impersonate Mohammed and preside over them in Heaven. The role of the 'double' is assigned to different delegates, one of whom is a Saxon who, having once been taken prisoner by Algerian corsairs, learned a bit about Muslims and Islam – but not enough! 'Having been a Christian, he was moved to speak to them of the Lord, and to say He was not Joseph's son but the Son of God; it was found advisable to have this man replaced. The office of the representative Mohammed is marked by a torchlike flame, visible only to Muslims' (*Universal History* 133). In the context of this chapter's analysis, we might read this playful passage as a proposition that mystery, like religion, has a universal aspect *and*, like the indissoluble connection for Muslims between Mohammed and religion, a sociocultural aspect.

'The Widow Ching, Lady Pirate' is a delightful example of a tale of Oriental material turned in the direction of opera bouffa. First, there is the subject matter itself, lady pirates, which Borges gently mocks in the story's opening: 'Any mention of pirates of the fair sex runs the immediate risk of awakening painful memories of the neighborhood production of some faded musical comedy, with its chorus line of obvious housewives posing as pirates and hoofing it on a briny deep of unmistakable cardboard' (*Universal History* 41). Then there is the author's selection of detail, which highlights the sensational and the archetypical: Widow Ching 'was a slinking woman, with sleepy eyes and a smile full of decayed teeth. Her blackish, oiled hair shone brighter than her eyes' (43). The crew of her vessel is a hardy, gambling lot: 'the[ir] fare ... consisted chiefly of ship biscuits, rats fattened on human flesh, and boiled rice,' and 'on days of battle,' 'gunpowder' mixed with 'their liquor.' 'With card games and loaded dice, with the metal square and bowl of fan-tan, with the little lamp and the pipe dreams of opium, they whiled away the time' (44–5). Finally, there is the staged, dramatic quality of the tale (as in 'Hakim of Merv') and the story-turning-into-story quality of the denouement. Describing the Widow Ching's surrender, Borges shows himself master of the *mise-en-scène*: surrounded by the imperial squadron flying 'airy dragons,' the widow Ching realizes that she has met her fate; she recalls the fable of the fox and the dragon, who concedes to the former's plea for protection even after 'long ingratitude and repeated transgressions,' and she determines to enter into the world of the fable, becoming herself part of the text. She throws down her swords, kneels down in a small boat, and demands to be rowed to the imperial flagship: 'It was dark; the sky was filled with dragons ... On climbing aboard, the widow murmured a brief sentence: "The fox seeks the dragon's wing"' (*Universal History* 48). The tale concludes then with this operatic gesture, with bits of history turned into legend. In *A Universal History of Infamy* Borges becomes perhaps the first Western writer since William Beckford in *Vathek* (1786) to realize the baroque possibilities of Eastern materials, which he then extends in his translations in other directions.

In our attempt to analyse mystery in these tales, different literary approaches present themselves. We can analyse its structure and dynamic; this approach tends toward a formalist, structuralist reading in which we look at mystery as an object. But such an approach becomes unsatisfactory because the boundaries of mystery exceed it. So we turn to an analysis of mystery as a discourse, as an event; this approach tends toward a phenomenological-hermeneutic approach, viewing the text of mystery as something incomplete that the reader must actualize in a performance. Throughout this chapter I have written 'Borges does this' or 'the tale is organized in this way'; this is a shorthand difficult to dispense with, and one that does convey a fundamental truth: there is a certain order of words on the page, and not another. However, it is the reader who actualizes and reconfigures the words (text), so it is the reader, just as much as the text (author), that is at the centre of mystery. The cultural aspect of mystery depends on an interpretive highlighting that derives from the concrete situation of the discursive event in conjunction with the reader's register of translation. This approach also meets its limitations, however; when mystery becomes, as it often does in Borges's texts, an inexhaustible and irresolvable interplay of concealment and revelation, then still another interpretive approach must be considered.

A third approach that is perhaps appropriate to mystery, in particular to Borges's treatment of it, is that of the 'traveling differential,' which explores incommensurabilities from within rather than without (Iser, *Range of Interpretation* 7–8). In this approach the reader seeks to comprehend the mystery through experiencing it. Borges himself seems to engage in this kind of interpretive translation and recomposition of the Oriental materials of his tales. In the preface to the 1954 edition of *Historia universal de la infamia*, he calls his composition 'baroque' and describes it as a 'style which deliberately exhausts ... all its possibilities and ... borders on its own parody' (11). He continues this line of thought, introducing a culturally specific, Eastern idea: 'The theologians of the Great Vehicle [in Buddhism] point out that the essence of the universe is emptiness. Insofar as they refer to that particle of the universe which is this book, they are entirely right. Scaffolds and pirates populate it, and the word "infamy" in the title is thunderous, but behind the sound and fury there is nothing. The book is no more than appearance, than a surface of images; for that very reason, it may prove enjoyable' (12). In the space of East–West intertextualities, the baroque and the Great Wheel meet, which is also the place of the reader's thought grasping the text of this world.

What and where is mystery? Borges translates it into the opposing registers of essence and emptiness. Mystery seems to promise a revelation, yet the revelation can be void of any significance; like the baroque, it may be a play of appearances. In its recursive process of concealment and revelation and its resistance to closure, perhaps mystery embodies something fundamentally Eastern. The nature of mystery would seem to lie in the play of signs and contexts, which is to say that it lies in the orientation of reader's experiences and expectations: to expect that there is something behind the mystery and that this something can be comprehended is a Western orientation; by contrast, to sense that behind the mystery there may be an incomprehensible emptiness is perhaps an Eastern one. For Borges – and for the reader – a travelling differential of suspense and deception, negation and affirmation moves the event of mystery forward, generating increasingly more refined differentiations while never arriving at a finality. The differential loses itself in the immeasurable, whose history these tales have just sketched. There is no end to mystery, and there is no end to its interplay of transcultural and culturally specific aspects – and that is because we enter from within. Mystery resembles Borges's definition of the aesthetic experience, which concludes his essay 'The Wall and the Books,' about legends surrounding the Chinese emperor Shih Huan Ti: 'Music, states of happiness, mythology, faces belabored by time, certain twilights and certain places try to tell us something, or have said something we should not have missed, or are about to say something; this imminence of a revelation which does not occur is, perhaps, the aesthetic phenomenon' (*Labyrinths* 188).[12] The play of presence and absence defines mystery, and for Borges, the reality that emerges through this aesthetic experience is the Orient.

'The very title of these pages,' Borges writes of the pieces in *Historia universal de la infamia*, 'flaunts their baroque character' (*Histoire universelle* 10). Using other terms that have become more popular today, we would say that these tales are postmodern in their playfulness, intertextuality, and self-reflexivity. In them the Oriental is something taken seriously – indeed it was a great inspiration to Borges – and something turned inside out, taken to the borders of parody. With this collection, written in the 1930s, Borges became the first Western writer to treat Oriental material in a postmodern fashion. Today we know that at the same time he was moving forward in that avant-garde, Borges was also looking back to the ancient world of mystery, Gnosticism, and Buddhism.

Aperçus of Other Orients

Gnosticism, Buddhism, the baroque and opera bouffa are registers of highlighting that I will single out in four pieces of Borges that reference and transform Oriental materials.[13] The first piece, 'El Apercamento de Almostásin' ('The Approach of Al-Mu'tasim') turns the book-review form into a meditation on spirituality and the enigma of infinity. The sources that Borges draws upon range from the purported Indian novel that serves as the inspiration for his reflections (i.e., *The Conversation with the Man Called al-Mu'tasim: A Game with Shifting Mirrors*), the Persian mystic Farid ud-Din Attar's *Parliament of Birds*, and Richard Burton's translation of the *Arabian Nights*. Borges describes the intrigue of *A Game with Shifting Mirrors* as the quest for a soul 'through the barely perceptible reflections cast by this soul in others': 'The nearer to al-Mu'tasim the men he examines are, the greater is their share of the divine, though it is understood that they are but mirrors (*Ficciones* 49). The Gnostic motif of descending and ascending mathematical mirroring recalls 'Hakim of Merv,' and as in other stories Borges gives the motif a transformative twist. Perhaps 'the Almighty is also in search of Someone, and that Someone of Someone above him (or Someone simply indispensable and equal)' (50). With neither beginning nor end to the chain, the seeker eventually becomes the sought. It may be all just a game; Borges accuses Mir Bahadur Ali, the Indian novel's author, of 'the grossest temptation of art – that of being a genius' (51). The profound and the trivial cannot be kept apart; like the title *Historia universal de la infamia*, there is perhaps only a lot of thunder, the proverbial sound and fury signifying nothing.

The second and third pieces, 'The Enigma of Edward FitzGerald' and 'Forms of a Legend,' treat Persian and Hindustani materials in a delightful inquiry into chance and interrelatedness; in these essays' transformations, life turns into an immense, timeless web of intersecting intrigues. How can one explain, Borges inquires, the 'collaboration' between an eleventh-century astronomer, Umar ben Ibrahim, and a nineteenth-century English writer, Edward FitzGerald, who transformed the astronomer's short verses into the *Rubáiyát*. Transmigration of souls, which Umar believed in, should not be ruled out as a possible explanation, given the alternatives: 'no less marvelous than these almost supernatural conjectures,' Borges states, 'is the assumption of benevolent destiny. At times, the clouds take the shape of mountains or lions; by analogy, the wistfulness of Edward FitzGerald, and a manuscript of yellowing paper [Umar's writings], in purple characters, forgotten in a vault of the Bodleian Library in Oxford, assume, for the good of us all, the shape of a poem' (*A Personal Anthology* 96). Which seems more astonishing, the bizarre workings of chance or the transmigration of a soul across eight centuries? As we know from *Qué es el Budismo*, Borges read the famous texts of Eastern religions and found limitless possibilities in the ideas of transmigration and reincarnation, which suggested to him a world in endless transformation where everything eventually turns into everything else. 'Any collaboration is mysterious,' he interjects. 'This one, of an Englishman and a Persian, was more so than any other, because the two were very different, and in life might not have achieved friendship; it was death and vicissitude and time that brought it about that one should know of the other and both become a single poet' (ibid.). Another essay, 'Forms of a Legend,' improvises upon Hindustani texts such as *Lalitavistara*, or 'The Detailed Account of a Game (of a Buddha).' '[F]or Mahayana Buddhism,' Borges remarks, 'the life of the Buddha on earth is a game or a dream, and the earth itself another dream' (ibid. 126). Borges passes these texts through the transformative prism of his own sensibility, yet it is not so much impressionism as an emergent Orient, neither subject nor object, that takes shape. The fusion between the spirit of Borges's writings and the concepts of Eastern religions interpreted from a Borgesian slant charms and captivates. Where Buddhism ends and Borges begins becomes a matter of perspective and accentuation, as in the legend of the man who set himself the task of mapping the world and ended up, inadvertently, drawing the lines of his own face. 'No one is extinguished in Nirvana,' Borges explains, 'for the extinction of innumerable beings in Nirvana is like the disappearance of a phantasmagoria which a magician at a crossroads creates by occult art; in another place it is written that everything is mere emptiness, mere name, including the book which says so and the man who reads it' (ibid. 127). It should be pointed out that Buddhism has a diversity of views; 'you do not find a unified front in the Buddhist teachings on the nature of the universe or the nature of the world,' the Dalai Lama points out (Hayward and Varela, *Gentle Bridges* 37). So again it should be emphasized that Borges is both translating Buddhism (i.e., the subject matter) and using certain aspects of Buddhist views that coincide with his own sensibility (i.e., the register) to comment on texts and the world (i.e., subject matter), underscoring the illusive, game-like quality that emerges from these Eastern concepts in the process of the translation. The collapse, or near collapse, of the subject matter into the register is precisely the intertextuality of the world that typifies the problematic of Borges's approach and viewpoint, where the Gnosticism, Buddhism, the baroque, and opera bouffa circulate between the poles of profundity and parody. Thus, the legend (of the essay's title) changes into self-exposing, mirror-like legend – 'I should not be surprised if my story of the legend were legendary,' Borges says, tongue in cheek (*A Personal Anthology* 127). But he has already told us the compensatory qualification: 'Reality may be too complex for oral transmission; legend recreates it in a manner which is only accidentally false' (ibid. 122).

A fourth and final piece, 'El Zahir,' again illustrates this near collapse of subject matter and register in Borges's improvisations and translations of Oriental materials. Not only in terms of themes, with the familiar Borgesian motifs of labyrinths, obsessions, and the search for an absolute, but also narratively speaking, the story contains both traditional and postmodern elements. In the first paragraph we are told that the Zahir is a coin, worth twenty centavos, and we are told of its transformations. In different cities throughout the East it has been, variously, a tiger, a blind man, an astrolabe, a compass, a vein in a marble pillar, and the bottom of a well. The Eastern ideas of reincarnation and interrelatedness take form in the Zahir and in Clementina Villar, of whom the narrator is enamoured. Clementina 'was in search of the Absolute,' the narrator explains. 'She was forever experimenting with new metamorphoses, as though trying to get away from herself; the color of her hair and the shape of her coiffure were celebratedly unstable. She was always changing her smile, her complexion, the slant of her eyes' (*Labyrinths* 157). Indeed, the tale has the obsessive quality of a love story, if one can speak of a love story turned into a philosophical and aesthetic quest. '[M]oved to tears' by her death, the narrator, after attending Clementina's wake, comes into possession of the Zahir, given to him as change when he pays for a drink in a bar. In Arabic *Zahir* means 'notorious' or 'visible,' the narrator claims; it stands for 'one of the ninety-nine names of God, and the people (in Muslim territories) use it to signify "beings or things which possess the terrible property of being unforgettable, and whose image finally drives one mad"' (161). In a still different sense, the Zahir embodies a 'repertory of possible futures' and the infinite in the finite (159).

Beginning with the banality of a twenty-centavo coin, this tale translates a romantic obsession into the registers of Eastern religion and philosophy. The narrator draws on Tennyson, who sees the world in a flower: 'Perhaps he meant that no fact, however insignificant, does not involve universal history and the infinite concatenation of cause and effect' (*Labyrinths* 163). The Romantic poet William Blake or Buddhist thought, as in these lines from the Avamtasaka, would have served equally well: 'To see in an atom, / And in each atom, / The totality of worlds / Is something inconceivable' (Ricard and Trinh, *L'Infini* 108). The subject matter and the register collapse; it is the story's magic (or folly) to show that seemingly unrelated things are interconnected in the weave and weft of history and fate, a dominant motif of *Historia universal de la infamia* as well the various Eastern sources upon which Borges draws. Does the reader interpret the mystery as a revelation or a deception? 'In the empty hours I can still walk through the streets,' the narrator concludes. 'In order to lose themselves in God, the Sufis [Islamic mystics] recite their own names, or the ninety-nine divine names, until they become meaningless. I long to travel that path. Perhaps I shall conclude by wearing away the Zahir simply through thinking of it again and again. Perhaps behind the coin I shall find God' (*Labyrinths* 164). In its dizzy movement from concrete to abstract, from finite to infinite, 'El Zahir' recalls 'Hakim of Merv' and 'The Approach of Al-Mu'tasin'; Gnosticism, Buddhism, and other Eastern thought serve as translational registers carrying the tales into a space of postmodernist game. The world is absorbed into the text. Subject matter and register collapse, and the liminal space or emerging reality – the Orient that the tale effectuates in the interpretive space linking author, text, and reader – becomes essence or emptiness. Behind the mystery we should not expect to find either subject or object; nirvana, Borges explains in *Qué es el Budismo*, also means extinction.

In sum, the fiction of Borges shows a double translation. Borges himself was orientalized by his readings of texts like *The Thousand and One Nights* and Buddhist scriptures; he translated himself toward the world of these texts. Using those registers of thought and conceptualization, he in turn postmodernized these Orients into a fictional landscape of enigma and paradox. Except for a single trip to Japan, at which time he was already blind, he never visited or lived in Asia, so it was principally through his enormous love of books that he absorbed and fashioned a sense of the Orient as a great book of stories, an intertext so extensive that it contains the world. This is an idea that has an ideological side, but for Borges, who was not interested in politics and did not turn his fiction in that direction, it tends more toward the pole of utopian and dystopian possibilities. The reader completes the text, but that does not mean that the reader has a 100 per cent say in interpreting a story. With Borges you must, to a certain degree, either take it or leave it, yet there may be still a third and more felicitous alternative: let your *karma*, so to speak, lead the way. Or, as Olivier Le Naire recommends in a review of recently published books about the author entitled 'Éternel Borges,' enter the labyrinth haphazardly: pick a book of Borges from the library shelf, open it randomly to any story, and let your pleasure and imagination be your guides.

2. 'Without Stopping': The Orient as Liminal Space in Paul Bowles

For Jorge Luis Borges, the Orient is a text; for Paul Bowles, it is an experience – an experience against the grain, an experience of transformation. Bowles is unique among North American authors, and perhaps among twentieth-century Western artists, for he distinguished himself not only as a writer of fiction but also as a composer of piano concertos, sonatas, opera, ballets, film scores, and incidental music for the theatre. During the course of these artistic pursuits Bowles also became the United States' pre-eminent expatriate, travelling and sojourning in Europe, Africa, Asia, and Central America, and living in Tangier, Morocco, for a period of more than fifty years. In his fiction and travel writings about North Africa (the Maghreb), Bowles brought a new perspective from the 'periphery' to American literature and contributed to bringing international attention to Maghrebine cultures by way of his numerous translations from Moghrebi into English and his collaborations with local writers and artists.

To use the rubric 'Orientalist' to designate the fascination with non-Western cultures and imaginaries that one finds in the writings of Jorge Luis Borges and Paul Bowles is to run the risk of being immediately misunderstood. The one thing I do *not* mean by calling Bowles an Orientalist is the one thing that Orientalism for the past twenty-five years has become a code for: racism and imperialist sentiment. In his landmark study *Orientalism*, Edward Said set up the equation that still remains in place, at least to a certain degree: Europeans – the West generally – have tended to reduce Asian, North African, and Eastern Mediterranean peoples and places to a set of essences and stereotypes. Some scholars have challenged this thesis, among them John M. MacKenzie, who in *Orientalism: History, Theory and the Arts* (1995) considers the transformation of the term, which in the wake of Said's influential work has become 'one of the most ideologically charged words in modern scholarship' (4). MacKenzie's own study, as well as those of other scholars – Dennis Porter, *Haunted Journeys: Desire and Transgression in European Travel Writing* (1991); Mary Louise Pratt, *Imperial Eyes: Travel Writing and Transculturation* (1992); Billie Melman, *Women's Orients: English Women and the Middle East* (1992); Lisa Lowe, *Critical Terrains: French and British Orientalisms* (1991) – have broken apart the monolith of Orientalism and shown its complicated contours and contradictions. Porter, for example, in his analysis of travel writing, has focused less on stereotypes than on the mixture of emotions bound up in travel and the traveller's incertitude and estrangement. Such writing may be interpreted as 'a form of experimentation at and beyond established limits'; rather than 'obliteration of otherness,' a 'self-transformation' of the traveller inevitably begins to take place 'through a dialogic engagement with alien modes of life' (quoted in MacKenzie 22). Similarly, Pratt, Melman, and Lowe have demonstrated the diversity within Orientalist discourses as well as the modifying effect of cultural encounters on individual identity. Scholars have pointed out the implication of Orient in Occident and the two-way nature of their dialogue and exchange; one need only consider, for instance, the contributions of Arabo-Islamic culture and civilization to European civilization during the Middle Ages. MacKenzie notes that Said acknowledges this interaction, but fails to draw out its consequences:

> [He] recognizes that the traffic cannot all be one way, that Orientalism was forming the West as well as the Orient. The East 'has helped to define Europe,' [and] has been an 'integral part of European *material* civilisation and culture,' a 'sort of surrogate and even underground self,' at times (as for the Romantics) even a means of regenerating the West. Thus the discourse of Orientalism seems to go further than merely highlighting the alleged superiorities of Europe. It can modify and therefore surely even challenge the West. Said never follows through the logic of this, that the example of the Orient can become the means for a counter-western discourse, that it can offer opportunities for literary extension, spiritual renewal and artistic development. Thus the Orient, or at least its discourse, has the capacity to become the tool of cultural revolution, a legitimising source of resistance to those who challenge western conventions, introspection and complacency. (*Orientalism* 10)

In short, there is, MacKenzie contends, 'a complexity of western approaches to the East' that Said's analysis does not take into account (xviii). These approaches resist ready classification. They may be mixed in their effects or have nothing whatsoever to do with racist sentiment and imperialist attitudes; they may go against the grain, and they may be primarily utopian rather than ideological. Representation and translation, we have said in the introduction, constitute two complementary yet opposing tendencies; the one identifies and clarifies, the other changes and reconstitutes. In terms of Paul Bowles's works, especially his travel writings and short fiction, how do these tendencies interact, and what part do his expatriate lifestyle and half-century sojourn in North Africa, as well as his dual profession as musical composer and author, play in the Orients that emerge in these works?

Bowles's works show a complex space of Orients with different aspects and significances – some intensely personal, others cultural and social in a larger sense – among which we certainly find the following. First, an artistic, inspirational aspect: Bowles drew inspiration from the terrains (cityscapes, landscapes) and the cultural juxtapositions and interactions of North Africa and other Eastern or East-West places. They were to him a muse of sorts. Furthermore, he found in them – this is the second aspect – a fertile ground in which to cultivate his particular existentialist and sublime sensibilities. I use the word 'sublime' in the sense of Jean-François Lyotard (who has borrowed it from the Romantics), as a combination of awe and terror: 'a fundamental disagreement between that which Reason can think and that which can be imagined or felt' (Zima, *The Philosophy of Modern Literary Theory* 178). Third, an alterity: for Bowles the Orient is *not* an occasion for composing fictions that demonstrate or are imbued with a sense of Western superiority; quite the contrary, he rebelled against and sought to escape from things North American and European. The Orient was a line of escape, an entryway into an 'underground self,' and a means by which the expatriate living in Tangier set himself apart from things Western. The Orient is thus a space of alterity that he transforms into a counter-Western discourse in his writings. Fourth, a nomadic aspect: although cultural binaries like East and West never disappear completely in his works, there is a sense in which he goes beneath and beyond them to touch his most profound subject matter: the terror and wonder of existence, both of which the nomad perhaps feels more deeply than the man sheltered at home. For Bowles the Orient is the sublime, a shifting of registers of apprehension that undermines the safe and the certain with the sinister. In the Maghreb he was to find a place that combined for him destiny, magic, and 'invisibility'; he never intended that his sojourn there become permanent, yet it extended from weeks to months to years, becoming a continuing act of cross-cultural translation of experiences. It is not by chance that so many of his works of the 1960s, 1970s, 1980s, and 1990s are in fact translations from various languages, especially Moghrebi; the translator is someone who puts him/herself in the skin of another person and experiences other lives. In this respect Bowles's autobiography *Without Stopping* could not be better entitled: his life journey moves from West to East, but the East, no matter how much it might be valued, is not the final destination. The Orient is itself not one term of a binary, but rather a liminal space, a place of translation and transposition into something else, call it a sense of the sublime or a nomadism. Non-European places (like the Maghreb) serve as the inspiration, the detonator, and the sustaining environment for Bowles's existentialist questioning and wandering. Perhaps more succinctly and exotopically[1] than any other Western author, he has evoked in his writings an end of modernity for which Oriental terrains are not only the setting but the vital inspiration.

Bowles's fascination with things Oriental, or with the non-Western and with non-patterned consciousness in general, should be placed in the context of his rejection of the American way – at least the America in which he grew up and from which, in 1929 while a freshman at the University of Virginia, he staged his first escape. In *Without Stopping* Bowles recounts/fictionalizes his fateful decision in memorable fashion:

> I got back to my room one afternoon at dusk and, upon opening the door, knew at once, although I had no idea of what it was going to be, that I was about to do something explosive and irrevocable. It occurred to me that this meant that I was not the I I thought I was or, rather, that there was a second I in me who had suddenly assumed command. I shut the door and gave a running leap up on the bed, where I stood, my heart pounding. I took out a quarter and tossed it spinning into the air, so that it landed on my palm. Heads. I cried out with relief and jumped up and down on the mattress several times before landing on the floor. Tails would have meant that I would have had to take a bottle of Allonal that night and leave no note. But heads meant I would leave for Europe as soon as possible. (77–8)

Paris was the first destination, although France and Europe came to serve as stops along the way to a more distant, culturally more complicated terminus: North Africa. In *Without Stopping* Bowles writes engagingly of his fascination with the Maghreb and of his preoccupation, in dreams, with the Strait of Gibraltar, at the entrance of which lies Tangier, where he ended up living most of his life. 'Since my early childhood it had been a fantasy of mine to dream a thing in such detail that it would be possible to bring it across the frontier intact,' he confesses (ibid. 165–6). Just as in Borges's 'Las ruinas circulares' ('The Circular Ruins'), which Bowles was the first to translate into English, the dream becomes reality. He was drawn to Morocco as if by the hidden springs of his unconscious, and the place became 'magical' for that reason, among others. It was a landscape in which he could move back and forth between East and West, and between the everyday and the sublime.

He was sceptical that a Westerner could penetrate the thought and experience of Eastern cultures, and his fiction recounts misunderstanding much as it presents any realization of an alternative, non-Western way of thinking and living. In his sojourn in North Africa and in his scepticism for the Western project of progress, Bowles found disturbing perspectives from which to observe and write about the post–Second World War, one in which everything had become implicated in everything else – the International Zone of *Let It Come Down* is a prescient metaphor of this – and in which Europe and America could never again be confident of the supremacy of their values. At a time of American hegemony in the decades following the war, Bowles exposed American and Western arrogance as a cultural debility, and showed the weakness of the Western viewpoint when confronted by an alien environment where the cultural and social props on which it depends vanish. It was Bowles's 'genius,' Gore Vidal comments, 'to suggest the horrors that lie beneath [the] floor [of our ramshackle civilization], as fragile, in its way, as the sky that shelters us from a devouring vastness' (Bowles, *Collected Stories* iv). Ahead of the times, Bowles scrutinized the kind of American vulnerabilities (i.e., a confident action orientation) that Fredric Jameson singles out in his foreword to Karatani Kojin's *Origins of Modern Japanese Literature*: '[Americans] need to cultivate a new kind of "national" inferiority complex of the superstate. We need to train ourselves to be vulnerable in some new and original sense, to be passive-receptive, weak, un-American, susceptible to boundless influence by currents from foreign countries and distant cultures' (xx). Certainly, the events of September 11, 2001, change the way that we read those remarks and probably too the way we read Bowles. In his fiction any discussion of the 'Orient as alternative way' must be connected with a scrutiny of Western values in the aftermath of the Second World War and the advent of U.S. hegemony. In as much as, at that time, American confidence rested on a reliance on action and a casting of cultural others in familiar American images, so Bowles's fiction of this period shows the inefficacy of action and evokes the strangeness of others, who elude attempts to set them within the pattern of a familiar world. The result is breakdown. The Orient acts as a detonator that sets off a collapse whose cause is a structural (intellectual and cultural) weakness in Americans abroad: the professor of 'A Distant Episode' (1945), Kit in *The Sheltering Sky* (1949), and Dyar in *Let It Come Down* (1952), among others. In this respect Bowles's work looks presciently forward; today these phenomena, of which certain vulnerabilities of Americans are but one aspect, are no longer abroad only; they are also found at home. So we should interpret not only what is *behind* his fiction but also what lies *in front* of it.

Bowles's critique of modernity goes hand-in-hand with his exploration of other, non-Western ways of apprehending and living in the world. As a sojourner, someone in-between, Bowles can be passive – un-Americanly passive, as Jameson might say – adopting the attitude of the observer, a kind of 'invisible spectator' (to use Bowles's own turn of phrase)[2] of the multicultural world about him. Exploring boundaries and debilities, Bowles simultaneously undermines 'white mythologies' of America and Europe and writes an end-of-modernity fiction.[3] By way of various techniques, his stories upset and overturn, questioning our beliefs in reason and the utility of action to resolve problems: the use of unusual and disorienting points of view, sinister atmospheres that bespeak a malevolence, landscapes that dwarf human presence and pretensions, the simulation of drug experiences and alternative states of consciousness, shocking turns of events and unexpected violence of a cruelty that snaps the imagination. 'I believe unhappiness should be studied very carefully,' Bowles has remarked; 'this is certainly no time for anyone to pretend to be happy, or to put his unhappiness away in the dark' (quoted in Sawyer-Lauçanno, *An Invisible Spectator* 299). Bowles often reverses Western perspectives, seeing the world not from a position of security and comfort but from insecurity and distress; 'how the inhabitants of alien cultures regard the creatures of our civilized world' is a key theme of his works, Gore Vidal observes in the introduction to the *Collected Stories* (iv). Here we have the suggestion of the inside and outside of Bowles's Orients: the inside is a movement toward transformation, toward a deepening recognition of others (i.e., non-Western cultures); the outside is a movement away from the values of modernity, of North America and the West, toward a nomad discourse, itself a translation with a horizontal movement that in principle need never cease.

What enabled Bowles to be so uncanny in his insights? It probably helps to have a mean father and to be an only child in a repressive, solitary environment; as Bowles recollects in his autobiography: 'Daddy was for unremitting firmness. This he called common sense. "It stands to reason," he maintained. "A kid will always go as far as you let him." [He], however ... overlooked the fact that at the age of five I had never yet even spoken to another child or seen children playing together' (*Without Stopping* 23). Bowles learned something about power right from the start, and he also learned about the necessity to fight back on his own terms and in his own ways. The young Paul, having taught himself to read – or so the adult recollects – enjoyed perusing newspaper reports and then locating the distant places mentioned on maps. He liked word games, and at age eight he wrote a story about a woman named Bluey Laber Dozlen: 'During her first year she has many illnesses and recoveries, several marriages and divorces, and becomes a spy. During the second year she learns to play bridge and smoke opium' (ibid. 35). After various adventures she hides away in Hong Kong, trying to elude a 'vengeful housemaid.' Daddypapa, Paul's paternal grandfather, who read in French and Spanish and who boasted, during a certain period in his youth, of never having slept twice in the same city, seems to have become a role model. The grandfather owned three houses on Seneca Lake in upper-state New York; when Paul visited he would admire the houses' exotic objects, such as Chinese lanterns, and revel in the sounds of the countryside, the 'song of the katydids' and waves lapping against the lake's cliffs: 'It was good to wake up in the night and hear that music all around me in the air,' he recalls (19). It is perhaps music in the largest sense that opens for Bowles receptivity and a range of shifting perspectives. Music is itself a translation almost 'without stopping'; it is the art par excellence of movement – in time rather than in space. So the composer, writer, and voyager meet in these metaphors of movement. Bowles's long sojourn in North Africa, coupled with his keen interest in its folk culture, especially its music, show a certain parallel. Perhaps it was, above all, this musical appreciation of Morocco that enabled him to appreciate other aspects of the country's cultural heritage. He often records his observations about place with a musician's ear; in a letter (spring 1935) to

William Treat Upton, he writes of folk music's importance to the reinvigoration of the Western art-song:

> Art-music will get what it needs not from new subjects to sing about ... nor from technical devices ... but from new ways to sing, which means that it will be increasingly conscious of folk-musics of all corners of the globe, particularly the now unfamiliar corners. The Italian idea will be one among scores of others. Singers will have to master the cante Flamenco, the difficult Chleuh songs, the Annamite lyrics, the Mexican, Cuban, and other Latin-Indian tricks, as well as the Central African declamation and the myriad of Arab innuendoes (to mention a few of the more important styles), in order to sing what should be written in the near future if the solo art-song is to be expected to remain in existence. (*In Touch: The Letters of Paul Bowles* 158–9)

Decades before 'world music' Bowles shows an insight into the direction that popular music will take in the second half of the twentieth century, and the reader wonders whether, without this musical sensibility, Bowles the writer would have been as open to or potentially comprehending of cultural differences. Another example merits quoting: in a letter of December 1947 to Peggy Glanville-Hicks, Bowles describes with a composer's ear the sounds of a morning in Fez, translating its 'music' into verbal representation:

> [T]he city ... lies below, very slowly disengaging itself from the ... mist and smoke, while a million cocks crow at once, constantly. There is also the faint sound of water in the fountains of the palace gardens ... I'm a great lover of natural sounds, and they have been present to fill the spaces which otherwise would have been only silence. Wind, water, birds and animals, and (here) human voices, make a fine auditory backdrop. The human voices make the most beautiful sound of all, when the muezzin calls during the night, especially the one for dawn ... They preface the actual *mouddin* with religious remarks, sung in freely embroidered florid style, each man inventing his own key, mode, appoggiatura and expressive devices. And when you have a hundred or more of those incredibly high, piercing, bird-like voices doing flamenco-like runs in different keys, from different minarets, against a background of cocks crowing, you have a very special and strange sound. (*Letters* 181)

When one listens to a place, as Bowles does here in Fez, one becomes less likely to impose on it the attitudes or stereotypes that one's own culture has prepared; to listen and hear is to enter a recursive cycle of translation of sounds into emotions and ideas. It is to enter a town, to wonder about its people, and to begin to appreciate their identities.

Voyages as Performance: Mimesis versus Translation

Voyages were part of Bowles's nomadic way of life, and they pervade his fiction, personal correspondence, and, of course, travel writing. His work is interesting in its own right as a challenge to Western attitudes and ways of thinking and as an exploration of Orients; here I want to consider it from the angle of travel-writing theory, especially from the dual perspectives of representation and translation. Bowles's fiction and travel writing use the figure of the traveller/sojourner and the narrative of his/her encounters in an alien place to reveal the limitations of the self; in these works Bowles views the individual less as an autonomous consciousness than as an interdependent relation that is incomplete and in need of continual (re)interpretation. Travel or voyage can be analysed as a performance (i.e., the manner of reacting to an environment and events): this process will be mimetic to the degree that the traveller responds in keeping with, and reinforces, his or her own cultural frameworks and prejudgments; it will be translational to the degree that he or she engages in a recursive loop of interpretation and is changed or transformed. On this point, Bowles's fiction converges from his travel writing: confronted by the new and the alien, his fictional traveller-protagonists tend to respond mimetically rather than translationally, and this often leads to failure, even cruelty and horror. For whatever reason – and one of them may simply be that Bowles, in the course of decades of living in North Africa, became himself a knowledgeable and open-minded traveller – his travelogues and essays of travel writing present many more instances where travel shows itself clearly as a translation that provokes repatternings and transformations of the traveller. Taken together, his fiction and travel writing critique a double illusion, individual autonomy and total cultural translatability, but they do this from different poles, one of them depicting travel as chiefly mimetic and the other showing it as rather more translational.

Mimesis reproduces, whereas translation repatterns: travel as performance can be viewed within this range of possibilities. In terms of mimesis, one initial question that we might ask, although it sounds trivial, is whether or not there is a difference between the responses of tourists (i.e., those who take a tour) and those of travellers (i.e., those who take an extended trip whose itinerary they have devised). We are all tourists at one time or another; in fact, it has become harder and harder not to be one, so I am not using this term automatically in a demeaning manner. However, tourists would seem to be less the authors of their voyages than consumers of a prefabricated script of sights and activities. The rationale, or generative desire, of the tour is largely imitative: tourists desire to see and do those things that others like them have seen and done. If the voyage as tour package does anything more than reinforce the tourists' identity and cultural and social predilections, it accomplishes this secondarily, because its primary purpose is to gratify the tourists' desires and to bring back their business another time. We might say that the tour as performative process operates at the conjunction of the tourists' sense of self, their idealization of their destination, and the spectacle of that place as it is presented and staged by the apparatuses of tourism within the locale. Tourism tends toward imitation; a cultural code is reproduced, though more subtlely than Umberto Eco would seem to suggest in his facetious observation that a visitor to Disney World 'must agree to behave like its robots' ('City' 479).

Tourism is mimetic, but travel as an extended, self-programmed voyage is also mimetic, at least to a degree; in the case of travel, it is simply more difficult to locate the model of imitation. To be 'on the road' does not mean to escape the bounds of cultural codes and frameworks, for although the road in travel literature has often been equated romantically with freedom, the travellers' embodiment in a particular culture and society affects the arrow of the compass and arrives with them no matter how distant their destination. The travellers' subjectivity, like the tourists,' is problematic; desire is not inherently independent, but rather it responds to someone or something at 'home,' that is, within the travellers' home culture and network of experiences. French philosopher René Girard contends that desire is always 'mediated,' and this mediation founds the intersubjectivity of human relationships; belief in a 'quasi-divine ego' and 'spontaneous desire' turns out to be an illusion. 'The objective and subjective fallacies are one and the same,' Girard argues; 'both originate in the image which we all have of our own desires. Subjectivisms, idealisms and positivisms appear to be in opposition but are secretly in agreement to conceal the presence of the mediator' (*The Girard Reader* 43). Tourists and travellers may be differentiated in other ways, however. Whereas tourists tend not to abandon their pre-voyage status and identity – in fact, the voyage takes its hidden meaning as an attempted reaffirmation, in one way or another, of an idealized model of that identity – travellers who sojourn sufficiently long in foreign places may adopt an imitative model shaped by the 'foreign' culture and society of their sojourn. This imitation might then become cross-cultural or transcultural, but it would need to do so by way of a translational process. For the traveller-sojourner, the voyage as performative process may lead to a transformed identity or an alternate lifestyle rather than a reaffirmation of an idealized self situated in the home culture.

The concept of mimesis may have a certain potential, then, to differentiate travel experiences and to clarify their significance. For an interesting illustration of this, I turn to the history of European relations with China during the sixteenth century and specifically to the life of the Jesuit Matteo Ricci. During that era, Europeans, whether merchants or missionaries, had had little success rebuilding relations with China established centuries before (in the thirteenth century by way of the papal emissaries and the precursors of Marco Polo) and thereby reopening the country to exchanges with the West. Only in the seventeenth century, with the missionary work of Father Ricci, did Europe begin to get a foothold in the Middle Kingdom, and then only because Ricci, who chose to dress like a mandarin and to learn to speak Chinese, visibly assimilated himself to the imperial culture and won the confidence of its authorities. It would seem that the insistence of earlier missionaries and travellers on sticking to the models of their home culture rather than adopting Chinese models of behaviour, at least in certain visible things such as dress and language for communicative purposes, played an instrumental part in the resistance of the 'foreign' culture to Western plans. 'The Italian Jesuit was ... the first to comprehend that Europeans would be able to make themselves acceptable to the Chinese only if they presented themselves as similar and shared with them a common culture,' Muriel Détrie explains:

> The key that finally permitted the opening of China was neither cannons nor merchandise nor money, but rather the European recognition of Chinese civilization and their submission to its conventions. In learning Chinese, in adopting mandarin dress rather than the robes of Buddhist monks, in studying the Classics that are the indispensable trappings of a learned person, Matteo Ricci succeeded in overcoming the Chinese mistrust and winning their acceptance and even respect. (Boothroyd and Détrie, *Le Voyage en Chine* 82)

This extraordinary example takes us beyond the limit of mimesis and into the domain of translation. For it would be more accurate to say that Father Ricci chose to translate himself – or at least visible aspects of his cultural allegiances – into the foreign culture, and in turn he was repatterned and transformed. When a traveller chooses to assimilate aspects of a foreign culture, this assimilation must pass by way of translation, because the frameworks of the home and the foreign cultures differ; they may contain correspondences, but they also contain incongruences that have to be negotiated.

A concept of travel as mimetic process has the advantage of dismantling the romantic notion of the traveller as free and autonomous, while it has the disadvantage of not being able to account for or deal with the imbalances and transformations that occur during the voyage, especially when travellers are receptive and responsive to their experiences and allow themselves to be pulled by the tensions between the home and foreign cultures to the degree that the process becomes recursive – and consequently modifying and translational. Travellers must shuttle, cognitively speaking, between 'the familiar and the alien'; as a mode of managing experiences, the 'recursive loop' dominates in such a situation, when the subject matter to be translated is culture itself and when, as in travel, the context remains open and constantly changes (Iser, *Range of Interpretation* 173–4). Various possibilities present themselves, depending on the receptivity of travellers and on their capability and willingness to enter a cross-cultural discourse and to engage in a translation of cultures. First, if travellers are relatively closed to foreignness and locked in a mimesis of their home culture, they will likely project their own frames of reference onto the foreign culture. This reproduction of the home culture short-circuits the recursive loop, although the loop cannot be shut down completely; to be in a foreign place is not the same thing as being at home, and the imbalance generated by the unfamiliar reconnects the circuits of the loop. Second, if the travellers – this time more open-minded – seek to chart the foreign culture, to bring it within their immediate reach but not interact with it or comprehend it in any depth, then much information about the culture that a recursive collecting of and reflecting on information might generate will be screened off or discarded. In this instance travellers attempt to deal with the foreign culture by setting up representational categories; the noise of the familiar thereby gets quieted, but resurges every time the categories, through new experience, become unstable. Third, if, however, the aim of travellers is 'to grasp otherness, then the operation will be powered by a positive feedback loop' (ibid. 103). This translation will be ongoing, modifying itself all the time. Representation/mimesis and translation counterpoise different tendencies, with the former aiming at a stabilizing of the foreign or the disruptively unfamiliar through categorization, and the latter tending toward a management of unfamiliarity through a recursive processing of feedback and the devising of increasingly more refined differentiations as registers of comprehension. The concepts of mimesis and translation, then, would seem to bring to the foreground basic processes of responding to the unfamiliar and the alien in travel and travel writing, to a detailed analysis of which the chapter now turns.

Voyages in Bowles's Fiction

Bowles's narratives of voyage de-romanticize the traveller and dismantle the modern belief in the individual as an autonomous self; in these stories, published during a period of the dissolution of European empires in the late 1940s and early 1950s, the imperial-colonial equation, which often worked to privilege and protect nineteenth-century European voyagers, breaks down, revealing the Western traveller's vulnerability in alien contexts. The barrier separating European and non-European, colonizer and colonized, weakens, no longer demarcating clear, unquestioned, unambiguous identities. Voyages split the Western self from its cultural, social base and set it adrift in another space where anything can occur. What often occurs is violence, because the world of Bowles's stories extends in one direction toward a naturalistic view of the individual at odds with society, with its reflex toward victimization and scapegoating, and in another direction toward an intersubjective view of consciousness whose desires and ambitions evolve mimetically in relation to those of others. When the individual – in Bowles's stories, the Westerner especially – becomes cut off from his cultural, social context, a possibility that travel in a foreign land always presents, he becomes disoriented and capable of a range of mimetic transformations. The egocentred point of view of the Western 'I' is dismantled and shown in all its vulnerabilities.

Several of Bowles's North African fictions, including 'A Distant Episode' (1945), a tale about the short-circuiting of home culture, use journeys to effect inversions from normalcy to disorientation and horror and to expose the fallacies of conceptions of the self as autonomous entity. The tale explores a transformation of consciousness, reflecting on how swiftly such a change can take place and how short is the distance between safety and rationality, on one hand, and captivity and madness, on the other. Individual identity is less firm and settled than we imagine; it can be cracked open and rendered formless with surprising ease, such a story seems to say. Exemplifying this demythification of identity, the plot runs as follows: an American linguistics professor returns to a Saharan desert town that he had visited ten years before; soon after his arrival he and a café waiter, who promises to show him where he can obtain some special souvenirs, go out for a walk. At nightfall the two men leave the town for the surrounding desert and canyons; the waiter turns back, but the professor continues on and descends a path into a gorge where he is suddenly attacked by dogs, knocked off his feet, and bound and gagged by members of a notorious desert tribe of the region, the Reguiba. The next morning, with one stroke of the knife, his tongue is cut out, and he is dumped in a bag and slung across the side of a camel. Days pass, a sack is put over his head and he is led away with a rope around his neck. Weeks and months transpire, by the end of which the professor has gradually become a buffoon who performs antics of idiocy at the *caravansérail*. In this fable-like tale, the tables are completely turned: power turns into powerlessness, rationality succumbs to the irrational. A tale of defamiliarization and horror, 'A Distant Episode' has the resonance of a parable about Western vulnerability and incomprehension; here the Orient is a world beyond, distant from Western ways of knowing and being.

We commonly think of travel as an act of power, for it is not the powerless who cross continents and oceans, but those who have the means and the ambition. Certainly this was true of the imperial period in modern Western history; this sense of power is sometimes unfounded, though. In 'A Distant Episode' the professor begins his journey within an illusion: that this region of North Africa to which he returns is a terrain in which his identity, his knowledge, and his money lend him a status and authority, a certain shield of protection. But identity derives from place and society, and in this place – distant from the safety of the hotel, much less from home in the United States – the professor is an alien, and he is not sufficiently imaginative to comprehend his vulnerability. His mimetic models lie in the home culture, not in the foreign place in which he journeys; his points of reference are the Western-style hotel and the town, not the unpoliced territory beyond it. He believes that the net of culture and society still protects him and fails to realize that he has crossed into a liminal space where signs and power relations have shifted. Even before his capture, the desert world seems to stun him, as if it is beyond his interpretative capability: he 'had come to the other side of the town, on the promontory above the desert, and through a great rift in the wall the Professor saw the white endlessness, broken in the foreground by dark spots of oasis' (*Collected Stories* 41). A traveller must constantly negotiate the distance (a kind of semantic blank) between his point of departure (the home culture) and his place of arrival (the foreign culture). The professor fails in this act of interpretation, and he pays for the failure. As he stands at 'the edge of the abyss,' his instincts tell him to return to the road and to home, but instead, he spits and then urinates into the depth below, where a nomadic community lives. Such as they are, these are his final acts of hubris, in imitation of a model of behaviour appropriate to the powerful and the protected, to the imperial not the post-colonial traveller. The professor continues walking toward an unmapped world that is in fact an emptiness within as much as outside him: 'Only the wind was left behind, above, to wander among the trees, to blow through the dusty streets of Aïn Tadouirt, into the hall of the Grand Hotel Saharien, and under the door of his little room. It occurred to him that he ought to ask himself why he was doing this irrational thing' (43). All the events that follow are steps into a different reality, which is always the direction of travel, but here the transformation is total because the traveller too, not just the landscape and the society, undergoes a radical, forced change. When the professor, a linguist, has his tongue cut out, he loses language – the power to reproduce the home culture – and with it his identity. In 'utter stupor' he is shocked into a state of mind that 'permitted no thought' (45). Without the capacity to reproduce his culture, which holds within it his identity, he devolves into a creature without volition; his captors string metal plates around his body and begin to train him to perform like a dancing bear. He obeys their orders and mimics their gestures: '[He] was no longer conscious; to be exact, he existed in the middle of the movements made by these other men' (46). He remains in this mimetic state until one day, while locked in a room, he hears someone speaking a vaguely familiar language, French, and at that point Western culture, if not the home culture per se, re-enters his existence: 'pain began to stir again in his being' (47). The pain intensifies, changing into a delirium and rage; this culminates when he sees something written in the vaguely familiar language on a calendar on the wall. With Western culture's return, he feels the hole within his being: he used to be somebody, someplace, but now he cannot speak and can only reproduce the gestures and expressions of an idiot. At the end of the tale, he breaks out of his confinement and races chaotically across the desert.

Mimesis functions in a noteworthy way in this story. The power of the imperial traveller derives from a reproduction of the home culture, including, among other things, its language. Deprived of that model – and this situation is shown symbolically in the story by the severing of the professor's tongue – he loses his culture and with it his identity. In hyperbolic form this is the existential plight of the traveller – unable to communicate with those in a foreign land, dressed in a manner that raises objections or hilarity, and isolated without a community. Elsewhere Bowles has remarked, after having observed a Moroccan brotherhood ceremony in which participants entered into trances, that 'a human being is not an entity and that his interpretation of exterior phenomena is meaningless unless it is shared by the other members of his cultural group' (*Without Stopping* 151). Interpreting 'A Distant Episode' from the perspective of the voyage as a performative process, one of whose poles is mimesis, highlights these questions about culture and identity; in addition, it also lends itself to a post-colonial reading that would go something like this. In this tale the tables are turned: not only do the powerful become the powerless, but the model of imitation is also reversed. In the colony, the colonized are expected to adopt the model of the colonizer; here the imperial traveller is forced to imitate not the colonized but a subhuman model, that of a trained animal. The professor's buffoonery may be interpreted as a more abased mimicry of the kind inherent in the imperial-colonial equation. Many of Bowles's stories treat the vulnerability of the traveller in an alien context; they demonstrate the idea that identity depends on a cultural reproduction, and that if that model is removed or shattered, the inner unity of individual consciousness goes along with it. His stories focus on Western travellers' (especially Americans') vulnerability, and as such they become counter-discourses, exposing and interrogating underlying cultural deficiencies rather than demonstrating and representing power.

Bowles's Travel Writing

Their Heads Are Green and Their Hands Are Blue (1957), subtitled *Scenes from the Non-Christian World*, contains travelogues and essays written during the 1940s and 1950s, a period when European colonies in Africa and Asia were struggling for independence or were experiencing their first decade of political autonomy. These essays treat the consequent changes and readjustments of cultural and social identity in several countries, including Morocco, Algeria, Ceylon, India, and Turkey. In the foreword Bowles places the collection within the context of a new, post-colonial world and indicates his own *points de repère* within it. Although the subject matter of the essay collection is cultural difference in the 'non-Christian world,' he immediately dismisses certain Western idealizations of traditional societies. He agrees with Lévi-Strauss that what travel often discloses to Westerners is their 'own garbage, flung in the face of humanity,' but he suggests that it would be a form of naive, cultural primitivism to condemn change and brand twentieth-century technology as evil (viii). Change, even in traditional cultures, is constant, Bowles reiterates, and Western travellers should not expect the exotic to remain so solely for their personal pleasure (vii–viii). He views the rapid assimilation of European ways and politically dictated change as the primary threats to the integrity of traditional cultures, which, in his words, 'are being ravaged not so much by the by-products of our civilization, as by the irrational longing on the part of members of their own educated minorities to cease being themselves and become Westerners' (vii–viii). Here Bowles sounds a bit like V.S. Naipaul; his remarks are not intended to be about any particular people, though, but about the traps that post-colonial governments have often fallen victim to. Continuing with his most direct and politically charged statement of the essay collection, he asserts: 'Many post-colonial regimes attempt to hasten the process of Europeanization by means of campaigns and decrees. Coercion can destroy the traditional patterns of thought, it is true; but what is needed is that they be transformed into viable substitute patterns, and this can be done only empirically and by the people themselves. A cultural vacuum is not even productive of nationalism, which at least involves a certain consciousness of identity' (ix). Cultures and societies must be allowed to evolve, he argues; identity is not something that can be programmed or imposed upon a population. *Their Heads Are Green and Their Hands Are Blue*, then, is about an incipient cultural vacuum and cultural conflicts at the advent of a post-colonial world.

Although the essay collection can be interpreted from the register of any number of issues in travel-writing theory, such as mimesis, metaphor, and monologic versus dialogic narration, I will focus on the tension between representational and translational processes in travel and travel writing. Two essays, 'The Rif, To Music' and 'The Route to Tassemsit' record journeys where music provides a theme and vehicle of translation; two other essays – 'Africa Minor' and 'A Man Must Not Be Very Muslim' – address representation and ideology. A fixth essay, 'Baptism of Solitude,' translates landscape into an existential, religious experience, and a sixth, 'All Parrots Speak,' extends the issue of difference of cultural consciousness to a lighthearted consideration of the hidden bond between humans and animals. This final essay may be read as a larger, meta-commentary on the possibilities for cross-cultural understanding that travel, from a utopian perspective, holds forth.

'The Rif, to Music' records an unusual journey; on behalf of the Rockefeller Foundation, Bowles spends six months crisscrossing Morocco, travelling twenty-five thousand miles collecting 'every musical genre to be found' there (84). The project seeks to plumb the country's rich folk culture, which, Bowles notes, has expressed itself primarily in music: 'the very illiteracy which through the centuries has precluded the possibility of literature has abetted the development of music; the entire history and mythology of the people is clothed in song' (83). Through music, we might say, the people have grasped and translated their sense of being in the world. Given that Bowles is himself a composer and is well versed in different sorts of ethnic music, music serves this traveller as a base of knowledge and a controlling familiarity from which the unfamiliar can be approached and apprehended. Here music serves as a paradigm of the culture itself, as Bowles suggests in the essay's opening paragraphs that treat Moroccan musical history from the Neolithic Berber, whose music was highly percussive and aimed at mass participation and a kind of hypnosis, to Arabic music, of a more contemplative nature and addressed to the individual (83–4). The music of the contemporary folk cultures of Morocco shows aspects of both types as well as their mixing. In general, music serves as a common language that facilitates cross-cultural interactions during the voyage. For example, when Bowles needs confirmation of the styles of some folk pieces he has recorded, he invites two Rifian maids to his hotel room to listen to the pieces; at first they are reluctant and demurely insist upon a chaperon, but they do enjoy listening to the music and quickly identify most of the pieces. When Bowles offers to pay them for their expert services, they are so pleased that they insist on washing some of his soiled laundry (102). In addition to being a common language that often facilitates cross-cultural interactions, music is itself a subject matter that demands translation. Bowles's encounter with a musician named Boujemaa ben Mimoun brings out this point; listening to the sounds of the *qsbah*, a long flute with a low register, Bowles remarks: 'In a landscape of immensity and desolation [like the Sahara] it is a moving thing to come upon a lone camel driver, sitting beside his fire at night while the camels sleep, and listen for a long time to the querulous, hesitant cadences of the *qsbah*. The music, more than any other I know, most completely expresses the essence of solitude' (112–13). In music one hears culture, and one touches existential registers; Bowles will develop this theme further in another essay in the collection, 'Baptism of Solitude.'

Travellers pass through changing landscapes; these landscapes, although they may be immediately and intuitively appreciated, must be translated in order to be understood, and in travel writing, they must be translated into written expression. Bowles often achieves this through ingenious pictorial comparisons that convey a sense of the incongruous, the surreal, and the sinister. The scene of Llano Amarillo is described in this way: 'Here and there, scattered over a distance which went toward infinity, was a herd of cattle or a flock of sheep. They looked as though they had been put there purposely to give the place scale. At first you saw nothing but the yellow flatness with the great cedar trees along the sides. Then you saw the dots that were the nearest sheep, then to the right the pinpoints that were cows, but smaller than the sheep, then far over to the left almost invisible specks that were another herd' (87). Similarly, the mood of the Moroccan town of Alhuecemos and its environs is captured in these words: 'The sea looked like lead. The town itself has a certain paranoid quality: the classic Spanish fishing village seen as in a bad dream. There is a vague atmosphere of impending disaster, of being cut off from the world, as in a penal colony' (97). Another brief passage describes a border town and the shock of transition from the traditional to the modern: 'It was getting dark as we went through Berkane, new and resplendent. The town was full of people, palms and fluorescent lights. After Nador it looked like Hong Kong' (118). In this essay, as in other travel writing, landscape is not something out there, something real to be copied; rather, it is a translation, something experienced and then transformed into words. Travellers do not copy reality; they interpret it, and in interpreting it they also add to it and remake it.

In terms of travel as translation, it is apparent that the subject matter of the journey is place, but place understood comprehensively – that is, the land, cultures, and society of the Rif region of Morocco, particularly its varieties of folk music. The register into which Bowles often translates his experiences and observations consists of Western – specifically North American – cultural attitudes, not only because this in part is his own cultural background but also because North Americans are implicitly the designated readers of the essays. As a traveller and narrator Bowles has a double identity, a *double je*; he is both an outsider – he is not Moroccan – and a sojourner within another culture. At the time of writing these travel pieces he had lived in Morocco and North Africa more than a decade, so to some extent he has already translated the subject matter that he will again be translating into the register of his Western readers. Yet during the course of the travelogue it becomes clear that he remains something of a stranger and struggles to comprehend the unfamiliar. The travel writer faces a predicament. On the one hand, he or she needs to remain open to experience in all its unexpected moments and contradictions, and to process that experience recursively, adjusting viewpoints and ideas according to feedback. On the other hand, experience, place, and people must be transformed into linguistic representations in order to be comprehended. Yet any representation stops the recursive loop of experience, stabilizing it in an attempt to capture its significance, if only provisionally; any representation eventually distorts.

Cultural phenomena and experiences of travel resist comprehension and translation, and that is partly what it means to travel, which is itself a dialogic process of distanciation and appropriation. As if to highlight the former, the estrangement of the travel experience, Bowles often makes a point of focusing on the incomprehensible and the misfitting, those things that seem *not* to make sense. The Moroccan attitude toward *kif* – leaves from the hemp plant that are dried and smoked for their drug-like qualities[4] – seems exemplary: the plant can be grown and transported legally, although it is illegal to sell it and to smoke it, with enforcement of these nuances depending on how 'the local authorities of each town feel about it' (*Their Heads* 90–1). Frustrating interactions with a hotel receptionist and government officials also fall into this category of misfitting elements, where differing cultural attitudes and practices remain incongruous: there is no apparent reason why, at the advent of an electrical power outage, the receptionist refuses to give candles to Bowles, petulantly denying that there are any in the hotel, but then, as if out of spite, giving some to Bowles's travel companion later in the evening. When a government official assures Bowles that there is 'no music in Figuig,' the author cynically comments: 'I understood that he meant he would be sure that we got none' (121–2). It is often difficult to 'read' others' moods and motives, or determine why another person responds in a certain manner. Even more so for a traveller in a foreign country: travel magnifies the incomprehensible. When

Bowles records these minor incidents and annoyances in his travel journal, he does engage in a reflection that sometimes leads him to alter his attitude or behaviour, so we could say that the traveller, during the journey, can be repatterned by his or her translation of the foreign culture. This process involves a feedback loop into which the new and unresolved disorder and the untranslatable elements of travel are recycled for further reflection and translation.

So we should think of travel as a translational process, not in the narrow sense of an immediate transposition of meaning, but in the broad sense of a recursive process that involves analysis, reflection, and revision – all of which have a transformative effect on the traveller and his view of the place in which he journeys. Sometimes the reasons for incongruous or puzzling exchanges or situations emerge only later, after further experiences and reflection shed new light on them; this is perhaps the case with the larger explanation for the overall meagre results of Bowles's recording project in the Rif, whose colonial history – the region having been a Spanish protectorate until 1955 – seems to play a role in the project's failure. Faced with the incongruous and the untranslatable, the traveller will often attempt to control the irrational and disorderly elements of experience by way of familiar narratives, rhetorical and thematic strategies, and categorical representations. Is this the case, we might ask, with Bowles's descriptions of squalor and dilapidation in the Rif? The *parador*[5] at Bab Berrett, with its bedrooms without doorknobs and its single out-of-order bathroom ('the place was so filthy that you didn't go into it'), provides one memorable experience and illustrates one tendency of representation in the travelogue: the highlighting of the repulsive and the absurd. Bowles recalls the night, years before, when he had to sleep on a makeshift cot in this particular bathroom; paying no heed to the out-of-order sign, French tourists pounded on the door and tried to break it down. Added to this were bugle calls from a nearby barracks and the gobbling of turkeys on the hotel terrace (*Their Heads* 89–90). In the essay the incongruous, the nonsensical, or the untranslatable is often dealt with through a similar thematic slant: life is full of absurdities and these are merely some of them, the travelogue implies. So the highlighting of the absurd within the travel experience functions as a stabilizing, thematizing strategy; this would seem to halt the processing of the incomprehensible or untranslatable in the feedback loop, but there turns out to be more to this strategy of selection and representation than at first meets the eye.

The description of squalor in Nador, a Rifian town near the Mediterranean coast, serves not to demean but to record a degrading situation whose cause, colonial/post-colonial tensions between Morocco and Spain, becomes clear only later in the travelogue. At Nador, Bowles and his two travel companions check in at the sole town lodging, Hotel Mokhtar (its name 'printed in crooked letters' above the door), which is even less inviting than the *parador* at Bab Berrett: 'we [were] so used to inhaling the stench of the latrines at each breath, but that first night it bothered us considerably. I flung my window open and discovered that the air outside was worse. The interior odor was of ancient urine, but the breeze that entered through the window brought a heavy scent of fresh human excrement' (105–6). The travellers find out too late that the town's open-air public toilets are located next to the hotel: 'at any moment during the day you can always see a dozen or more men, women, and children squatting in the trenches' (107).

Nador and the Hotel Mokhtar are described as disagreeable places, but the travelogue incorporates their representation within a larger process of detection. The primary cause of the town's difficulties, which lie less in the nature of a Moroccan town than in the political tensions and infrastructural pressures that colonial/post-colonial tensions have brought to the region, soon becomes apparent. Bowles explains that the stationing of thousands of Spanish troops – the Mediterranean Spanish colonial port of Melilla is not far away – and the retaliatory stationing of thousands of Moroccan troops has overburdened Nador's resources:

> There are many more people here than there should be. Water has to be got in pails and oil tins from pumps in the street; food is at a premium and all commodities are scarce. Dust hangs over the town and refuse surrounds it, except on the east, where the shallow waters of the Mar Chica lap against the mud, disturbing the dead fish that unaccountably float there in large numbers ... Nador is a prison ... When the beaches are full of the hundreds of desperate-looking Spanish and Moroccan soldiers who roam the streets, the only place for new arrivals to sit is in the chairs put out under the palms by the café-keepers. They sit there, but they stare down the boulevard and order nothing. At night it's a little less depressing because the thoroughfare is not at all well lighted and the intense shabbiness doesn't show. Besides, after dark the two military populations are shut into their respective barracks. (107–8)

What emerges in this essay on the Rif and music, with its passages that express disgust, is a link between colonialism and an absence of development and progress in the region. The travelogue establishes this link tangentially, by way of highlighting the sordid and thematizing banal absurdities. One incident in particular exemplifies this disgust better than others, without diminishing it rationally through analysis. The author wearily spies, caked to the bottom of a pail of murky drinking water that the hotel management has provided Bowles and his travel companions, a dirty rag: the memory of having drunk the water in the pail creates a nausea that perfectly conveys the essay's mood. It is perhaps not by chance that, in the travelogue's final pages, the travellers are biding their time in the border town of Oujda, close to which the struggle for independence in French Algeria rages. Colonialism is *not* the subject of this essay – music is – yet the consequences of colonialism intrude and speak by default. The colonized Moroccan countryside has not been developed – provided with electricity, drinking water, sanitation – and thus recording folk music in the various towns and villages of the Rif presents insurmountable difficulties. In Oujda, Bowles and his companions are restricted in their movements by the bombardments in neighbouring Algeria. All these complications, which are linked to colonialism or which cannot be disassociated from it, play a part in the recording project's dismal outcome: 'The Rif is finished, and I managed to record only in two places,' Bowles resignedly concludes (127). The ironic merit of this travelogue is that it has accidentally 'recorded' something else, so to speak. The travellers went looking for music; they found instead a social and political reality. What would be the impact on the travelogue – by its generic nature free-wheeling and uncensored – if the uncomplimentary passages pertaining to the Moroccan Rif, with their descriptions of filth and squalor, were deleted? It would certainly lose its power to evoke the predicament of rural, post-colonial Morocco; the travellers can leave, but the inhabitants must stay. The Rif travelogue also illustrates the tension between the traveller's translation of cultural experience, which never ends, and its representation, which must always artificially bring it to an end. The former involves a recursive loop of analysis, while the latter employs familiar narrative, thematic, and rhetorical strategies to order the disorderly and to make sense of the nonsensical – if only by calling, and representing, it as 'absurd.'

In 'The Route to Tassemsit,' a counterpart to 'The Rif, To Music,' Bowles and a Canadian travel mate journey southwest of Marrakesh to Tiznit and then to Tassemsit, a remote feudal-like town where, the travellers are told, political power belongs to a nineteen-year-old girl, the town's reigning 'hereditary saint,' and to her family's chauffeur. 'C'est très délicat,' a colonial French pharmacist cautions Bowles: 'One false move, and the story of Tassemsit can be finished forever' (*Their Heads* 177–8). Bowles treads lightly, although the travelogue makes a point of underscoring his false assumptions and mistakes, especially regarding the recording project; in this sense it shows a recursive process of interpretation in which travellers engage in order to understand the unfamiliar worlds they encounter. The unexpected and the accidental can be revealing, and Bowles highlights just these sorts of things: he has an eye and a sensibility for the incongruous and the absurd – in other words, for those elements of travel that cannot be immediately translated into a facile understanding. By its very title *Their Heads Are Green and Their Hands Are Blue* suggests that something lies beyond the reach of Western ways of framing and comprehending the world, and it is this that he seeks to witness and capture fleetingly in his recordings of Moroccan folk music. His plans often go awry; about his own overly ambitious intentions to record numerous musicians and groups he laments: 'During the next few days I discovered how unrealistic my recording project had been. We visited at least two dozen villages in the region, and made no progress toward uncovering an occasion where there might prove to be music' (170). The most interesting journeys rarely resemble a straight line, but rather a straying from the path that itself attempts to process the unexpected, the accidental, and the disorderly; the direction of the journey then resembles a path through a labyrinth. In any open system where entropy enters, a feedback loop will be needed to process information and re-establish a balance within the circuit of translation. It might be argued that Bowles's highlighting of his biases, errors, and misjudgments – which demonstrate an attention to feedback – enhance his narrative credibility; the final episode in the essay demonstrates this point. He is treated to an amazing evening of music and dancing, which his host, Monsieur Omar, insists on tape-recording but in an apparently technically flawed manner: 'As the shrill voices and the drumming grew in force and excitement, I became convinced that what was going on was indeed extraordinarily good, something I would have given a good deal to record and listen to later at my leisure. Watching my host in the act of idly ruining what might have been a valuable tape was scarcely a pleasure' (186). The 'final irony,' Bowles continues, is that 'the spoiled tape ha[d] to be given to me, so that I c[ould] know in detail what I failed to get' (187). He is sure that the tape has been botched, but when he listens to it he is astonished to discover that it is flawless. He accepts the 'joyful mystery': 'It is always satisfying to succeed in a quest, even when success is due entirely to outside factors' (188). Here, and elsewhere in the essay collection, a narrating self exposes the bias and misjudgment of a narrated self; an aspect of travel writing as translation, this split between narrator and narrated is one of several rhetorical techniques used to achieve a discourse that is finally non-orientalizing in its treatment of its often controversial subject matter. The technique engages a larger mode of travel as translation: a recursive feedback loop in which a mistake or a failure to comprehend an experience leads to some readjustment of one's attitude or position, and then a reinterpretation of a situation or event. In the narrator-narrated split, it is the identity of the traveller that undergoes constant adjustment and readjustment.

Bowles's representation of landscapes and his observations (before Islamic fundamentalism became a late-twentieth-century phenomenon) on the malaise and discontent of young Muslims and Africans constitute two representational-translational aspects of this essay. For the travel writer, to represent is to stop the flow of experience and to make of it a picture; once the picture is in place, it reverses the flow of experience and holds the writer and the reader in the grasp of its insight or distortion. Much of the time, we can never say with certainty which is which. As in other essays of the collection, Bowles describes landscapes with a pictorial eye and poetic sensibility, translating them into the framework of North American perspectives. The emptiness of a rural highway, for example, is partly conveyed through a comment that it lacks even billboards (*Their Heads* 159). The oasis city Marrakech is implicitly compared with a Far West (North American) town: 'When the wind blows, the pink dust of the plain sweeps into the sky, obscuring the sun, and the whole city, painted with a wash made of the pink earth on which it rests, glows red in the cataclysmic light' (161). Another rural place, Tafraout, recalls the bad lands of South Dakota, and a descent into a canyon suggests – this time with a more literary turn – 'Persephone going along a similar road each year on her way down to Hades' (168, 177). All of this shows, again, that for the traveller, landscapes do not exist until they are captured (held still) in metaphors and images. Bowles's eye for the incongruous and the absurd (at least this is often the direction of the translation and representation) finds a perfect specimen in a mid-twentieth-century personage – the radio-man – too striking to be an exaggeration. 'Moulay Brahin is militantly of his epoch,' Bowles observes; 'his life is almost wholly abstract.' Prostrate on a mattress, he spends his day with his head linked to a short-wave radio, listening to international broadcasts; he knows what 'Sékou Touré said to Nkrumah about Nasser' and where and what the Nigerian representative to the United Nations might be doing: 'The radio is never silent save for a useless five minutes now and then while he waits impatiently for a program in Cairo [or] Damascus or Baghdad to begin' (164–5). For Moulay Brahin the radio is neither entertainment nor information, but a 'metaphysical umbilical cord'; it is a way of existing and feeling. The register into which Bowles translates this idiosyncratic behaviour shows the author's search for an understanding that exceeds the banal: no, he suggests, this young man is not looking for relief from boredom, nor is he trying to keep up with events in the world for information's sake. The nowhere into which Moulay Brahin projects his energies and identity signifies the deracination of young Moroccans, Bowles surmises (165). The same malaise apparent in 'The Rif, to Music' – the delayed effects of colonialism – shows again in this vignette from 'The Route to Tassemsit,' but with this twist: the post-colonial appears not as a lack of modernization but as a nervous in-between, neither traditional nor modern.

Three other essays in the collection merit analysis because they pose questions about representation in travel writing; all three show a tendency to essentialize cultural characteristics and, thereby, to control the flow of experience, although at least one of the essays succeeds in bringing a complexity to the material through dialogic, multi-voiced perspectives. Written in the context of the colonial-independence debate of the 1950s and the discovery of Morocco by the North American and European tourist industries, the first essay, 'Africa Minor,' renders Bowles's sense of the essence of North Africa such as the region might be perceived by Western travellers if they were to look and listen with openness and imagination. 'What do you expect to find here?' Bowles queries the stream of Americans who in the 1950s have begun to pass regularly through Tangier; their response is characteristically Orientalist – 'a sense of mystery' – to which Bowles replies poetically, though in a style vulnerable to *carte postale* vulgarization: 'They find it in the patterns of sunlight filtering through the latticework that covers the souks, in the unexpected turnings and tunnels of the narrows streets, in the women whose features still go hidden beneath the *litham* [veil], in the secretiveness of the architecture.' And if the travellers listen – as Bowles does with his composer's and ethnomusicologist's ear – they find mystery in the calls of the muezzins, the beat of the *darbouka* (a hand drum), and other Eastern sounds of the city (*Their Heads* 24–5). In this essay, whose title ironically echoes the French 'l'Afrique mineure,' a phrase employed by one of the colonial administrators who hounds Bowles during his travels in Tunisia, the author not only evokes a magic of place but also gives an aperçu of the people's life and the region's diversity and cultural richness. Bowles is clearly not a traveller whose goal is to seek out 'architectural wonders'; people are the point of his travels: 'North Africa, without its tribes, inhabited by, let us say, Swiss, would be ... a rather more barren California,' he explains to those who would view the inhabitants only as part of the decor and spectacle (vii). The Maghreb fascinates, and a salient question raised by this particular essay is the inverse of the question raised by descriptions of squalor in 'The Rif, To Music': does the traveller orientalize not by demeaning others, but rather by idealizing Morocco and the Maghreb?

A passage in *Without Stopping*, which recounts Bowles's first voyage to Morocco, may throw some light on this question; the passage does not so much idealize as chart an existential rapport between place and consciousness:

> Always without formulating the concept, I had based my sense of being in the world partly on an unreasoned conviction that certain areas of the earth's surface contained more magic than others. Had anyone asked me what I meant by magic, I should probably have defined the word by calling it a secret connection between the world of nature and the consciousness of man, a hidden but direct passage which bypassed the mind ... And now, as I stood in the wind looking at the mountains ahead, I felt the stirring of the engine within, and it was as if I were drawing close to the solution of an as-yet-unposed problem. I was incredibly happy as I watched the wall of mountains slowly take on substance, but I let the happiness wash over and asked no questions. (125)

Even though Bowles's attitude sours in the 1970s and 1980s[6] – Tangier becomes less magical to him – in this passage he connects Morocco (and the Orient) with a prospective identity; he sees in it something of what he will become or what he admires – and this is also what other Westerners see and seek, a transformation in its liminal space. He describes this liminal space poetically, correlating the change of day to night with a contemplative moment in which the hustle and bustle vanishes into the purity of existence – into a music: 'For long hours I sat in the patio listening to the sounds of [Fez],' he writes in 'Africa Minor,' 'sometimes hearing faint strains of music ..., watching the square of deep-blue sky above my head slowly become a softer and lighter blue as twilight approached, waiting for the swallows that wheeled above the patio when the day was finally over and the muezzins began their calls to evening prayer' (*Their Heads* 34–5).

If Bowles idealizes Morocco, it is not in the manner of a popular Orientalist fantasy nor in any of the senses of the term 'idealization' that David Spurr employs in *The Rhetoric of Empire*. He does not, for example, attempt to fit Morocco into 'the fabric of Western values,' many of which he has already abandoned. Nor can a personal sense of magic and fate be linked either with an idealization that rationalizes a colonial mission (as in T.E. Lawrence's *Seven Pillars of Wisdom*) or one that compensates for guilt, transgression, and loss (as in Dominique Lapierre's *The City of Joy*) (Spurr, *The Rhetoric of Empire* 128–9, 132). Bowles's intent is to differentiate the Maghreb from other places in the world, and to explain the spell it has cast on him. In other essays he describes unpleasant and repulsive aspects of daily life there, but in this particular essay he allows himself to dwell on scenic beauty, cultural richness, the people's hospitality, and their manner of living life with pragmatism yet mysticism and dignity. Bowles is acutely aware that the issue of how he is representing the Maghreb is very touchy, if not, finally, *the* issue with which he must contend. He incorporates statements by Moroccans and others that challenge his own dominant viewpoint; he modifies his generalizations with counter-examples. Thus, the essay develops a dialogic, multivoiced texture, as in a discussion of positions from different perspectives; in this way Bowles gets beyond the idiosyncratic and essentialist and discovers attitudes that reveal the cultural difference between Moroccans and others (e.g., North Americans). 'Truth is not what you perceive with your senses, but what you feel in your heart,' a Moroccan interlocutor, objecting to Bowles's depiction of illiteracy in the country, complains. When Bowles defends his representations as 'objective truth,' a Moroccan lawyer friend smiles bemusedly and adds, as one might explain something to someone who doesn't know any better: 'That is statistical truth. We are interested in that, yes, but only as a means ... For us, there is very little visible truth in the world these days' (*Their Heads* 32). In traditional Maghrebine society the most important things are often hidden, and some are too sensitive to be written about.

A case in point are Brotherhood gatherings, which may feature mutilation, trances, and the eating of scorpions and broken glass. 'To me these spectacles are filled with great beauty,' contends Bowles, 'because their obvious purpose is to prove the power of the spirit over the flesh' (27–8). In response to this a Moroccan interlocutor pointedly inquires:

'Are all the people in your country Holy Rollers?' adding, 'Why don't you write about the civilized people here instead of the most backward?' (31–2) Identity in post-colonial Morocco would seem to be the larger question and sensitive issue that provokes friction between the expatriate Bowles and some Moroccans. 'One reason ... the city folk are so violent in their denunciation of the cults,' he explains, 'is that most of them are only one generation removed from them themselves; knowing the official attitude toward such things, they feel a certain guilt at being even that much involved' (28–9). I read 'Africa Minor,' then, as an essay that engagingly mixes the autobiographic with the ethnographic; through its willingness to treat controversial material (e.g., the Brotherhood societies) and its dialogic, multivoiced commentary, it escapes the idealizations of the *carte postale* and includes within itself a recursive appraisal and reappraisal of its observations and points of view.

International travel writing runs the risk of stereotyping ethnic groups, societies, and nations, and in this collection Bowles has unavoidable recourse to terms such as 'Moslems,' 'Jews,' 'Moroccans,' 'Turks,' 'Egyptians,' and so forth that may lead to essentialization of cultural characteristics by arresting the translating of the traveller's experience with categorizations. The essay 'A Man Must Not Be Very Moslem' (1953) measures gradations of religious belief and social change and addresses indirectly the issue of stereotyping and biased representation. The dialogic character of the essay, which records the differing impressions of the author and a Moroccan travel-companion (Abdeslam) of 1950s Turkey, enables it to offset, if not to overcome, tendencies toward Orientalist portraiture. In its determination to modernize, Turkey 'has turned its back on the East and Eastern concepts,' Bowles observes, 'not with the simple yearning of other Islamic countries to be European or to acquire American techniques, but with a conscious will to transform itself from the core outward – even to destroy itself culturally, if need be' (*Their Heads* 61–2). The conservative Abdeslam – today we would call him fundamentalist – is shocked and irate at the scope of secular revision taking place in this Mediterranean neighbour. When he asks two Turks how many times they pray each day, they respond with a muffled laugh. Abdeslam is told that in Istanbul, unlike Morocco, mosques are open to non-believers – even Western tourists may visit them, and vagrants sleep in them – that pork is eaten, that tobacco has replaced *kif* in the pipes smoked in cafés, and that Ramadan has been reduced to a day – and all this he views with displeasure. He causes a scene at a local restaurant when he demands that the bill be written in Arabic; the baffled waiters call the restaurant's manager, who points out that in Turkey, which has officially committed itself to modernization, a man can go to jail for insisting that his wife wear a veil, or even for writing in Arabic (66). 'A man must not be *very* Moslem,' the manager politely cautions. Reading this essay after the events of September 11, 2001, or simply within the context of the rise of Islamic fundamentalism in the late twentieth century, gives one a sense of the scope of the cultural alienation that has proliferated in Islamic countries in just a few decades.

Whereas Abdeslam considers Turkey's modernization and modification of certain aspects of Islam as apostasy, Bowles for his part notes some advantageous changes that have occurred:

> The Turks are the only Moslems I have seen who seem to have got rid of that curious sentiment ... that there is an inevitable and hopeless difference between themselves and non-Moslems. Subjectively, at least, they have managed to bridge the gulf created by their religion, that abyss which isolates Islam from the rest of the world. As a result the [Western] visitor feels a specific connection with them which is not the mere one-sided sympathy the well-disposed traveler has for the more basic members of other cultures, but is something desired and felt by them as well. (74)

Interpreting Turkey from a modern viewpoint, Bowles distances himself from Abdeslam's radical disgust with the country's secularization, yet he admits that he is 'not exactly sure' where he stands in this 'philosophical dispute' (66). The combination of the two differing viewpoints makes for an ambivalence that Bowles draws out at the end of the essay, where he at once acknowledges secular Turkey's achievement while implying its default: Turkey's cultural transformation has been imposed rather than arrived at through an evolution of people's attitudes: 'The old helplessness in the face of a *mektoub* (it is written) is gone, and in its place is a passionate belief in man's ability to alter his destiny. That is the greatest step of all; once it has been made, anything, unfortunately, can happen' (81–2). He then points out the sincerity of Abdeslam's emotional response, and intimates an intuition that his companion's zeal may distort but cannot negate:

> Abdeslam is not a happy person. He sees his world, which he knows is a good world, being assailed on all sides, slowly crumbling before his eyes. He has no means of understanding me should I try to explain to him that in this age what he considers to be religion is called superstition ... Some-

thing will have to be found to replace the basic wisdom which has been destroyed, but the discovery will not be soon; neither Abdeslam nor I will ever know it. (82)

So although this essay begins with a kind of Orientalist classification, its overall treatment of Islamic diversity and the conflict between tradition and modernity in complex countries like Turkey and Morocco, which look toward Europe as well as to the Middle East, puts it ahead of its time. Decades before the advent of late-twentieth-century fundamentalism in the Islamic diaspora, Bowles dramatizes something of the inner turmoil that must certainly be at least one of its principal underlying causes. What a distance separates this essay about secularization from, for example, Salman Rushdie's short story of faith gone bezerk, 'The Prophet's Hair' (*East, West*), yet 'A Man Must Not Be Very Moslem' shows how the road was already being paved to another kind of fanaticism. After September 11, 2001, this essay as well as the entire collection of travel essays takes on an additional interest as a historical background to a foreground that we oftentimes, in our contemporary limitations, cannot see beyond.

In 'Baptism of Solitude' Bowles takes the subject matter of North African landscapes, here the desert landscapes of the Algerian Sahara, and translates them into the register of religious experience, especially mysticism. The essay has a double thrust: a historical and anthropological contextualizing of a 'vanishing' Sahara, changing due to political and economic pressures, and the translation of the desert into an existential experience of the absolute. The Orient is a liminal space, and the translation/transformation works in two directions: both from man to desert and from desert to man. 'Here, in the wholly mineral landscape lighted by stars like flares, even memory disappears,' Bowles comments; 'nothing is left but your own breathing and the sound of your heart beating. A strange, and by no means pleasant, process of reintegration begins inside of you, and [you] have the choice of fighting against it, and insisting on remaining the person you have always been, or letting it take its course. For no one who has stayed in the Sahara for a while is quite the same as when he came' (*Their Heads* 129). The desert repatterns, stretching the traveller's consciousness across its vastness and incommensurability. 'Baptism of Solitude' is perhaps the most satisfying essay in the collection because its author is obviously writing about a subject that inspired and fascinated him. The French-Algerian war, with its deleterious effects on the cultures of the Sahara, would eventually interfere with Bowles's sojourns there, though never completely sunder the spiritual connection that he felt with the desert. 'Before the war ..., under the rule of the French military, there was a remarkable feeling of friendly sympathy among Europeans in the Sahara,' he explains. 'It is unnecessary to stress the fact that the corollary to this pleasant state of affairs was the exercise of the strictest control over the Algerians themselves, a regime which amounted to a reign of terror' (129). Bowles goes on to note that from the European point of view 'the place was ideal. The whole vast region was like a small unspoiled rural community where everyone respected the rights of everyone else. Each time you lived there for a while, and left it, you were struck with the indifference and the impersonality of the world outside' (129).[7] Although the desert in Orientalist discourse is often a place of intrigue, adventure, and sexual abandon, in this essay it is viewed more in the tradition of the anthropologist (e.g., Théodore Monod) – or rather, the anthropologist, poet, and spiritual searcher all rolled into one.[8] Bowles's intense poetic response to the landscape and his interest in North African folk cultures enable him to touch particulars that stereotypes oversimplify and blur. Especially with North American readers in mind Bowles remarks: '[T]here is a popular misconception of the Sahara as a vast region of sand across which Arabs travel in orderly caravans from one white-domed city to another' (133). His travel essay seeks to counter this stereotype, revealing the variety of the desert, both its landscapes and its peoples, many of whom, of course, are not Arabic.

Because the time frame of the essay is colonial, two of these non-Arabic, European groups are the French military and the Pères Blancs. The commandants of the former were often gracious hosts to the desert traveller, while the latter, Bowles notes, were even more 'extraordinary.' They embody an ideal not totally different from Bowles's own sojourn as a writer/composer in Morocco: 'There was no element of resignation in their eagerness to spend the remainder of their lives in distant outposts, dressed as Moslems, speaking Arabic, living in the rigorous, comfortless manner of the desert inhabitants. They made no converts and expected to make none' (131). Their life in the desert modifies their sense of Christian spirituality, making it something hybrid; they acquire a 'certain healthy and unorthodox fatalism,' which complements their basic beliefs and helps them comprehend the people among whom they live. Other desert groups of which Bowles takes note are the inhabitants of the M'Zab, a community of five towns following rituals that include pre-Islamic elements, and the *imochagh*, or Touareg. The latter are the so-called veiled men, their veils serving a practical as well as identifying function: to conserve the breath's moisture and thus prevent nosebleeds produced by the desert's dryness. Bowles compares the religious attitude of the inhabitants of the M'Zab to a 'puritanism ... carried to excessive lengths,' and thereby he translates their tradition into an idiom more understandable to North American readers of the 1950s.

In his representation of the Sahara as an existential experience, Bowles the traveller engages in a translation of place – sand, sky, wind – into a phenomenology of fundamental elements and forces of being-in-the-world. The opening sentences of 'Baptism of Solitude' focus on the 'stillness' of the Sahara, which Bowles compares to a 'conscious force' that minimizes and disperses sound (128). Whether during the daytime or at night, the sky has an intensity that carves its impression on human consciousness. In these and other passages, Bowles does not personify the desert so much as translate it into a human response, while showing the mutual implication of subject and object – the desert taking on the existential solitude of the individual, the individual taking on the silence of the desert. Because Bowles seeks to translate extremes or absolutes or incommensurabilites, he speaks of the Sahara as uncompromising. 'Man is hated in the Sahara,' he warns; 'one feels it in the sky, in the stones, in the air ... But of course that can be exciting. Where life is prohibited, it becomes a delectable forbidden fruit, and that is the feeling that one gets here: each instant is a begrudged one by an implacable tyrant' (*Letters* 189). All of Bowles's works, the travel essays as well as the short fiction and the novels, translate what Kant, and more recently Jean-François Lyotard, would call the 'sublime.'[9] This is a particular aspect of the Orient for Bowles, a translation unlike any other. Although Occidental voyagers have typically viewed the Orient as something to be penetrated, conquered, and possessed, what matters to Bowles is the desert's transformative effect on individuals, especially those who suffer from the spiritual maladies of twentieth-century civilization. His attitude toward the Sahara exemplifies aspects of a larger counter-Western and nomad discourse, with its deflations of power and ceaseless movement toward the untranslatable:

> There are probably few accessible places on the face of the globe where one can get less comfort for his money than the Sahara ... Everything disappears eventually – coffee, tea, sugar, cigarettes – and the traveler settles down to a life devoid of these superfluities ...
> Perhaps the logical question to ask [is] ...: Why go? The answer is that

when a man has been there and undergone the baptism of solitude he can't help himself. Once he has been under the spell of the vast, luminous, silent country, no other place is quite strong enough for him, no other surroundings can provide the supremely satisfying sensation of existing in the midst of something that is absolute. He will go back, whatever the cost in comfort and money, for the absolute has no price. (*Their Heads* 143–4)

Bowles's translation of the Sahara as an existential experience arises in part from a tradition. Another spiritual vagabond in the Algerian desert, Isabelle Eberhardt, whose letters and travel writing Bowles translated, also felt the appeal of 'le grand Silence du Désert.' For her, as for Bowles, the desert is both harsh and beautiful: 'O Sahara, Sahara menaçant, cachant ta belle âme sombre en tes solitudes inhospitalières et mornes!' ('Oh Sahara, menacing Sahara, hiding your beautiful dark soul in your inhospitable and sad isolation'; *Œuvres complètes I: Écrits sur le sable*, 319, 338). Although their descriptions might be considered by some readers as Orientalist – Eberhardt seeks, as she herself says, a 'vie tout orientale' – this Orientalism is hardly the ethnocentrist, racist one that Said decries. Rather it is a response to and a critique of modern Western civilization, with its diminishing returns of distractions, gadgets, comforts, and luxuries for those who can afford them – and, we can add, its conversion of the Sahara from a 'baptism of solitude,' as it was for Bowles some fifty years ago, to a playground for tourists in their four-wheel-drive vehicles.[10] Bowles's attitude is not one of superiority in the face of the less developed, but of respect for people who manage not only to survive but also to create unique cultural identities within the desert's harsh space.

'All Parrots Speak' is a light-hearted departure from the meditations of 'Baptism of Solitude.' Its subject, Bowles's affection for pet birds during the course of his Central American travels, would seem to have little to do with vignettes from 'the non-Christian world,' and yet, when read from a certain perspective, this essay fits perfectly. Often having both green and blue feathers and crowns, parrots are just as exotically other as the 'jumblies' of the epigraph to this travel book, whose title alludes to the imaginary 'others' of an Edward Lear poem:

Far and few, far and few,
   Are the lands where the Jumblies live;
Their heads are green, and their hands are blue,
   And they went to sea in a Sieve. (*Their Heads* iv)

So among essays about cultural difference, why not an essay about the difference between humans and animals? And besides, in the Orient of the imagination, things are never quite as they seem. In the *Arabian Nights*, for instance, metamorphosis and magic are the rule: humans transform into animals and animals become human. In this vein, 'All Parrots Speak' records Bowles's voyage into the realm of parrot language and parrot consciousness. About one of his feathered travelling companions he explains: '[The bird] did indeed speak its own language, something that no philologist would have been able to relate to any dialect. Its favorite word, which it pronounced with the utmost tenderness, was "Budupple." When it had said that several times with increasing feeling, it would turn its head downward at an eighty-degree angle, add wistfully: "Budupple mah" and then be quiet for a while' (147). As it turns out, Bowles has gotten to know more than one parrot and has had to translate their differing behaviours and languages: a Mexican *cotorro*, for example, engages in a conversation that sounds like 'an old-fashioned rubber-bulbed Parisian taxi horn run off at double speed' (149).

In the essay's final paragraph, Bowles the composer-author elaborates a deeper reason for his affinity with parrots:

> The spoken word, even if devoid of reason, means a great deal to a lonely human being.
>
> I think that my susceptibility to parrots may have been partly determined by a story I heard when I was a child. One of the collection of parrots from the New World presented to King Ferdinand by Columbus escaped from the palace into the forest. A peasant saw it, and never having encountered such a bird before, picked up a stone to hit it, so he could have its brilliant feathers as a trophy. As he was taking aim, the parrot cocked its head and cried 'Ay, Dios!' Horrified, the man dropped the stone, prostrated himself, and said, 'A thousand pardons, señora! I thought you were a green bird.' (157)

Although we should not try to extract a moral from this delightfully light piece of unorthodox travel writing, to become 'parrot-conscious,' as the author says, is a bit like being initiated into another culture (146). The process of translating and understanding parrots contains some of the same elements as travel; turned into writing it is a representation that repatterns the traveller, who engages in a recursive process of grasping and failing to grasp completely something alien and perhaps finally unknowable. After reading 'All Parrots Speak' one will never again think of these feathered creatures in quite the same way. And that is also a criterion of good travel writing: because travel writing not only records, but also translates and transforms the world; reality is added to and the world becomes not smaller but larger.

3. The Living Labyrinth: Hong Kong and David T.K. Wong's *Hong Kong Stories*

Perhaps it is Dante who tells us the most, allegorically, about contemporary urban places: every city has its cultural imaginary – its Heaven, Hell, and Purgatory – because every city is not only a material locale but also a network of lives, and all the events of those lives, in interaction narratively with one another. These stories, like the subways, auto routes, and skyscrapers of the city, reach upward and downward, and finger out along the distances of a plane in all directions; no story is simple, each has a present (and past) linked with other stories, and each has different possibilities of development and of prospective finality. It would take a god to oversee and comprehend it all, while we can only exist within the actual moment and its branches of recollection and anticipation. We are accustomed to thinking of cities spatially, rather than existentially or intertextually as situations and narratives. In this respect the Internet provides a new metaphor, as Antoine Picon emphasizes in these remarks about the new 'ideal cities' of the Internet and the notion of place as event:

> [A] city organize[s] itself around immaterial exchanges of information and the interactions that they provoke. This ensemble of exchanges and interactions can approximate a system of events. It is more in time than in space, in the heart of this dense network of occurrences and conceivable scenarios, where the contours of the ideal contemporary city take form. ('Ville idéale' 246)

The notion of city as events – specifically as unfolding narratives – is an idea that I will explore in this and the subsequent chapter, which attempt to reorient certain concepts that underlie post-colonial literature. To discover this reoriented, narratized city – one's identity immersed within it, as well as the city's emergence from one's identity – the reader as city dweller needs to be a detective of the labyrinth of texts and their transformations of which the city is constituted. To become familiar with a city takes more than a physical tour of its neighbourhoods and visit to its famous sites; it takes a mapping of the reality that emerges in its narrative events of the personal and the individual as well as the collective.

Initial Questions

In 'Traveling Cultures,' James Clifford writes: 'I find the work I'm *going towards* does not so much build on my previous work as locate and displace it' (97). Amid the migrations and cultural and social upheaval of the twenty-first century, many people can identify with Clifford's observation. I find something of my own life in these larger migrations and events; ten years ago I could not have imagined living in Asia, much less writing about Hong Kong fiction in English, specifically David T.K. Wong's short stories. Two things are immediately at stake before I can begin: first, defining the positions from which I write and, second, defining what I might be able to write about. Claims of identity are politically and culturally sensitive matters in contemporary Hong Kong. One has to be careful about who one claims to be and how one addresses others; the forms and the frames of encounters are very important. So I begin by stating the obvious, that I am not an insider, a native to Hong Kong; rather, I am someone situated 'to the side,' so to speak, although not totally outside. Having lived here for several years, I write from a position that is somewhere between that of a traveller and a permanent resident; I have the small privilege, for example, of bypassing the tourist line at the immigration checkpoint and proceeding to the (often shorter) residents' line, itself adjacent to but distinct from the permanent residents' line. I am neither traveller nor citizen, but what Roland Barthes calls a 'sojourner,'[1] a person who occupies an intermediate space, 'posited between two strong statuses' (*New Critical Essays* 117). The sojourner, he argues, is a 'tourist [I would say 'traveller'] who *repeats* his desire to remain'; in this repetition he runs the risk of becoming like Lieutenant Loti – the hero of Pierre Loti's Oriental novel *Aziyadé*, about whom Barthes circumstantially writes in this particular essay – 'the paradoxical being who cannot be classified' (ibid. 118). Lieutenant Loti is adrift, and *Aziyadé* is the novel of the drift. Today, unlike in the nineteenth century of Loti, we live in a world where immigrants and sojourners are no longer a small minority. Identity has many more gradations than it had for Loti, and my claims in this chapter are more than those of a tourist who has visited China or of the traveller who has lived there and wants to share his thoughts with the people back home. Hong Kong is part of me, and I am part of it – in a sidewise manner.

In reflecting on my own status, I wonder whether Hong Kong too is not also an inside-sidewise place where a belated post-coloniality has produced a problematic status, neither independent from nor identical with mainland China – nor with the West, for that matter. Perhaps Hong Kong was the twentieth century's first virtual post-colony. Certainly, however, the entity about which I write is a 'Hong Kong' best put in quotation marks. It is a recursive system and a collection of narratives themselves part of a larger cultural imaginary; it is a physical and virtual space, the locus of seven million inhabitants with their memories, hopes, and ambitions as well as an idea that others beyond its boundaries have about a place that they may only know in the context of a film or a fiction.

Translation would seem to be the rule. People of Hong Kong have constant recourse to it when they interact with mainlanders, Taiwanese, and Westerners; to interpret Hong Kong or write about it one must also, no matter who one is or what status one has, translate it into an array of diverse registers. As a place that is at once inside and to the side, with its own tilt toward China, Taiwan, Southeast Asia, America, and Europe, what value systems enter into play in a post-colonial Hong Kong, and about what, to whom, and for whom can a Chinese Hong Kong author who writes and publishes in English speak? To answer these questions this chapter has recourse to interpretation as translation in a double sense: as the perspective of this reader of Hong Kong fiction, a transposition of my (Western) literary, cultural imaginary by way of an understanding that is situated to the side of the Hong Kong narratized in these texts; as the perspective of the stories themselves, whose author translates Hong Kong (a difficult to define, sideways city/place) into a cultural imaginary itself neither East nor West. These translations are at once autobiographical and heuristic. In both, something particular is translated into a cast of representations; even so, perhaps for Hong Kong it is the untranslatable that always sets its mark on every attempt at translation and always has the last say.

There are lots of Hong Kong stories – too many in fact to ever be countable or classifiable. So the initial questions that one might ask about Wong's collection – whose stories? which Hong Kong? from whose perspective? and whether or not Wong is a 'Hong Kong writer,' whatever that term might mean today in heterogeneous, globalized societies where all locales have been de-localized to a lesser or greater degree – cannot be immediately answered, unless one states perfunctorily that Hong Kong writers live in Hong Kong and write in Chinese about Special Administrative Region – related subject matter. Wong fails this test, but perhaps only someone who fails can make a claim as a Hong Kong writer, the city being not only an inside but also a heterogeneous, sideways place vis-à-vis both China and the West. Contemporary Hong Kong is more than any single ethnic or political element, no matter its size or significance; Hong Kong is also, in part, all other places in the world, to which it is linked through economic interests, language, history, and family ties, though it takes part in all these places tilted or shifted in a particular manner.

Born and educated in Hong Kong, residing in London, David T.K. Wong brings a culturally mixed perspective to his stories. In this regard he resembles many other post-colonial writers who have the advantage of what Mikhail Bakhtin calls an 'exotopy,' a vision from the 'outside' that overcomes the limitations of a point of view situated 'inside' a particular locale or culture:

> There exists a very strong, but one-sided ... idea that in order better to understand a foreign culture, one must enter it, forgetting one's own, and view the world through the eyes of this foreign culture ... Of course, a certain entry as a living being into a foreign culture, the possibility of seeing the world through its eyes, is a necessary part of the process of understanding it; but if this were the only aspect of this understanding, it would merely be duplication and would not entail anything or be enriching. *Creative understanding* does not renounce itself, its own place in time, its own culture; and it forgets nothing. In order to understand, it is immensely important for the person who understands to be *located outside* the object of his or her creative understanding – in time, in space, in culture ... In the realm of culture, outsideness is a most powerful factor in understanding. It is only in the eyes of *another* culture that foreign culture reveals itself more fully and profoundly (but not maximally fully, because there will be cultures that see and understand even more). (*Speech Genres* 7)

Although we can readily grasp the sense of this concept, the world has changed in the more than half a century since Bakhtin made these observations, and exotopy may no longer have the same meaning or validity. Culturally speaking, it is harder today to delineate where 'in' and 'out' are: in a world of interdependencies or within the intertexts of cultural imaginaries, can there be an outside? Yes, certainly, particularly if the cultural imaginary depends on the password of a language competency for entry; I will never enter very far into the Chinese cultural imaginary except by way of a sideways movement, by way of translation, that is. Conversely, even if we contend that a cultural imaginary has no outside because it brushes up against or touches all other imaginaries as well, that would not erase completely the advantage of mixed perspectives as a limited form of exotopy. Today it might be more accurate to translate the term 'exotopy' as 'to the side' rather than as 'outside.' 'The entire world is being creolised, all cultures are being creolized in their contact with one another,' Édouard Glissant argues (*Introduction à une Poétique du Divers* 21).[2] Writing some seventy years after Bakhtin, Glissant provides a new, dynamic perspective on the network of languages and cultures; we live in a chaotic 'tout-monde,' he contends, where interactions of languages and cultures mark our consciousness. Wong, like many other post-colonial writers, situates his work in the world of these cultural and linguistic interactions, exchanges, tiltings, and shiftings. His Hong Kong stories, while remaining 'local,' criss-cross this larger cultural and linguistic imaginary. Although these sideways (exotopic) perspectives carry with them a certain awkwardness and strangeness, this effect does not negate the complex, labyrinthine interrelatedness that ought to serve as the base of any cultural mapping of world cultures, and that is why it would be better not to think of these sideways perspectives as 'outside' in a narrow sense.

In addition to these advantages of exotopy, there are also some disadvantages of any cultural identity that exceeds the limits of a particular locale: the lack of an indigenous community of readers. For a Hong Kong author like Wong, who writes in English and lives in Britain, the question of audience never disappears, consciously and unconsciously shaping the act of a writer's writing for, in the case of Hong Kong, a hard-to-identify or even somewhat phantom public. Who is going to read fiction about Hong Kong when the people here themselves do not read it? Well, at least most do not read fiction in English, preferring Chinese texts. So these initial questions, then, about which Hong Kong stories – which Hong Kong, and which perspective? – turn out to be sticky ones. How does Wong's fiction contend with the issues that these questions raise? His 'writing of Hong Kong' would seem to combine (1) an exotopic or 'sideways' perspective – that is to say, he does not write as an insider per se, but as someone who stands at one remove – and (2) a reliance on a broad cultural imaginary that cuts across and includes transcultural narrative materials and metaphors. He mixes 'Eastern' with 'Western' elements; he works with popular themes and common situations in the Occidental literary traditions, but at the same time he ironically and satirically comments on and transforms certain notions about Hong Kong – notions or myths that Westerners like me often harbour about this place when they first arrive. He is an ironist and satirist, drawing on materials from colonial Hong Kong issues and situations; he is not a realist writer in a narrow sense, but rather seeks to tap and translate the (trans)cultural imaginary of Hong Kong, writing stories with a contemporary bite yet archetypical in that they constitute typical stories/situations in the lifetime of the city's continuously evolving identity. Some of these common Hong Kong narratives treat the role of chance or luck in a person's life, money, the conflict of tradition (the old) and modernity (the new), family ties and responsibilities, inequalities and discrepancies, success through hard work, and immigration. When we try to define the Hong Kong of the story collection, we find that it is perhaps better to think in terms of situations and events rather than place. Hong Kong emerges as a certain predicament, a certain range of obstacles and choices; it might be compared to a theatrical performance or a labyrinthine game. Wong offers both a critique of the present as well as a certain anticipatory projection of the city's future identities. In fact, the reader cannot conceive of Hong Kong identities that would be limited to a present moment, that do not have some elements of memory and of anticipation and hope; however, a contemporary moment – particularly the transition in 1997 from colony to Special Administrative Region (SAR) – does seem to shape the meanings of the events of several of these stories. Both Wong and the reader, then, engage in translations: for Wong, the year 1997 provides a privileged register of interpretation of city life; for Western readers, the focus shifts from present to future, to encounters with prospective and anticipatory identities emerging from the stories' narratives. Given Wong's register of translation, then, the collection encourages us to look forward, not backward. 'What will Hong Kong be tomorrow?' is the question that the reader often asks. The traditions of Hong Kong are not viewed as meaningful in themselves or in isolation, but in an interrelationship with the present and future; they are interpreted or take their meaning in the light of present situations and future possibilities.

Interpreting Post-colonial Hong Kong

How can we grasp or talk about Hong Kong? One response to this question is Ackbar Abbas's *Hong Kong: Culture and the Politics of Disappearance* (1997), which may be the most penetrating analysis in English of the contemporary city/SAR. His study examines a city whose identity eludes any easily defined category. Hong Kong people are not British, nor are they culturally and politically identical to Chinese mainlanders; they are, Abbas comments, 'a bird of a different feather, perhaps a kind of Maltese Falcon' (ii). He then elaborates some of the city's 'unusual and even paradoxical features.' First, an 'uneasy relationship' exists between Hong Kong's '"floating" identity' and its need 'to establish something more definite in response to current political exigencies' (iv). In the future, it 'will increasingly be at the intersections of different times or speeds,' yet its 'port mentality' (a place of transience) must be complemented by a stable identity vis-à-vis mainland China. Second, Hong Kong's celebrated vitality has a 'decadent' quality – decadent because it is 'an energy that gets largely channeled into one direction,' that is, it is primarily economic (iv–v). When people's aspirations (e.g., for political independence) are blocked, then these will take other forms: 'the citizens' belief that they might have a hand in shaping their own history, gets replaced by speculation on the property or stock markets, or by an obsession with fashion or consumerism' (v). Third, the status of culture in contemporary Hong Kong has radically changed. Before the Sino-British Joint Declaration of 1984, Hong Kong citizens tended to think of culture as an imported commodity; today the 'imminence of [the pre-1997 mentality's] disappearance' has 'precipitated an intense and unprecedented interest in Hong Kong culture' (vii). 'The change in status of culture in Hong Kong can be described as follows,' Abbas speculates: a movement 'from reverse hallucination, which sees only desert [i.e., Hong Kong does not have its own culture], to a culture of disappearance, whose appearance is posited on the imminence of its disappearance' (vii). To clarify this convoluted point Abbas quotes Louis Aragon, who, writing in the 1920s about the disappearing Parisian arcades, remarks: 'It is only today, when the pickaxe menaces them, that they have at last become the true sanctuaries of the cult of the ephemeral' (viii).

In Abbas's view, binaries such as East/West, traditional/modern, and colonial/post-colonial do not enable us to discern the nature of culture and society in contemporary Hong Kong. Facts and reality do not accord. The city's post-coloniality began at least a decade before 1997, when people found themselves thinking and acting in a way different from the thought and behaviour that distinguished the period of British rule before the Sino-British Joint Declaration of 1984; nor, Abbas emphasizes, did colonialism necessarily come to an end with the closing of British rule in 1997. It survives in certain aspects of globalism that fixes the SAR in a new kind of colonial dependency. Hong Kong's challenge – in Abbas's words, the challenge of the 'postcolonial subject' – is 'to survive a culture of disappearance by adopting strategies of disappearance as its own, by giving disappearance itself a different inflection' (xiv–xv).[3] What this might mean is not evident. Whether Abbas intends to do so or not, his analysis brings an analogy of disappearance and groundlessness – an analogy that becomes prominent with Nietzsche in the late nineteenth century – to bear on Hong Kong's cultural crisis of the late 1980s and 1990s. As a response to and commentary on this analysis, in the following paragraphs I will consider post-colonial strategies of identity construction and the manner in which they do *not* – or only partially – fit the Hong Kong context. I will then put forward some metaphors that may better chart the nature and dynamics of the city/SAR in the first decade of the twenty-first century.

Since the 1950s, throughout the world, different strategies of resisting and overcoming a mutant colonialism in an emerging post-colonial epoch have been put forward; none of them, however, seem completely applicable to Hong Kong. Abbas, for example, dismisses what he calls 'the temptation of the local, the marginal, [and] the cosmopolitan,' or the 'fallacies of three worldism, two worldism, and one worldism' (xi). Let us look more closely at what constitutes these strategies and how Hong Kong constitutes an exception. Localism, or nativism, emphasizes radical difference and makes its most persuasive argument in a context in which the values of an ethnic group or a cultural locale are undermined or attacked by values perceived to be alien or external to the group or locale. Francophone colonial writers of the early and mid-twentieth century – Aimé Césaire, Léopold Senghor, Franz Fanon, and Albert Memmi, to name just a few – often formulated their arguments within this context and under these circumstances. Although the nativist argument became less popular in the 1980s and 1990s, it persists in distorted form in fundamentalist religious and cultural movements, and in the writings of certain influential post-colonial writers such as the Kenyan Ngugi wa Thiong'o, whose *Decolonising the Mind: The Politics of Language in African Literature* (1986) and *Moving the Centre: The Struggle for Cultural Freedoms* (1993) contend that imperialism is still very much alive and that its effects on native cultures, at least in certain regions of the world, are devastating. '[T]he biggest weapon wielded and actually daily unleashed by imperialism,' N'Gugi writes, 'is the cultural bomb,' the effect of which is 'to annihilate a people's belief in their names, in their languages, in the environment, in their heritage of struggle, in their unity, in their capacities and ultimately in themselves. It makes them see their past as one wasteland of non-achievement and it makes them want to distance themselves from that wasteland' (*Decolonizing the Mind* 3).

Language is a key in countering the ill effects of imperialism and re-establishing a society's identity: 'The choice of language and the use to which language is put is central to a people's definition of themselves in relation to their natural and social environment, indeed in relation to the entire universe' (ibid. 4). For this reason, N'Gugi, who made his reputation during the 1960s and 1970s as an anglophone author, now prefers to write and publish in his native African language, kikuyu; in the same vein, he advocates teaching African languages and cultures at the tertiary level as a road to creation of a different, non-Western identity for today's East Africans. The concept of radical difference opposes globalization (which it perceives as a mutant colonialism) with efforts to nourish a strong native/local culture, one able to resist different sorts of imperialism and homogenization in world capitalist culture. The cultural conflicts, social precariousness, and fundamental inequality about which N'Gugi writes apply most dramatically to contemporary sub-Sahara Africa, although he also intends a broad application of this assessment of the damaging effects of imperialism. Does N'Gugi's argument have much force in today's Hong Kong? It does have some. Politically, the 'North' (i.e., mainland China) can never be ignored; culturally, the influence of Japan – its high-tech products and its department stores, for example – is strong here, perhaps just as strong as that of England and the United States. Similarly, in a bilingual environment,[4] in Hong Kong as in post-colonial Africa, there are crucial issues about language education that must be resolved. In the Hong Kong of David T.K. Wong's short stories, tradition (i.e., the privileging of native/local values) is the subject of several stories, but in them tradition sometimes immobilizes and suffocates rather than heals or wisely guides. If we accept the localist notion of fixed places, then all value-and-identity construction must take place somewhere, in some locus, yet the nativist argument has been diminished by the problematic nature of locales today and by the critique of cultural essences that post-structuralism and post-coloniality have brought to bear on it.[5]

Cosmopolitanism makes another sort of appeal – in Abbas's dismissal, the temptation of 'threeworldism' (*Hong Kong* xi). 'No one today is purely *one* thing,' Edward Said writes in *Culture and Imperialism*. 'Labels like Indian, or woman, or Muslim, or American are no more than starting-points, which if followed into actual experience for only a moment are quickly left behind' (336). Said's statement, which echoes those of James Clifford and other cultural anthropologists, encapsulates the core idea of this second framework of identity and value construction, that is, hybridity and syncretism. 'Imperialism consolidated the mixture of cultures and identities on a global scale,' Said explains. 'But its worst and most paradoxical gift was to allow people to believe that they were only, mainly, exclusively, white, or Black, or Western, or Oriental. Yet just as human beings make their own history, they also make their cultures and ethnic identities' (ibid.). Indeed, perhaps the defining characteristic of post-coloniality is its sense of diversity and plurality within individual cultural identity. Whereas coloniality emphasizes black-versus-white divisions and separations, post-coloniality emphasizes the inevitability of mixing and the construction of new identities. 'It is from [a] hybrid location of cultural values – the transnational as the translational,' Homi Bhabha writes, 'that the postcolonial intellectual attempts to elaborate a historical and literary project' ('Postcolonial Criticism' 439). Hybridity as a framework of identity and value construction is most compelling in dynamically multicultural contexts; it is much less compelling, however, where one culture or a cluster of related cultures is predominant, as is the case of Hong Kong, which is not multicultural in the same sense, for example, as the Mediterranean basin or the Caribbean – or even Singapore. Hong Kong and Singapore are often compared, but culturally they are quite distinct. In Singapore, although Chinese inhabitants predominate (75 per cent of the population), the ethnic origins of this Chinese popoulation are quite diverse. Furthermore, Malays and Indians constitute two other sizeable groups in a state that also includes a mixed non-Asian presence; English is the language of government, but Chinese Mandarin, Malay, and Tamil are also official languages. Conversely, in Hong Hong the Chinese population is much larger and more homogenous. Ninety-eight per cent of Hong Kong's inhabitants are Chinese, the overwhelming majority coming from Kwangtung province or Hong Kong itself; the remaining 2 per cent are split between Asian and non-Asian inhabitants. Cantonese Chinese is the primary language; although English continues to have an official status, it is neither heard nor spoken to the degree that it is in Singapore. So a Chinese culture, a particular Chinese culture, dominates here as no single culture does in Singapore or these other exemplary regions.

Still, Hong Kong is – and has the ambition to be even more so in the future – an international place where Eastern and Western cultural elements coexist. They coexist sometimes gracefully, sometimes awkwardly, and often without much visible interaction, like the diversity of cultures displayed in stores in a Hong Kong shopping mall, with everything from Marks & Spencer, to Suzuya, to the Disney Store and the very Chinese 'wet market.' Things fit together here in their own particular way, from one neighbourhood and shopping mall to the next. In themselves, neither the concept of localism nor that of cosmopolitanism, then, would seem an adequate framework for analysing culture and identity construction in Hong Kong.

Furthermore, Abbas's own conceptual rubric – 'culture of disappearance' – may already have become *caduc.* The 1997 phenomenon has come and gone; as Hong Kong passes through economic hard times in the first decade of the twenty-first century, it is struggling to define itself in new ways, not to hang on to something that is disappearing or has passed. Hong Kong is, above all, a system of interdependencies and a culture and society of linkages. It might be conceived of as a living labyrinth of networks in a recursively operating system, itself linked to other systems; it is almost wholly by way of the recursive management of its multifarious linkages that it maintains itself and generates an identity. At each linkage is the challenge of a liminal space, which has 'to be ported over through continued interaction between unities that are separate' (Iser, *Range of Interpretation* 126). This portage ranges from transactions of material goods to human translations of communications and imaginaries. The recursive system modifies its behaviour in response to 'noise,' disruptions or perturbations, such as the return/handover in 1997 and the current economic crisis; it is always in transition and never reaches a terminus, except to make another linkage. If Hong Kong is soul-less, as some people charge, it is perhaps because it is alive and real, wholly occupied in interacting with and mapping the contours of its world:

> Mapping reality in terms of recursively operating systems is pertinent insofar as there is no given reality other than the one made to appear by the systems. If reality as a structured order were to exist, systems as a mode of

construing it would be redundant. Therefore [biologist Francisco] Varela states: 'All of this boils down ... to a realization that although the world *does* look solid and regular, when we come to examine it there is no fixed point of reference to which it can be pinned down; it is nowhere substantial and solid.' At best the world can only be disclosed as an emerging phenomenon, to be fathomed by recursively operating systems. (ibid. 129)

Yet 'Hong Kong has a soul,' declares an announcement for a recently published, ambitious anthology, *City Voices: Hong Kong Writing in English, 1945 to Present* (ed. Xu Xi and Ingham, 2003). Between the two positions there may be no grounds for argument, finally, because most people would agree that these stories and poetic expressions are testaments and aspects of this place and are part of its reality. For many, Hong Kong is home; for others, it is a haven or place of sojourn. At a more abstract, symbolic level Hong Kong might be conceived of as a network of systems, a living labyrinth; at each turn of its paths its inhabitants adjust themselves to and discover a reality that emerges from a testing – a posing and solving of problems – and a recurrent translation.

Hong Kong Stories

Although tiny on a global scale of measurement, Hong Kong cannot be easily rendered; 'in its amorphousness and diversity [it] often strikes one as being made up of an *anthology* of lifestyles' (Abbas, *Hong Kong* 117). David T.K. Wong's *Hong Kong Stories* would seem to address just this aspect of the city; composed of thirteen stories[6] of a popular and sometimes melodramatic and farcical subject matter, the collection delineates the city less by descriptions of static places than by dramatizations of predicaments and tests – of the labyrinths, so to speak, within which the characters must find their way or tentative resolutions of the problems they face. An anthology of the city's diversity, the collection presents a range of characters and professions, socio-economic classes and values: colonial administrators, a tycoon, a policeman, a trade negotiator, a jockey, a lawyer, illegal immigrants and construction workers, a bartender, journalists, a nightclub hostess, intellectuals, a typesetter / night watchman, communists and capitalists, a sinologist and a collector of chicken-blood seals, a housewife, and an honourable councillor split between his public Western identity and his private Chinese identity. This range of personages constitutes a readily graspable aspect of the collection as fictional anthology of a city, while diverse and recurrent predicaments and challenges to individual and collective identity and values present a less obvious, though profound, one.

Given its variety and its dispersed publication (stories originally written and published over a period of years), the collection cannot be reduced to a single, overall theme; given that qualification, what I find most interesting in *Hong Kong Stories* are the situations and value systems that these stories sketch and ponder. The values do vary from story to story, but one can make some generalizations about the entire collection, which narrates the city as an anthology of situations. Pragmatic values take precedence over transcendent values; the latter, French philosopher Gilles Deleuze argues, tend to demand obedience, whereas the former tend to encourage thought, the capacity to find new solutions to problems, and a sense that the individual can determine a part of his destiny.[7] Whether or not we accept Deleuze's distinction – I do not entirely agree – it is a useful one for discussion of certain stories in this collection. The book's dedication – to Hong Kong – and its epigraph ('May its spirit of freedom, irreverence and enterprise remain forever intact') would seem to celebrate pragmatic values mixed with a certain orientation toward utopianism and Western individualism. Those characters in Wong's stories who live according to transcendent values, whether Eastern or Western, eventually become paralysed and unable to resolve a crucial problem in their lives. In these stories, then, Wong, the city's most prolific short-story writer, translates Hong Kong into the register of a particular set of values, which reference a tradition but which also project a prospective identity.

The labyrinth is a metaphor of struggle and pragmatism. The man in the labyrinth seeks to survive, to find his way out one way or another; he tries different strategies to achieve this end. Cultures too face threats and must struggle to survive, for culture is itself a strategy, Homi Bhabha elaborates, with both transnational and translational aspects: 'It is transnational because contemporary postcolonial discourses are rooted in specific histories and cultural displacement ... Culture is translational because such spatial histories of displacement ... make the question of how culture signifies, or what is signified by *culture* a rather complex issue' (quoted in Valdés, *Hermeneutics of Poetic Sense* 72). David T.K. Wong's stories treat both of these aspects of Hong Kong culture, representing a struggle for survival in various literal and figurative senses. At least five of the thirteen stories deal overtly with questions of tradition and honour in a postmodern world where these values have an increasingly marginal place. The past can serve as a guidepost, but it may also deceive, torment, and render false in the context of the changing complications of the present. The story 'Blood Debt' raises a question echoed in other stories: 'what [is] the use of precepts about justice and loyalty and honour in a hostile world?' (*Hong Kong Stories* 43) There is a certain ambivalence in Wong's answer: in this story, for instance, a respect for one's elders and traditions leads Chief Inspector Hung into an ethical trap; to extricate himself, he chooses honour, but he pays with his life. Hence, the story's ironic title refers to the promise that Hung makes to his father, little knowing at the time that he will pay dearly and in an unexpected manner for his filial piety, a primary value in Hong Kong and Chinese society. 'We owe the Ma family a debt of gratitude,' Hung's father explains. 'If not for Uncle Ma, we would be unable to earn a living. Debts of money can sometimes be overlooked, but debts of gratitude must be repaid. That is the Chinese way. You must help the Ma children ... Should you in later life find yourself in a position to do them a service, you must not hesitate' (43). Decades later, Hung remembers these words and his obedience to them leads him into a moral labyrinth, symbolized by the Hong Kong ghetto:

> The patched-together shelters, made with corrugated metal sheets, salvaged bricks, planks, plywood, tar paper and a variety of handy materials, shared with flies, mosquitoes, cockroaches and rodents, seemed as mean and dispiriting as ever. Electric wires, dangling like festoons from overhead cables, evidenced the continuing theft of electricity. The odours of stale food, hemmed-in humanity and rotting garbage soured the air.
>
> The sights, sounds and smells dragged him back to the past. The treacherous turnings and random hazards of the encampment had once been a daily gauntlet he had to run. (36–7)

Life in Hong Kong can resemble a maze, and for those who are poor, the opportunities the city offers – and flaunts with its neon lights and luxuries – can seem illusory. 'We'll never escape from here,' Ma the Second laments; '[t]he promises of the city are just there to torment us, like a mirage' (47). The Ma family turn to crime and prostitution as a way out of their social caste; they enlist a reluctant Hung in a scheme that turns out to be profitable for both parties. In this story traditional values are treated ironically in that, first, they lead Hung into a trap and, second, they lead to an act of futility. Inspector Hung does not resolve his ethical crisis; he commits a kind of suicide, saving his professional reputation but leaving others to clean up the mess and enact a justice that the story has already called into question by highlighting inequalities. For a traditional value to remain valid in a contemporary context, it must continue to evolve and meet the challenge of the new.

Three related stories – 'Voices in the Heart,' 'The Chicken Blood Seal,' and 'Anniversary' – treat traditional values and ideological value systems either with ambivalence or with implied disapproval. The first of these stories appears to praise the values of resistance and revolt in the face of authoritarianism. 'Winning does not always equate with success, nor defeat, failure,' Uncle Poon, the patriarchal figure of 'Voices in the Heart' counsels (191). This is a lesson that Keung, the story's protagonist, learns only after long years of feeling that he has abandoned those who put their confidence in him when he was sent, at the age of fifteen, on a journey from Canton to Hong Kong 'to help set up clandestine supply lines' for the Communist party (190). In Hong Kong, Keung must battle for his daily survival; forgetting his political mission and personal ambitions, during the next forty-five years he puts his nose to the grindstone, working as a typesetter and a night watchman. The story ends with Keung's decision to return to Canton to pay tribute to Uncle Poon and his wife Red Hope, and in so doing to confront the Chinese government that has 'betrayed' communism's ideals (201). Keung imagines shouting his final judgment to all who will listen: 'Is it not time to ask why we are so filled with hatred and violence? Is it not time to demand of our leaders where cruelties and fratricides are leading?' (202) Keung knows that the Red Guard will knock him down and smash his spectacles, but that does not matter: 'If a single person could be moved to ponder, then hope would remain alive and he would have fulfilled his destiny' (202). This conclusion would seem a personal redemption, but there is an aspect of futility as well as heroism in his imagined defiance, and that is perhaps the key point: the defiance is not manifest; it remains an idea, a kind of nostalgic resolve, not a completed action that has an effect and consequences. Keung's life story breaks in two, divided between a utopian ambition and an economic struggle for survival. The former has the quality of a wish; the latter, of a fatalism.

A certain futility also moves as an undercurrent in 'The Chicken Blood Seal.' Although this is primarily a story about a generation gap and a conflict of values between Soong, who stands for Chinese tradition, and his son, a successful banker who stands for modernity, the larger question that the story poses concerns Hong Kong's future: will that future take shape with a knowledge of the past to guide it? Whether in China, dominated by an ideology that is destroying the family and traditional values, or in Hong Kong, where capitalism fosters greed and selfishness, a new 'Dark Age' has arrived – that, at least, is Old Soong's analysis of the contemporary Asian world. The story's narrator, a British expatriate who becomes a sinologist thanks to Soong's inspiring tutelage, wonders whether generations formed by such different circumstances and exigencies can possibly share the same values. At the end of his commemorative recounting of the old man's life, the narrator ponders the chicken blood seal that Soong has inscribed for his recently born grandson:

> The [Chinese] characters read simply: 'To go far is to return' ... I wonder whether the grandson will be able to decipher that ancient script. If he can, what meaning will he draw from that message? If he cannot, will those archaic and incomprehensible characters launch him on an intellectual and spiritual odyssey as magnificent as his grandfather's? (241)

'The Chicken Blood Seal' is rich with ambivalence. Soong is admirable, but he has a 'faraway look' in his eyes and he lives – in his son's judgment – out of touch with the world, among a museum of dead things. His utopia has a pathologic quality, unresponsive to situations and predicaments that test its range of accommodation. The narrator's attitude toward Soong and Chinese tradition is consistently respectful, yet his description of the son's frustration and turmoil shows that he also comprehends that tradition can harm if it does not evolve and make itself vital and responsive to the contemporary moment. For Soong, has not 'the old way' become a withdrawal from life rather than an engagement with its changing demands and challenges? The story concludes with a final ambivalence: Soong leaves his magnificent collection of seals not to his son, but to the British Museum and other art foundations in England, an ironic repartee to bulldozing, ultra-modern Hong Kong, where remnants of the past become harder and harder to find. This story suggests that the crisis, then, is two-fold: a tradition without contemporary responsiveness confronts a modernity that is short-sighted and sterile. The society moves within this labyrinthine dilemma.

'Anniversary' focuses on the often unpredictable cumulative effect in contemporary Hong Kong of two value systems, Chinese traditional values and Christian morality; their combination frames the predicament that Mei-ling confronts in her unhappy marriage and ensures that Kwan, her dear friend, will be unable to throw aside his own scruples to come to her aid. As in other stories, appearances differ from reality; this inversion constitutes a consistent register of translation throughout the collection. Thus, in Kwan's as well as society's eyes, John Sham (his name immediately raises suspicion) and Mei-ling are the ideal couple: not only are they 'popular, charming and devoted to each other,' but they are also 'socially prominent and active in the charitable work of the Catholic Church' (243). Their marriage has a secret flaw, though: John's sexual impotency and Mei-ling's guilt and frustration as a woman. Her Catholic morality combined with her Chinese dedication to her husband impede her finding a resolution to the marital crisis; she feels suffocated by moral standards inappropriate to her dilemma, yet she is incapable of altering her situation. She eventually commits suicide, slashing her wrists with her husband's razor blade, 'to end her life in mortal sin' (256–7). To the Western reader, accustomed to the idea of divorce and other practical resolutions of such marital difficulties, the story's ending is melodramatic. Perhaps only an Asian reader (steeped in the enormous importance of children in the perpetuation of a family's identity) can appreciate the depth of Mei-ling's turmoil and predicament as a woman and wife. Her rigid morality – a Chinese devotion and a Christian sense of sin and guilt – ensures that there can be no non-destructive way out of desire's impasse. The story retains a certain disturbing quality, like the *faits divers* in the *South China Morning Post* about suicides that the Asian economic crisis had helped spawn. In this and other stories Wong succeeds in narratizing particularities of the city and the lives of its inhabitants as situations that resonate in a cultural imaginary at once specific to Hong Kong and Asia yet intersecting with other more Western ones.

A second group of stories, including 'Hammer and Tong,' 'Uncle Tuck,' and 'Crippled Sunday,' specifically treats East-West cultural conflict and cultural hybridity. The author, although himself a product of Hong Kong and London, of Chinese and British cultures, views the notion of cultural mixing with a certain scepticism. 'Hammer and Tong' farcically recounts the transformation of a young Chinese civil servant who rises from his humble village origins to become an exemplary junior officer – too exemplary, in fact, for senior administrators who begin to fear his scrutiny of their sometimes illegal management of funds. To refine his manners (i.e., to teach him 'to pass the port') – and to get him out of the way – they send Tong to Oxford for special training, where he westernizes himself far beyond the expectations of his superiors. He falls under the charm of a Swedish student of anthropology who convinces him that he must liberate himself from his colonial masters.

He resigns his Hong Kong post and causes a scandal when the tub in which he is bathing with his Swedish girlfriend crashes through the upper floor into the kitchen of a genteel Oxford boarding house. Hammer, the deputy financial secretary and Tong's superior, imagines with horror the popular press headline, one that might well have appeared in the now defunct *Hong Kong Standard*: 'Sex in Bath Lands Hong Kong Official in Chicken Soup.' With a touch of the wackiness of Benny Hill, 'Hammer and Tong' takes polite, farcical revenge on all those who would advocate one culture's assimilation of another and pokes fun at the hypocrisy of colonial morality. Do the British really want the Chinese to be like them? No, the unstated conclusion would seem to be that they simply want them to learn to play the game, even when they themselves conveniently break the rules. A less direct and more theoretical approach to the story would highlight the character of Tong as a cross-cultural translation; depending on one's interpretation of his motivation and behaviour, he either succeeds at parodying and ridiculing his British masters, or he shows the limitations of translating one culture into the register of another. Again, although this story is light-hearted, it narrates a situation that finds a resonant place in the cultural imaginary of Hong Kong as former colony and crossroads between East and West.

It has been said that in Hong Kong you can't switch identities fast enough; from a different perspective than 'Hammer and Tong,' 'Crippled Sunday' also explores the psychological processes and social drama of cross-cultural translation. An entrepreneur and distinguished public figure, Leung Shing-Chee, the story's main character, cultivates a Western modernity with aplomb, yet on Sunday, when at home and away from the public eye, he exchanges his pinstripe jacket for a Chinese suit and shoes, and transforms his character, even his physical features. The look of his benign, crooked smile and comic nose metamorphose into a serious (and menacing) expression: that of a 'prize-fighter on the point of achieving a knockout.' In sum, Leung seems to be two different persons: the modern 'corporate wizard' is 'at heart a traditionalist, harbouring deep attachments to roots and continuity' (261–2). Why, the reader wonders, does Leung engage in this ritual of cross-cultural transformation? The motivation lies, the narrative suggests, deeply seated in his childhood, where the themes of deception and self-reliance were inculcated. Early in his life Leung's father teaches his son to distrust the world: he instructs him to jump from the cockloft of the family grocery store, but at the last moment he withdraws his arms and allows his son to fall to the ground, which leaves him permanently crippled. 'You trusted me and I let you down,' the father explains. 'I did that to teach you something important. We live in treacherous times. It is dangerous to put too much trust in anyone. Even those dearest to you are capable of betrayal' (264). The mistrust that this betrayal engenders lies at the core of Leung's success as well as his failure; by dint of hard work and clever calculation, he proceeds to conquer the business world and the colonial public domain. Superficially, Leung would seem to epitomize a perfect mastery of the etiquettes of East and West, yet the translation and social transformation is of a Dr Jeckyll–Mr Hyde order. In this translation, one culture's interrelationship with the other becomes unrecognizable, blotting out the commonalities that certainly exist between them. This leads to a binary world of deception, absolute difference, and unbridgeable gulfs, symbolized by the unfatherly father who allows his son to fall to the ground, crippling him. Leung becomes two very different persons, one on weekdays, the other on weekends; without a middle ground, a liminal space across which these different identities exchange congruencies, he becomes untranslatable, even to himself. In 'Crippled Sunday,' then, Wong shows scepticism toward the notions of hybridity and cultural assimilation – we see the same scepticism and the same patterns of mixed dressing and 'a fateful fall' in 'Hammer and Tong.' Is it Leung's Chinese body that resists a total assimilation into Western culture, or is his split personality a consequence of his will to conquer two different worlds no matter the personal cost? Leung's failures – to produce an heir, for example – might also be thought of as urgent communications, in the sense that Nietzsche uses: 'we question the body and reject the evidence of the sharpened senses: we try, if you like, to see whether the inferior parts themselves cannot enter into communication with us' (quoted in Karantani, *Origins of Modern Japanese Literature* 93). Leung as fictional character may be interpreted as a metaphor for problems of translation and the clashes and conflicts of styles and values that Hong Kong brings into existence – and leaves unresolved. As I have suggested, one might read this story as a popular rewriting (with postcolonial touches) of different Western mythic material, from Faust to Frankenstein to Dr Jeckyll and Mr Hyde, all tinted with the colouring of the specific lens of the Hong Kong cultural imaginary.

The story 'Uncle Tuck' takes a totally different view from 'Crippled Sunday'; it celebrates translation and cultural mixing, with its protagonist exemplifying the spirit of 'freedom, irreverence, and enterprise' to which the author has dedicated this short-story collection. Tuck embodies East and West, combining something of the legendary San Tuck, 'the fighting monk from Shaolin Temple who was never above breaking his vegetarian vows for a good feed, and Friar Tuck, that jolly companion of Robin Hood' (173–4). His life is a performance in the best sense of that word: to paraphrase *international situationniste* Guy Debord, 'Le plus grand art, vivre' (see Dachy, 'International situationniste'). An-Shan, Tuck's nephew and the story's narrative reflector, recalls his uncle's bits of wisdom, outrageous acts, and genius for unconventional living, and thus duly honours him (upon his death) with gaiety rather than sadness. Jazz, not dirge, graces Tuck's funeral; defying time, the deceased, by bequest, throws a post-mortem party. Overall, the story has a nostalgic, commemorative quality as if Tuck's death, and the hybrid, East-West genius that he exemplifies, prefigures a larger event, the end of an epoch in Hong Kong. Perhaps this is one reason why, on *Hong Kong Stories*' book jacket, the infamous '1997' appears in red letters on the front page of the newspaper that a rickshaw driver is idly reading. The entire collection can be read as a farewell – a commemoration to an Uncle Tuck–like Hong Kong that has passed away but, as in the post-mortem party, comes back from the dead; these stories are just as much about an anticipatory, future identity of the city as they are about its colonial past. Like other stories in the collection, but perhaps more overtly so, 'Uncle Tuck' takes the moment of political transition (i.e., the 1997 handover/return to China) as a focus to translate the city into a utopian narrative of its multicultural heritage and an anticipatory future where cultural diversity constitutes a hope and strength.

A third group of stories, of which I will briefly mention five – 'The Cocktail Party,' 'Miss Tsushima,' 'Dead Cert,' 'The Revolt of Grass,' and 'Szeto's Bar' – dwell on moral and ethical complications and the twists and turns of fate in contemporary Hong Kong. Life in the city has a labyrinthine quality; things are never quite what they seem, and one rarely achieves one's ends by moving directly in a straight line. Each story features some act that conceals a truth or breaks a cultural taboo, social convention, or governmental law, as if the situations that make up Hong Kong have themselves a shadowy as well as a transparent quality. In a metaphorical sense, this is part of the city's yin and yang. In 'The Cocktail Party,' a middle-aged entrepreneur, K.B. Woo, recalls the reception at which he first met the twenty-year-old Lulu, who, during the past five years, has been the libidinal flame of his life. A married man, with a simple, uneducated wife selected for him by his father, had he lived in another time he would have taken Lulu as his concubine, K.B. surmises, but in colonial Hong Kong, morality intervenes: 'everywhere that they went the British had to spread their obsession with monogamy like a contagion,' he bemoans (31). A man of cosmopolitan tastes, he wines and dines Lulu and tutors her in the entrepreneurial spirit, so much so that he later learns that it is she who has been managing him. K.B. may be the master of the 'multifarious uses' of the cocktail party, but in the end it is Lulu who concocts the most ingenious fête – to introduce K.B. to her future husband, another aging entrepreneur with whom she has been trysting on Wednesdays while meeting K.B. on Fridays. He is duly humbled, but he recognizes that Lulu is not to blame, for her principles of getting ahead in the world are exactly the ethics that he himself has taught her. What makes the end of this short story work so well is K.B.'s refusal to mope when Lulu stands him on his head; he understands that sadness is not compatible with his life of practical decisions and action. In defeat, he still affirms the values by which he lives. Are K.B.'s and Lulu's values Hong Kong's? The collection does show the effects of money on people's moral sense, but it also breaks down stereotypes about Hong Kong as a 'capitalist jungle.' The Western image of the city/SAR equates it with money-mindedness and crass materialism; *Hong Kong Stories* dismantles this stereotype because it shows that money is also something human and complex and almost always other than itself. I think of a passage in Jorge Luis Borges's 'The Zahir':

> [T]here is nothing less material than money, since any coin whatsoever ... is strictly speaking, a repertory of possible futures. Money is abstract ...; money is the future tense. It can be an evening in the suburbs, or music by Brahms; it can be maps, or chess, or coffee; it can be the words of Epictetus ...; it is a Proteus more versatile than the one on the isle of Pharos. It is unforeseeable time, ... a coin [that] symbolizes man's free will. (*Labyrinths* 159)

Wong's collection is quite interesting in its different depictions of the effects and meanings of money. Certainly there is nothing crass, for example, about K.B.'s attitude toward money; he uses it like a magic carpet to transport Lulu to Paris and to shower her with flowers and gifts.

The story 'Miss Tsushima' mixes various themes, but seems primarily about traditional (Asian) values in the contemporary world. Its plot again recounts a tryst between a middle-aged man and a young woman, but here the encounter leads not to an affair but to a strange absolution and an affirmation of transcultural, humanistic values. Yung, a Hong

Kong trade negotiator, and Miss Tsushima, a translator and liaison assigned to aid him during his conference participation in Japan, share an intimacy; what Yung does not understand is that Miss Tsushima, who is engaged to be married very soon, allows herself to be seduced by him as a way of atoning for the crimes that her father committed during the Second World War. To explain the story in such a straightforward manner, though, depletes it of its subtleties and its intimations of unconscious forces guiding the behaviour of Yung and Miss Tsushima, and directing them toward a moment of larger-than-individual comprehension. The author depicts this in haiku-like images. The trees in Kyoto, where Yung and Miss Tsushima spend the day sightseeing, are full of blossoms, flowers that will be rent by the first rain. 'Is that not the law of nature, Yung-san?' Miss Tsushima inquires. 'Petals must fall sooner or later from even the most beautiful blooms. Is it not the very transitoriness of things that makes life precious?' (72). When the rain arrives and does its expected damage, Miss Tsushima cannot resist being overwhelmed with sadness: the 'petals fell as if with a sigh, like so many white, wounded butterflies' (72). Yung feels that he is witnessing a 'sacrilege.' Certainly on one level of interpretation, this scene enacts a sacrifice, one that will be repeated in a different form when Miss Tsushima offers her virginity to Yung. What motivates her action is not sexual desire, but a deep sense of an individual's implication in the actions and destiny of one's ancestors. Yung tells Miss Tsushima that his father, a pharmacist seeking to aid an ailing friend, was executed by the Japanese military for smuggling medicine into an internment camp (75). Upon hearing this story, Miss Tsushima bows deeply and asks for forgiveness. Yung does not make an immediate connection between her bow and their intimacy later in the evening; two weeks before her marriage she sleeps with a man other than her fiancé in order to, as she says, 'repay a debt, to atone' for her father, who, during the campaign in Nanking, engaged in a fury of looting, rape, and murder (78). The experience marked him permanently, leaving him mentally imbalanced and suicidal. 'I thought if I atoned ... for my father's crimes, by offering you what is most precious to me and what only can be offered once,' she explains, 'the gods might take pity and grant my father peace. It was a silly idea, I now realize, but I meant no harm' (81).

Among other things, 'Miss Tsushima' is a kind of disguised morality play about memory and individual responsibility; the present is unable to forget the past, it suggests, and this is an awareness that twentieth-first-century global society often lacks. To find one's way through the labyrinth of today's interconnected world, Jacques Attali argues in *Chemins de sagesse: Traité du labyrinthe*, memory is crucial (180). One problem with globalism as a concept is that it seems devoid of a time sense, a historical sense of the strata of human experiences that must be comprehended and commemorated in order for the world to become truly global in its knowledge and sensibility. In 'Miss Tsushima' it is a fragment of a very particular Hong Kong / China and a very particular Japan that reaches a new understanding. Global and international interrelatedness must be viewed as a labyrinth with hidden passages like those that Yung and Miss Tsushima intuitively and then consciously follow. They actualize a potential that exists in the world today, but this global potential can only be tapped through millions of individual, local encounters, all of which have their own specificity. It is also interesting to read this story from a more abstract perspective; unlike 'Crippled Sunday,' which appears to deny that differences can be translated, this story, by way of the translator Miss Tsushima, asserts interrelationships and responsibilities that cross common barriers of time and space, unimpeded by generational differences and national frontiers. In this sense, human values have both a transcultural and translational component.

'Dead Cert,' 'The Revolt of Grass,' and 'Szeto's Bar' concern the struggle for survival and dignity in a world ruled by autocratic decree on one side of the border (mainland China) and the 'green-eyed monster' on the other (Hong Kong). In these stories the protagonists enter a maze of moral complications; through their actions they must construct a new value system and a new sense of their identity. Above all, they must struggle to survive. In 'Dead Cert' Tiger Yang overcomes numerous handicaps; through a fighting spirit and an acquired understanding of the unwritten rules of racing he becomes a champion jockey. Being a jockey involves more than riding horses, however; it also involves, Tiger is told, taking account of people's motivations and the effect of money on them. If a jockey ever wants to win big, Tiger's mentor explains, he must be prepared to betray everyone (88). Tiger plans carefully for the perfect moment; he is sure, riding Dead Cert, that he is going to pull it off, win a bundle of money, and then retire in high style. Chance – or is it destiny? – has the final say, though. During the race a horse falls in his path; hurled to the ground, Tiger meets life's only sure outcome. (As an aside, it is perhaps worth noting that a Hong Kong jockey died in this manner in March 1999, only the second in the city's racing history; was Wong thinking of the first when he wrote this story?) To a certain extent, life in *Hong Kong Stories* is a gamble and a game, just as writing these short stories, all of them about different Hong Kong people with different fates, is a writerly game. In this sense, they are popular entertainments with satiric, melodramatic, and even operatic touches.

In 'Dead Cert,' we can readily understand Tiger Yang, a little guy trying to beat the (corrupt?) system; we also understand Yun, the proletarian hero of 'The Revolt of Grass,' an illegal immigrant who tries to pull his family in mainland China out of poverty. Yun enters a political and economic labyrinth, playing a high-risk game in the hope of eluding the Hong Kong immigration authorities long enough to recross the border and take care of his family's needs. He is betrayed. The foreman of Yun's work crew arranges a police raid of the construction site a few hours before paytime so that the illegal workers will be rounded up and the construction company will not have to dispense their wages. When the police arrive, Yun is laying bricks on the twenty-sixth floor, so there can be no escape from the fate awaiting him below. 'A blade of grass survives storms better than a tree braving the wind,' Yun's father has counselled (96). Following this wisdom, Yun has often submitted, humbling himself in the face of authority. But this time his anger, long held within, breaks; he chooses to ignore the commands shouted at him on police bullhorns and rests on a ledge throughout the night rather than descend and surrender. 'He felt as if he were poised on the edge of the world, charged in some inexplicable way with defending his fellow men from some encroaching darkness ... His tiredness fell away and he felt unaccountably refreshed. He did not know what tomorrow would bring but he knew if he clung to his perch long enough he would be rewarded by the sight of a new dawn' (112). It is in the spirit of modern existentialist heroes that Yun disobeys, rebels against authority; he chooses, and therefore takes charge of his fate. He will go to jail and eventually be extradited, but he has not been broken as a human being, as an individual. It might be argued that Yun's decision is also a pragmatic one, because in the long term his self-esteem is more precious than any wages lost during several weeks or months of detention. What values does Hong Kong make available to its citizens – and to those, on the other side of the border, who are not its inhabitants but who are drawn into Hong Kong's stories? 'The true city,' Spinoza remarks, 'offers citizens the love of freedom instead of the hope of rewards or even the security of possessions; for "it is slaves, not free men, who are given rewards for virtue"' (quoted in Deleuze, *The Deleuze Reader* 76). To disobey can be a first step towards freedom, and even the lowliest can rebel, the story's title affirms. 'The Revolt of Grass' highlights a latent, prospective identity, allegorized by Yun, that the city, Wong would seem to suggest, might embrace and develop as a counterweight to the 'green-eyed monster.' This story tends, then, toward utopian values.

'Szeto's Bar' puts into play the different value systems that inform the collection – tradition, East-West hybridity, pragmaticism, and modernity – without seeking to resolve them into simplistic formulas. Like 'The Revolt of Grass' and 'Voices in the Heart,' the story is an anti-capitalist tale (there are also anti-communist tales in the collection), for the demands of money and success pull the story's two lovers, Yuen and Ching Ching, apart. Childhood sweethearts who plan to marry, they are separated by Yuen's decision to accept a scholarship to study in the United States and by the death of Ching Ching's father, which forces the mother to take the children to Singapore; the family departs without leaving a forwarding address, and Yuen and Ching Ching fall out of touch. In order to support the family, she becomes a dance hostess; years later, Yuen meets her again by chance, though now she is known as Jade Lotus, queen of the Hong Kong dance halls. The clock cannot be turned back; their respective fates cannot be recast. Hers is a great, though tainted, success, and he is a cynical journalist who drinks too much and whose salary is much too low to support a social celebrity and her family. Still a traditional Chinese woman within, Ching Ching views herself as a fallen, albeit successful, businesswomen who must cater to the rich men who pay for her services. When Yuen interferes, believing that he is defending her honour, he unwittingly sets in motion events that lead to her death.

This sentimental love story is set within the framed tale of Szeto and his bar, which are mentioned in three of the collection's other stories; it is Szeto, for example, who gives Uncle Tuck's magnificent funeral oration. The balding bartender is an unorthodox mixture of businessman, psychologist, and philosopher; he allows his customers the freedom to indulge in drink to their heart's content – to become merry or sad, it matters not to him – and the only rules in his bar are practical ones that apply to its smooth functioning: no unescorted women and no passing out from alcoholic excess. If a customer drinks too much and collapses, Szeto has him dragged to a dark room, itself a kind of labyrinth for the inebriated. A clever system of locks ensures that any bungler will remain there until moderately sober, at which time he will eventually open the door and find his way down the alley, itself a final, minor humiliation: 'the departure w[ill] be undignified, involving unpleasant navigation through a back alley cluttered with overflowing garbage bins, discarded containers and colonies of stray cats' (114). Opposed to Szeto's pragmatism is Yuen's romanticism and sadness. Yuen regrets his decisions and grieves the loss of the woman that he has loved. Intensified by alcohol, this sadness and romanticism decompose his character; he deteriorates physically and morally. Yet Yuen's telling of his story to Szeto has a therapeutic effect; in the end Szeto comforts him with what could be interpreted as an affirmation of a cultural value (i.e., a belief in everlasting love) or an illusion that suits a lover's romanticism. In listening to Yuen's story, Szeto has understood the client and the problem and has responded in a way that allows Yuen to be reconciled with his grief and to leave the bar with dignity. Rather than impose his own values, Szeto performs an act of translation; he translates Yuen's story and situation into a pragmatic that mixes Chinese with Western values. He also allows the ambiguities to remain in place.

Having looked briefly at several stories, I would like to return to the questions that I posed at the beginning of the chapter and respond to them by way of a discussion of the collection's characterization, transcultural and translational aspects, and rewriting of notions and myths of Hong Kong as seen 'from the side' (that is, not solely from a nativist perspective). One angle from which *Hong Kong Stories* can be analysed is characterization: to what degree do its personages possess an interiority, a self-reflection, or conversely, to what degree are their identities limited to the social roles that they perform? In 'Gender Constructs and Chinese Womanhood,' Kwok-kan Tam states: 'In the Chinese tradition, the formation of selfhood is not based on the construction of the ego as self-identity ... As demonstrated in *Daxue* ... the process of the "cultivation of personal life, regulation of the family, ordering the state, bringing peace throughout the world" ... prescribes a strong sense of communitarianism, in which the self is just a relational self-role. In Confucianism the self is described always in relation to others, but never as a separate category' (4–5). (As an aside we might note that, interestingly, here we have stated a traditional Eastern concept of interdependence and interrelationship that would seem compatible with twentieth-century phenomenological and hermeneutical philosophy, on the one hand, and with theories of relational forces in modern physics, on the other.)[8] One could argue that Asian texts that conform to such a tradition could be classified as 'Oriental,' whereas texts that depart from this tradition could be classified as showing an Occidental influence. For example, contemporary texts by Asian writers that assign 'established discourse roles' (such as 'mothers, daughters, wives, girl friends') and established 'discourse positions' (such as 'marginal, passive, dependent') (Ho, 'Women in Exile' 31) to female characters might be considered Eastern as opposed to Western. In this regard *Hong Kong Stories* seems to me a book split along gender lines: it is chiefly Oriental in its female characterization, yet Occidental in its male characterization. This is not true for every personage, of course, but this seems to be the collection's tendency. Female characters are absent from several of the stories; in others, females have minor and traditional roles. They are chiefly supportive, as is Red Hope in 'Voices in the Heart,' the wife who seeks to reconcile father and son in 'The Chicken Blood Seal,' Mei-ling the frustrated wife in 'Anniversary,' and the wife-back-in-China in 'The Revolt of Grass.' Red Hope and Adelaide (Tuck's wife and An-shan's secret flame in 'Uncle Tuck') are two versions of the female who provides moral inspiration and gives physical comfort. With the possible exception of 'Miss Tsushima,' whose heroine is Japanese not Chinese, none of the stories focuses exclusively on a female character; as in Szeto's bar, it would seem that unaccompanied women are not allowed.

We also see another form of this principle in the various stories' framing devices. There must first be a male character who establishes the space within which a counterpart female character can then exist; in 'The Cocktail Party,' for instance, it is K.B.'s story that frames Lulu's; in 'Miss Tsushima,' it is Yung's story that frames Miss Tsushima's, and in 'Anniversary,' Kwan's story frames Mei-ling's. The assignment of characters' professional identities shows a similar female dependency on male authority. Only three women, Miss Tsushima, Lulu, and Ching Ching, have a professional identity; Lulu and Ching Ching enter the entrepreneurial world of Hong Kong and achieve a certain success, but both must use their bodies to help them find their place. Lulu gets her boutique by way of her sexual relationship with K.B., and Ching Ching uses her beauty and charm to transform herself into Jade Lotus, the queen of the nightclubs, and thus is able to support her family. The Hong Kong of these stories, then, is not primarily a woman's place, though females are important to its male characters; the women are, variously, supports and sources of desire and inspiration. Although this aspect of the collection may reflect the social landscape of a Hong Kong of the 1970s and 1980s, it might also be interpreted as a residue of Oriental myths that are still part of the cultural imaginary of this East/West place. Perhaps Wong's own vision, as a male, takes control of his pen; or, more to the point, the stories may show Wong's sense of popular Western notions about and expectations of Hong Kong and Asian women.

Of course, women are everywhere present in contemporary Hong Kong; they occupy the full range of positions, from government officials to business executives, professors, drivers, and construction workers.

In the male characters we find, conversely, a tendency to occidentalize motivations and actions. I think, for example, of Uncle Tuck, Yun of 'The Revolt of Grass,' Tong of 'Hammer and Tong,' Tiger Yang of 'Dead Cert,' and Yuen of 'Szeto's Bar.' In these characters we see something of the modern Western individualist striking out against authoritarian and bureaucratic systems. When we consider the male characters of these stories in relation to success and failure, we find that traditional (Asian) values such as diligence, hard work, loyalty, and obedience are often ineffectual. The world is perilous, the situations and characters of *Hong Kong Stories* assert; the 'rules of the game' change rapidly and unpredictably, and sometimes there are no perceivable rules. Characters with dominant traditional values may place themselves in opposition to such a treacherous and precarious world, but they usually do not intervene in it or struggle against it, or perhaps they intervene or struggle in the wrong way. Tong, of 'Hammer and Tong,' gets himself into trouble because he does his job so efficiently, inadvertently exposing the questionable practices of his seniors; Yun, the illegal worker of 'The Revolt of Grass' raises suspicions when he lays his bricks with care and attention to the final product. Inspector's Hung's filial piety entraps him in criminal activities that ruin his career; Old Soong's loyalty to traditional values isolates him and distances him from the needs of his son; Kwan's fraternal loyalty impedes him from responding to the predicament of Mei-ling, his friend's wife. Generally speaking, the short-story collection affirms other qualities and values, such as cleverness, tough mindedness, a capacity to adapt to change and modernity, creativity in the living of one's life, and a capacity for generosity. It is interesting that in this story collection about an Asian place and people, readers' sympathies are rarely on the side of the law; in a social context in which authority is still the dominant regulator of individual behaviour, Wong would seem to view a capacity for disobedience, revolt, and nonconformism as vital in today's world. We see here an aspect of the transcultural value system – a mix of East and West – that moulds Wong's fiction of Hong Kong; we also see, perhaps, a translation of Hong Kong for a Western readership. At least ten of the thirteen stories focus on individuals who rebel against or break a cultural proscription, social convention, or law. If only in a minor key, Tong, K.B., Miss Tsushima, Yun, Uncle Tuck, and Keung are all rebels, at some point in their lives breaking either taboo, convention, or law. Betrayal is also a recurrent theme in the collection; like revolt and law-breaking, betrayal depends on a certain interiority and self-reflection. A character who rebels or who betrays must be given a sense of self in order to account for the motivation for the rebellion or betrayal. In these two aspects of *Hong Kong Stories*, then, we see features of a westernization of the subject matter, or an inverse orientalization that structures Chinese male characterization in Wong's work. Anarchy is not Wong's implied stance, but the stance is definitely a modern Western one: in a hostile, unstable, bureaucratic order, individuals must sometimes take a stand; otherwise, they will be brushed aside in a world that rapidly changes with no consideration to good behaviour and past virtue. In an authoritarian, bureaucratic society individuals are always in danger of losing their interiority and becoming totally externalized. They become routines, conventions, duties, 'the people,' statistics, and so forth. The author, we recall, dedicates his collection – 'To Hong Kong. May its spirit of freedom, irreverence and enterprise remain forever intact' – with this peril in mind. 'Freedom,' 'irreverence,' 'enterprise,' 'individualism': these words provide the translational key for interpreting the Hong Kong that Wong composes. Certainly it is more a Hong Kong of situations and value systems in conflict and at ironic play than one viewed pictorially (as tourists experience the city) or spatially, as it is often represented in glossy post cards of its imposing skyscrapers along the Central waterfront.

Contemporary Hong Kong is many things. Historically, it has been principally three things: 'a transit point between China and the world, refugee haven, and site of belonging for many of its local inhabitants' (Ho, 'Women in Exile' 44). Wong's collection portrays each of these aspects of the city/SAR, but it also responds imaginatively, putting 'Hong Kong' in quotation marks, translating/transforming something spatial and impossible to grasp into narratives of the city's prospective identity and futures. These localized, realist stories dip equally into the mythic and the transcultural, exceeding boundaries by following intertextual linkages into other cultural imaginaries. This chapter has foregrounded two related notions of Hong Kong as a network of narratives and as a society of linkages, because culture is not only something in place, but also something fluid, throwing out 'lines of flight,' to use Gilles Deleuze's phrase, in multiple directions. In this sense, identity and culture are 'rhizomes'; they are dimensions or 'directions in motion.' Conceived of as a rhizome – itself a living labyrinth – identity and culture have 'neither beginning nor end, but always a middle [milieu]' (*The Deleuze Reader* 34–6). In the living labyrinth, reality takes shape along the networks of communication, linkage, and exchange, but to be comprehended it requires a translation into words and narratives; stories then feed back recursively into the thoughts and activities of all those who have the labyrinth as their home, whether permanently, as a haven, or in sojourn. Hong Kong may be tiny, yet 'Made in Hong Kong' embraces the world. Although some people will say, 'Nothing is made here; everything just passes through,' others prefer to put the accent on the future and its possibilities: 'Everything, the whole world, is already here, in the making.'

4. Where is Place? Locale and Identity in Kazua Ishiguro's *When We Were Orphans* and Ricardo Piglia's *La ciudad ausente*

> They proceeded toward the imposing castle, on whose frontispiece was written: 'I belong to no one – and to everyone. You were here before you entered this place, and you will still be here after you leave.'
> Denis Diderot, *Jacques le fataliste*[1]

The Presocratic thinker Zeno, who in the words of philosopher of science Karl Popper constructed some of the 'most searching and ingenious defensive attacks in the history of Western philosophy,' had this to say about the concept of locale: 'If place exists, where is it? For everything that exists is in a place. Therefore, place is in a place. This goes on to infinity. Therefore, place does not exist' (quoted in McKirahan and Card, *A Presocratic Reader* 77). The argument is sophistic, but the question is more difficult to answer than it first may seem. Place and identity might be compared to two parallel trains in a railway station. For a passenger seated in one of the trains and looking into the windows of the other, determining which train is actually in motion at the beginning of a journey can be deceptive. Imperfect though the analogy may be, the main idea is clear: we commonly think of place as fixed, yet it is finally no more fixed than an individual's identity. The changes that a locale undergoes contribute to our sense of changing, evolving identity, and vice versa. We find this idea at the dawn of Western philosophy, in Presocratic philosophers such as Heraclitus and Cratylus. One cannot step twice into the same river, Heraclitus famously argued, challenging those who contended that everywhere everything is the same. Not to be outdone, Cratylus rebuked this conservatism, remarking that one could not step even *once* into the same river. The world is in flux, so much so that place and identity cannot be permanently located; the river is never the same, so how can it bear the unity of a name – or so seems to be the point of objection behind Cratylus's retort.

What is true of the river is also true of the individual. One is never the same person; one is always, in a sense, partly absent. In *101 Expériences de philosophie quotidienne* (*101 Everyday Experiences of Philosophy*),[2] Roger-Pol Droit, in one of his language and thought games, asks readers to look for their 'I.' This leads to a strange and paradoxical search, not for the least of reasons because 'I' belongs to everyone in societies where English is spoken, yet this 'I' cannot be found: 'You will never find the "I" in your body,' Droit explains. 'None of your cells have survived a ten-year period. None of the elements that make up your body have remained the same. To what, then, will this "I" refer? To the form? The ensemble of structures? The organization? Thought remains (or such is the classical response). Everything changes, but not your memories, your sense of continuing to be the same, identical in spite of the alterations. But there as well, you will never put your finger on the "I." You will find only thoughts, sequences, memories, association of ideas, and desires that are affected by what you call the "I"' (25). Whether for objects, such as the river of Heraclitus's celebrated remark, or subjects, such as the 'I,' the world is in flux; the world *is* flux. Both place and identity are hard to find.

This chapter, which builds on the discussion of Hong Kong as narrative and situation in chapter 3, and serves as a bridge with the discussion of identity as interrelationship and virtuality in chapters 5 and 6, has at once a banal and an ambitious intention: to explore the notion of place in a way that goes against the grain, so to speak, thinking about it not as a residence of people and conglomeration of buildings and objects, but rather as a series of filters and lenses through which we view the world. I want to consider place less as a geographic entity, with its materiality and factuality, than as an ensemble of experiences and ideas, some shared with a community, others private and idiosyncratic. In this sense, place has an aspect not of something 'out there' to which one refers with certainty, as one refers to a location on a map, but rather of something constructed by consciousness and then believed in, in more or less the same way that one views one's image in a mirror. In each place we see something that reflects both who we are and who we are not; in each, place and identity meet and meet differently each time. In general, then, I want to take a less travelled approach to the popular assumption that place is outside and identity is within. Continuing along this line of thought, the chapter will consider the relationship between place and identity in some contemporary literature, especially the recent work of Kazua Ishiguro (*When We Were Orphans*, 2000) and Ricardo Piglia's *La ciudad austente*, translated into English as *The Absent City* by Sergio Waisman (2000). We can say that place and identity are interrelated; the question is, in what way?

At the beginning of Western philosophy, with Presocratic philosophers such as Heraclitus and Pythagoras, place and identity constituted key topics of inquiry. They have continued to be throughout the intellectual history of the West – during the modern period, in the eighteenth and nineteenth centuries, for romanticism, for example, and again later in the nineteenth century, for naturalism. In the twentieth century, existentialism, among other philosophies, called into question the notion of individual identity as an autonomous entity, replacing it with the notion of relation, in one form or another. Similarly, place has also become diffuse; the more we try to localize it and isolate it, the more it exceeds the borders assigned to it. It has been displaced not only by the processes of globalization, but in other ways as well. Place recedes from us, spreading into consciousness, blending or transforming into an attitude, a recollection, an ambition, among other things. The Dublin of James Joyce's *Ulysses* and *Finnegans Wake* transforms place in a wholly new way. This is also the idea that informs Italo Calvino's reflection on urban spaces, *La città invisibili* (*Invisible Cities*): 'Cities are a collection of many things: memories, desires, signs of a language; [they] are places of exchange, as all books of economic history explain, but these are not only exchanges of merchandise, but exchanges of words, desires, and souvenirs as well' (Preface to *Les Villes invisibles* vi). Taking the form of a conversation between the celebrated Oriental traveller Marco Polo and the emperor Kubla Khan, Calvino's delightful tale contains many thought-provoking reflections on the concepts of place, identity, time, and space, so much so that it has been taught in urban-studies departments in North American universities as well as in literature and language courses in universities around the world. The tale is postmodern in its insistence that place is a text, and as with any text, it is narration and relation that distinguishes it; it is also postmodern in its sense of the displacement of all particular places into a place that is itself a simulacrum, a semblance that partakes of reality but does so incompletely. Marco Polo says to the Khan: 'It is known that names of places change as many times as there are foreign languages; and that every place can be reached from every other place, by the most various roads and routes, by those who ride, or drive, or row, or fly' (*Cities* 137). To which the Khan replies: 'I think that you recognize cities better on the atlas than when you visit them in person' (ibid.). 'Traveling, you realize that differences are lost,' Polo responds: 'each city takes to resembling all cities, places exchange their form, order, distances, a shapeless dust cloud invades the continents' (ibid.). Today one does not even have to travel to realize that, in one sense, differences between places are disappearing. At the beginning of the twentieth-first century, place has been displaced in at least a double sense. First, each place has begun to look like all places, each an imitation of an anonymous other, which in turn is itself an imitation of some idea of modernity. Technological reproduction, as Walter Benjamin explained, and globalization work together to generalize, to essentialize, each place into all places.[3] I recall a passage in Ricardo Piglia's *The Absent City*, about place and politics and television:

> 'Faces and faces that appear and look at each other and get lost again and are substituted by new faces that appear and look at each other and get lost again.'
> 'It swallows up faces,' said the man who had spoken first.
> 'But the mirror is always there,' the other man said ...
> 'Now, the truth is ... that television is a mirror.'
> 'Exactly ... A mirror that holds onto faces.'
> 'It has all of them inside and when you look at it you see the other's face.' (75)

Each place becomes like all other places because, in part, the situations of living whether here or there repeat like 'faces' in mirrors and on television screens. Second, and this has a different effect from the first phenomenon, places have become 'creolized,' that is, made particular and different by a process in which 'external' or 'foreign' elements become included within an identity, mixing with it and changing it. Another way of describing this is to say that a place, like a person, has the capacity to migrate; a place can turn up where it is least expected, like the inexhaustible Chinatown, which can be found in almost any major city, no matter the continent. There seems no end to its reach; it is global, yet its impact on each context is of a sort particular to that context. Each Chinatown differs from others, and yet they are all Chinatown. Landscapes can also take on this ambivalent quality of difference and sameness. In the short fiction 'Utopía de un hombre que está cansado' ('Utopia of an exhausted man'), Jorge Luis Borges writes: 'There are no two hills that are the same, but anywhere on earth the plains are one and the same. I was travelling on a road in the plains. I wondered whether I was in Oklahoma or in Texas or in the region that literati call the pampas' (*El libro de arena* 69). Borges begins this story with an epigraph explaining that 'utopia' derives from a Greek word that means, paradoxically, no place or nowhere. (The word 'outopos' may also denote a 'place of ideal perfection'; hence, the radical ambiguity of utopia as place derives from its etymology, among other things.) Everywhere, anywhere, and nowhere all share the same incomplete reality of being unpresentable but conceivable. About the presences and absences of place, Italo Calvino is likewise certainly right: all cities are invisible cities. (And this idea of place as virtuality will be developed even further in Piglia's *The Absent City*.) There is more to cities and to a place than meets the eye or that can be represented; this chapter tries to explore the possibilities of that insight, linking it with contemporary reflections on postmodern and post-colonial identity.

Existentialist Orientations

It goes almost without saying that there are a number of approaches to the topic of place and identity in contemporary, especially postmodern and avant-garde, literary works; what I would like to do here is frame these reflections within an existentialist tradition, which itself grounds certain postmodern and post-colonial strategies of reading and interpreting texts. The Presocratic philosophers, in particular Heraclitus, are arguably the first existentialists in the Western philosophic tradition. Heraclitus's emphasis on the dynamism of the universe and on the 'continual newness of all things' appeals to a modern sensibility with its embrace of motion and its belief in progress (Friedman, *The Worlds of Existentialism* 17). Given that existentialism comprises a plurality of philosophies and sometimes radically different positions, it is necessary to indicate which of its aspects are being singled out or highlighted in this chapter's treatment of place and identity.

Here are four fundamental emphases. First, existentialism focuses on the concrete, on the flux and reflux of particular existence, within which we live in uncertainty and unknowing. Far from understanding the world, or ourselves in it, with each step we take we encounter questions without answers ('des pourquoi sans réponse'; Foulquié, *L'Existentialisme* 46). We keep this disquieting and destabilizing aspect of our lives at bay by (thankfully) not thinking about it constantly, the same way that a commuter on a train or in the subway represses the anxiety of time by reading a newspaper or occupying him/herself with anything other than thinking about his own limited existence; on an everyday basis, we often manage the arbitrary and impenetrable nature of reality simply by ignoring it or by filling it with other kinds of partial realities. We tell stories – and invent other realities.

Second, our consciousness is bound to the world, which it cannot and does not transcend. This idea has been expressed in a variety of ways by various existentialist thinkers. For Husserl, consciousness is always consciousness of something. Existence implies a dependence on, a situatedness in, the world: to be is to be somewhere. In simplified form, this is Heidegger's concept of *dasein*. In Sartrean terms, this bond between consciousness and world is expressed in the concepts of 'l'en-soi' and 'le pour-soi.' The former term designates the something, the 'quelque chose,' that constitutes the materiality of thought, which Sartre describes as 'massive' and 'opaque to itself,' devoid of any consciousness. Paradoxically then, consciousness depends on world (this massive and opaque 'something'), yet world receives its significance or is brought into existence by consciousness (Foulquié 68–9).

Third, consciousness interprets the world; there is no world for us without it. In terms of place, Ralph Singh of V.S. Naipaul's *The Mimic Men* draws an interesting distinction: 'All landscapes eventually turn to land, the gold of the imagination to the lead of reality' (10). In these lines the difference between 'landscape' and 'land' roughly corresponds to a division between a human intervention in the world and something outside of or untouched by this intervention. For human beings, however, there can be no outside in that we are always implicated in our interpretations of the world, transforming the 'land' into a 'landscape.' In another Naipaul story, 'A Flag on the Island,' the narrator remarks: 'All landscapes are in the end only in the imagination; to be faced with reality is to start again' (149). Naipaul expresses well the notion that place, in addition to its 'thingness' or materiality, is informed above all by a human intervention, though this intervention is unstable and unsustainable. The subject is always implicated in thinking about the world, French philosopher Gabriel Marcel explains: 'To think of something as existing is to think of oneself as the perceiver; it is to extend one's experience in such a way that it includes even that which remains outside of itself' (*Journal métaphysique* 15–18; quoted in Foulquié, *L'Existentialisme* 38). Consciousness mediates, makes sense of, even composes the world (i.e., the 'en-soi'), as described poetically in the following passage drawn from Simone de Beauvoir's novel *L'Invitée* (1943):

> She left the office ... the dark corridors attracted her. When she was not there, the smell of dust, the shadows, the desolation of the solitude, these things did not exist for anyone, they did not exist at all. And now she was there, the red of the carpet pierced the obscurity like a timid night light. She had this power: her presence uprooted things from their unconsciousness, she gave them their color, their odor. She walked down one floor and pushed open the hall door; it was as if she had been given this mission – to bring things into existence, this deserted room, in the middle of the night. The iron curtain was lowered, the walls smelled of fresh paint; the red velvet armchairs were inertly aligned, as if in waiting. Suddenly they were no longer waiting. And now she was there and they stretched out their arms to her. They watched the scene masked by the iron curtain; they called Pierre and the ramp lights and the crowd gathered. It would have been necessary to stay there forever in order to perpetuate this solitude and waiting. (10)

In this passage place is actualized, or brought into a humanly ordered existence, by consciousness (the 'pour-soi'). Although we commonly think of the world as if it existed outside of the consciousness of beings, place cannot be disconnected from the individual's perception and comprehension of it; it is this consciousness of the world, of place, that gives it its reality. Yet here we enter one of those absurdities – of existence, or simply of existentialist thinking if you like: on the one hand, affirming a world separate from the self, or consciousness, leads toward an illusion, yet on the other hand, the self is not something substantial, not a complete reality, but rather a reflection – at least that is how Sartre conceives of it. In *Being and Nothingness* (*L'Être et le néant*) he asserts: 'Consciousness, being-for-itself, ... is the nothing by which there are things' ('Le pour-soi ... est le rien par quoi il y a des choses'; 502; quoted in Foulquié 77). To know the world is to know it by way of consciousness, which is itself, paradoxically, a 'rien.' For Heidegger, consciousness 'is a being for which there exists within itself the question of its own being' ('est un être pour lequel il est dans son être la question de son être') (quoted in Foulquié 79). Sartre extends this thought, stating: 'Consciousness is a being for which there exists within itself the question of its own being in as much as it implicates a being other than itself' ('La conscience est un être pour lequel il est dans son être question de son être en tant que cet être implique un être autre que lui' (*L'Être et le néant* 29; quoted in Foulquié 79).

These definitions of consciousness lead to and overlap with a fourth point, or concept: relation and intersubjectivity. Consciousness is a 'rien' in the sense that it depends on 'l'en-soi,' on otherness, as the mediator to arrive at an authentic relationship with the world. The word 'otherness' here designates not only the consciousness of others but also place, or the world. 'It is not in some retreat that we discover ourselves,' Sartre argues; 'it is rather in the streets, in the town, in the middle of the crowd, thing among things, man among men' (*Situations* 1: 34–5; quoted in Foulquié 71). Elsewhere in the same work, he reiterates that a human being is finally an ensemble, a 'situation': 'Man is only a situation ... Totally conditioned by his class, his salary, the nature of his work, conditioned even in his emotions and his thoughts' (*Situations* 2: 27–8; quoted in Foulquié 59). To be situated is to be located within a network, within a relation; an individual makes choices, although he makes those choices not autonomously but rather within a network of relation where individuality is itself referenced and framed by otherness. We discover ourselves through others, insists Karl Jaspers, who conceives of this otherness in terms of communication or personal attachments between human beings in which the other becomes a 'toi.' Perhaps we see the world chiefly through the eyes of others, through the prejudgments of the epoch in which we live. In *Truth and Method* Hans-Georg Gadamer argues that these prejudgments constitute an individual's sense of history and reality (276–7).

Otherness and relation may also be discussed as a place. A place alters in conjunction with the person or persons with whom the place is associated. Without place (inseparable from any situation), identity dissipates into subjectivism. Because existentialist philosophy privileges the concrete and the particular as opposed to the essential, it can be interpreted as fundamentally relational and relativistic in its focus: 'The world is ... not this rigid and valid reality, the same for everyone, that people commonly believe. It varies according to the individual, according to the society and the historical époque' (Foulquié, *L'Existentialisme* 70). Certainly in this sense, then, place is not fixed, but dynamic and relational; it is concrete, situated in the framing and signifying mechanism of individual consciousness, which is itself informed by community, culture, and the historical moment. Today, under the impact of globalization, each place – especially urban spaces – tends more and more to be a reproduction, a copy of something else that is also a copy.

Still, a counter-phenomenon is equally prevalent: each place, no matter how much it resembles other places, is still marked by difference and diversity, if only because a place varies according to the individual experiences that compose it and narrate it. The Oriental city Irene, explains Italo Calvino's Marco Polo, deserves many, not one name:

> For those who pass it without entering, the city is one thing; it is another for those who are trapped by it and never leave. There is the city where you arrive for the first time; and there is another city which you leave never to return. Each deserves a different name; perhaps I have already spoken of Irene under other names; perhaps I have spoken only of Irene. (*Cities* 125)

This seems another way of saying that, from the experiential perspective of the subject, one cannot step twice into the same river; perhaps we cannot step in it even once, for neither the subject nor the river has any sameness.

Existentialism, with its focus on concrete experience rather than essences, defamiliarizes place and identity, allowing us to think about them from new perspectives. So one response to the question 'where is place?' is that place is experiential; it is intra-subjective, and thus blends into desire, memory, and particularity of perception. Just as consciousness from a Sartrean point of view dissolves into a reflection, so too place when defined as situation actualized by consciousness dissolves into this same reflection. In Calvino's *Invisible Cities*, Kublai Khan and Marco Polo reach the end of a long sumptuous conversation, in which the former suggests that both of them are simply two drunken men who have mistaken the junk heaps and discharge of the world for treasures of the Orient. To this conjecture, Polo replies: 'Perhaps all that is left of the world is a wasteland covered with rubbish heaps, and the hanging garden of the Great Khan's palace. It is our eyelids that separate them, but we cannot know which is inside and which is outside' (104). Polo's reply acknowledges the role of consciousness in the composition of place; it suggests, however, a division between 'inner' and 'outer' that this chapter tries to avoid or at least minimize. Place has a consubstantiality; it is at once matter and matter shaped and given significance by consciousness, just as the lens of a camera frames the world, bringing it into an order at once imposed and composed and actualized by the viewer. Like the workings of consciousness illustrated in Simone de Beauvoir's *L'Invitée*, this framing and viewing of the world brings things into light. It unconceals and awakens.

A second response to the question 'where is place?' or 'what is place?' – is a postmodern one: place is a language within language. If place is a text, though, it is a hypertext composed of signs that can be read in different orders and from numerous perspectives. Of the traveller who arrives in the city of Tamara, Calvino's Marco Polo observes: 'The eye does not see things but images of things that mean other things: pincers point out the tooth drawer's house; a tankard, the tavern ... Your gaze scans the streets as if they were written pages: the city says everything you must think, makes you repeat her discourse' (*Cities* 13–14). The city imposes its presence, but we compose within and choose from among its possibilities; we reconfigure it and add to its reality. Like a book, a place too must be read or interpreted in order for it to exist concretely for any particular person, and this reading transposes it into fragments of innumerable narratives. Place is like a book, yet it is somewhat like the book of sand in the eponymous short fiction of Jorge Luis Borges, 'El libro de arena.' When the narrator of the tale tries to flip back to the illustration on a page that he has just looked at, he is unable to find it. Its pages, and the material they contain, change incessantly, and thus the book, a finite object, becomes infinite; it is a hypertext in which the arrow of time cannot be reversed by rereading the story, which simultaneously reconfigures it (changed this time) and provokes the awareness of its absence. Our habits and routines give a place its location, make it finite, yet place can be just as mercurial – and destabilizing – just as inexhaustible as this fictional, infinite book, which the narrator, after sleepless nights, decides to replace randomly on a bookshelf in the basement of a library.

A third response to the question, where is or what is place – one appropriate to the age of post-colonial immigration, television, rapid transport, the Internet, and economic globalization – is that place is a hyperspace because each place references and is linked with many other places. We live in all of these places. For travellers like Marco Polo, post-colonial emigrants/immigrants, or just everyday television viewers and email users, place becomes complex, multi-dimensional. In *101 Everyday Experiences of Philosophy* philosopher Roger-Pol Droit recommends exercises designed to alter our sense of place, one of which is to enter the space of a painting. Upon imaginatively entering the painting, one discovers that one has wandered into a realm whence there is no return. So one lingers, while at the same time continuing to live in that other place that is one's world. 'One finds oneself, therefore, permanently, in several spaces,' Droit comments. 'And that is why the arts intensify existence' (196). We find this idea in the poetry of William Blake and

William Wordsworth, among others: the space where we live is always here but it can also be there. In the world, and in a labyrinth, each space resembles other spaces. So, like a voyager, the person in a labyrinth begins to live in several spaces at once. This chapter's epigraph from *Jacques le fataliste* alludes to this overlapping of space, which one can easily experience. Try, for example, thinking about place – not just any place, but all the places that exist in the world, not only cities but apartments, subway stations, cafés, corridors, basements, balconies, culs-desac, every space from the tiny to the vast. The effect of the exercise, extended to twenty or thirty minutes, will vary, but one effect may be this: a sense that the place where you are is not simply one among an infinite number of places, but an infinity of places. That place, your consciousness, contains all the others as well (ibid. 60).

It is difficult to budge the conviction that subjectivity, our identity, is something within us and that place is somewhere outside of us. Yet it might be argued – and in a sense this is the defamiliarization or the inversion that existentialist philosophy enacts – that place is equally 'within' and identity is equally 'outside.' Identity and place are consubstantial: both are material, yet both are shaped by the reflection that is consciousness. For Calvino's Marco Polo, the world is a mirror of negations: looking into it, the individual, the traveller, 'recognizes the little that is his, discovering the much he has not had and will never have' (*Cities* 29). Travel, sojourn, and immigration accentuate this experience of negation or defamiliarization because travel disrupts the lenses that give us a sense of stability, of belonging in a particular place. Deprived of routines and familiar presences, the traveller, sojourner, or immigrant may experience a kind of primal existential connection, feeling temporarily without identity and without a place of belonging yet more aware of a being-in-the-world. As soon as consciousness localizes or familiarizes a place, it shapes and informs this presence with its dispositions, memories, and motivations. When we inhabit a particular place, we bring these dispositions and motivations to it; the various lenses of our consciousness transform it into a narrative of our life.

For an individual, what is a place, then? A place is the conjunction of one or more of these lenses and the material world. A particular place is an ensemble of lenses that shape and tint; these lenses are superimposed on the existential condition of embodiment, or being in the world. We might draw an analogy with vision and the experience of seeing colours. The world is without colour; it is we who colour it. Our colouring of the world is a lens superimposed on our fundamental existence. The analogy, like all analogies, is partly false in that, for most people, being in the world cannot be separated from the colouring of it, but the idea here is that colour as a lens resembles those other lenses, our prejudices and motivations, that are superimposed on our fundamental embodiment in the world. All of these underlie our narratives, or stories, of the place that is our life.

La ciudad ausente / *The Absent City*

Before turning to an analysis of *When We Were Orphans*, I am going to take a detour to consider one of the most innovative and enigmatic reflections on locale and identity in contemporary literature, Ricardo Piglia's *La ciudad ausente* (1992) / *The Absent City* (2000). This novel / critical reflection – for it is indeed something of both fiction and literary theory – also illuminates concepts of translation and rewriting and the language environment in which we live today. (Édouard Glissant would use the term 'tout-monde' to describe this network of intersecting languages.) During the course of the past twenty-five years Piglia has become a principal figure of avant-garde Latin American fiction; in 'Detective de laberintos literarios,' Caleb Bach of the popular magazine *Américas* points out that Paglia is generally considered the top writer in Argentina today, a country with a rich literary tradition that includes Jorge Luis Borges, Roberto Arlt, Julio Cortázar, and Macedonio Fernández, to cite a few well-known twentieth-century authors. In 1967 Piglia received a prize from the Casa de las Américas for the short-story collection *Jaulario*; in 1975 he won a prize in a short-story competition whose jury consisted of Borges, Augusto Roa Bastos, and Marco Denevi. In 1997 he won the Premio Planeta for his novel *Plata quemada*. In addition to these works, he has also published three other short-story collections, including *Nombre falso* (1975), translated into English as *Assumed Name* (1995), and two other novels: *Respiración artificial* (1980) and *Plata quemada* (1997).

La ciudad ausente, which Piglia has also adapted into the libretto of an opera, is well known in the Spanish-speaking world and admired for its 'combination of literary innovation and poignant sociopolitical reflection' (Waisman, 'Introduction' to *The Absent City* 1). In postmodernist fashion the novel mixes different genres of fiction and registers of language, such as detective fiction, love story, picaresque adventure/investigation, imaginary travel fiction, dystopian/utopian fiction, cyberpunk and science fiction; in Borgesian fashion (shifted in the direction of

Thomas Pynchon's *V* and *Gravity's Rainbow*), it constructs labyrinthine plots that seem to move in two different directions: toward chaos and disconnections, on the one hand, and toward a utopian assertion of rhizomic interrelationships and connections, on the other. The messages that the reader draws from its varied and unusual stories, often arranged in *Arabian Nights* interlocking units, seem full of both the sinister and ominous as well as the deeply hopeful and inspirational. It goes almost without saying, then, that the novel's plots resist facile summary; to describe or summarize its 'story' is itself an act of interpretation and translation that shifts its text into another register of comprehension. In the introduction to the English translation of the novel, Sergio Waisman gives this sketch of its plot:

> Junior, the son of English immigrants in Argentina, is a newspaper reporter trying to solve the mystery of what is happening in the city of Buenos Aires ... The world in which Junior operates is a futuristic Buenos Aires, in which the map of the city is constructed by a series of fictional narratives. The intrigue of each of these stories ... multiplies as they intersect each other (like streets and avenues of a city) and unfold to make up the enigma of the text (the written, as well as geographic and political text) that Junior is trying to solve. (3)

One of the most ingenious and memorable aspects of the novel is its heroine/writing machine, Elena, a mechanical, computer-like Scheherazade who composes the stories that make up the novel and relate the city as roads of intersecting narratives. The novel is highly literary and intertextual; the character/machine Elena, for example, alludes to Elena Obieta, the wife of Argentine writer-philosopher Macedonio Fernández, while Macedonio is also (the name of) a principal character in the novel. The novel constructs these parallel or hypertextually linked worlds, where fiction and fact cross-reference. When Elena the character becomes terminally ill – an occurrence that finds a parallel in the life story of Elena Obieta – Macedonio programs her memories into the writing machine, which provide the raw narrative material for the stories that she composes. Housed in a museum, the mechanical Elena resembles 'a phonograph with all sorts of cables and magnets inside a glass box' (37). In addition to these elements of science fiction and romance, political intrigue reminiscent of Kafka's *The Trial* and *The Castle* also informs the novel, lending a certain sinister and conspiratorial quality to its atmosphere, at least in some of the stories; at other times a wackiness and absurdity, counterpointed by a tenderness and inspirational imaginative touches, define its complexly textured mood. Piglia's debt to Borges and Joyce, and his cross-referencing of a library's worth of other authors, including Dante, Poe, Kafka, Defoe, Robert Louis Stevenson, Swift, William Burroughs, and Thomas Pynchon, are apparent. Piglia dips into biblical stories and Greek and Roman myths and draws upon the nuclei of numerous intersecting narratives and themes of the Western and world's literary imaginaries.

An aspect of the novel that I want to look at more carefully is its recomposition and reorientation of material from *The Thousand and One Nights* in the story entitled 'The Girl.' Elena the writing machine composes stories by transforming narrative frameworks and story nuclei, and in 'The Girl' she transforms materials from the principal framed tale of *The Thousand and One Nights*, the story of King Shahrayar and Shahrazad. Elena's recompositions appear to follow, Junior the newspaper reporter/investigator claims, a basic set of logical yet unpredictable operations, exemplified by her rewriting of Edgar Allan Poe's 'William Wilson.' When Poe's tale is fed to Elena, she turns it into a story entitled 'Stephen Stevensen':

> At first they had tried to make a machine that could translate texts ... In spite of its imperfections, everything that followed was already synthesized in that first story ... We had wanted a machine that could translate; we got a machine that transforms stories. It took the theme of the double and translated it. It makes due [*sic*] as well as it can. It takes what is available and transforms what appears to be lost into something else. That is life. (37)

In this commentary we find again some important ideas about translation and rewriting that we have touched on in earlier chapters: first, a translation moves across registers (or between a subject matter and a register, if we stick with Iser's terminology), and the registers may be 'higher' or 'lower,' or situated in a context quite foreign and alien to the original text. (Actually, the register is always 'to the side,' since there is no outside against which a translation can be measured; in this sense 'higher' and 'lower' would make sense only subjectively or consensually.) Second, there is always a space across or gaps that must be filled (the transformation 'of what appears to be lost into something else'), and this liminal space drives the translation. Third, any translation or transformation presupposes nuclei and a network of potential relationships, yet because languages are different and because there are no one-to-one correspondences, a translation (like Elena's recomposition) is always a 'making do' as best one can. There are elements of chance, surprise, and serendipity that enter the recomposition; Piglia refers to this element in narrative terms when he remarks, in the 'Afterword': 'I like this idea of a plot that is like a street in which you open the door and suddenly your life is completely different. It is there, perhaps, that my decision came of using the city as a metaphor for the space of the novel' (142). All plots and all narratives are translations in the basic sense that life experience is translated into intrigue; in the literary, cultural imaginary these intrigues are connected in expected as well as unexpected (hyper-related) ways. What translation reveals, we might say, is the inexhaustible and often surprising labyrinthine networking of languages and literary and cultural imaginaries. One can always move to the side, but as in a labyrinth, the untranslatable, like a wall, will eventually force the translation to reorient itself and change directions. The fourth point worth noting is that translation and life are equally events or performances; nothing is certain, and each portentous moment holds the capacity of suddenly opening out onto a completely different street. Our identity and our place are just as much unstable as stable, just as much virtual as realized/acualized.

In the following description and analysis of Elena the writing machine's story 'The Girl,' I will highlight four topics: (1) language and the performance of the reader/translator/liver of life; (2) the internet of stories of the literary imaginary; (3) the lost or the absent; (4) the dynamic, transformative nature of place and identity. The famous framed tale of the *Arabian Nights*, which 'The Girl' translates and transforms, recounts the cuckolding of King Shahrayar, who consequently takes revenge on his wife and virgin girls of his kingdom. Deflowering and then killing the girls the morning after, Shahrayar's appetite for revenge seems insatiable, until the vizer's daughter, Shahrazad, intervenes, surviving the king's rage by placating him with the suspenseful, interlocking stories that she tells night after night. Through narratives, she educates, cultivates, and cures the king of his lust for revenge; she saves her sisters and the kingdom. In our literary imaginary Shahrazad symbolizes the power of storytelling, and she is present (in oblique, disguised form) in innumerable tales that translate/transform this basic story of healing and education through the virtualities of narrative. (Readers of Isabel Allende's *Cuentos de Eva Luna* [1989] will recall that Allende chooses an epigraph from *The Thousand and One Nights* to incorporate this message of storytelling's power into her own *cuentos*.) Like

Elena the writing machine's translation of 'William Wilson' into 'Stephen Stevensen,' 'The Girl' features some obvious correspondences with the framed tale of the *Arabian Nights* as well as some inversions, reversals, and improvisations (the 'making do' technique). She translates the story into a contemporary register that mixes psychotherapy with mechanics, linguistics and world literature, myth, and English history; the prose ranges from the scholarly to the sentimental, from the technical to the wacky and tender. (In his register switching, Piglia recalls Thomas Pynchon, though the writing is more elegant and lyrical and much more compact.) Laura is the Shahrazad figure, but in this case it is she who is ill and must be cured. She suffers from hallucinations that the doctor calls 'extravagant references,' and what this amounts to is a kind of autism. Laura lives in her own world, projecting herself outward into people and, especially, objects: 'The world was an extension of herself; her body spread outward and reproduced itself. She was constantly preoccupied by mechanical objects, especially electric light bulbs. She saw them as words, every time one was turned on it was like someone had begun to speak. Thus she considered darkness to be a form of silent thinking' (47). Believing that her soul lives in an electric fan, when her mother turns off the fan one afternoon, Laura experiences difficulties with language, being unable to use personal pronouns and finally to select words or speak at all; she can only make a vague sort of clucking sound. She undergoes electrical shock treatments, but all to no avail.

After a mystical Polish pianist, a Madame Silenzky (an allusion to W.B. Yeats's *A Vision*?), attempts to cure Laura with music therapy – 'Music is not an experience, it is the pure form of life, it has no content, it cannot frighten her' – her father steps in and begins telling her short stories (49). Here we see one of the reorientations of the *Arabian Nights*' framed tale, with the male figure representing caring and cure through narration. At this point 'The Girl,' which is already a tale within the novel itself, becomes a further tale within a tale; the process continues in a somewhat dizzying fashion, as in the *Arabian Nights*, with the father's recounting of a story of William of Malmesbury, from the *Chronicle of the Kings of England*. This is the story of the Roman noble and a ring, a love story about a statue that comes to life; recounting the tale has a beneficial, soporific effect on the poor girl, so the father tells a variation of this story the next day – this time a German compilation from the twelfth century – and continues to do so. 'Every day, in the early evening, the father would tell her the same story in its multiple variations. The clucking girl was an anti-Scheherazade, she heard the story of the ring a thousand and one times at night by her father' (50). At this point another reversal of roles takes place. Laura begins to speak, uttering her own recomposition (with hints of the post-colonial) of the story of the noble, the statue, and the ring: 'Mouvo looked at the night. Where his face had been another appeared, Kenya's. All of a sudden Mouvo was in a corner of the house and Kenya in the garden and the sensorial circles of the ring were very sad' (50). Laura's behaviour here and the trajectory of her illness and cure suggest an important concept that Macedonio programs into Elena the writing machine's authorial tendencies: identity depends on narration, and narrating one's own story (as well as one's own interpretation of others' stories) not only actualizes the self but protects one from having an identity imposed from the outside. Laura's behaviour might be interpreted then from different perspectives, as resistance as well as self-development and entry into a broader human network of culture and community. She must learn to navigate the network of stories in her own way (that is, by telling *her* versions of others' versions of the story of the noble, the statue, and the ring). So every night, Laura, slowly building her own language and narrative repertoire, tells/translates to her father the same story, in all its variations, until she gets to the final recomposition, her version of Henry James's 'The Last of the Valerii' (51). She finishes the story, and then steps out of the narrative into her own life: she asks her father to buy her a golden ring.

Junior interprets this story that Elena the writing machine has just told him as a tale of love and of 'the power of stories, the song of the girl looking for life' (51). The reader will recognize that this tale is also a fictional variation of Elena's own life story, of Macedonio's love for his terminally ill wife and his attempt to give her life by programming her memories into the writing machine. Identities transform – and now, in the twenty-first century, humans translate themselves into machines, and machines become human-like, almost with their own identities. Stories too translate/transform into other stories. Elena is Elena, as well as 'the eternal One, the river of stories, the endless voice that kept memory alive' (41). The story 'The Girl' transposes the gender relationships of the framed tale of the *Arabian Nights*: 'The girl lives again thanks to her father's stories. To narrate,' Junior draws out the moral, 'was to give life to a statue, to give life to someone who is afraid of living' (51-2). Within the museum that houses the writing machine, Junior finds a photo of Elena (Macedonio's wife) and Macedonio's manuscript under protective glass panels. A passage of the manuscript that seems to sum up all the variations of love in all the stories that Elena the writing machine recounts – from father to daughter and then from daughter to father – as well as Macedonio's love for his wife and his vision of composition and narratives, reads: '*To escape toward the indefinite space of future forms. The possible is what spreads forth into existence. That which can be imagined occurs and goes on to become part of reality*' (emphasis mine) (52). Here we encounter the utopian strain of this wonderfully varied and complex novel.

'The Girl' and *The Absent City* are full of riches, yet experiencing them involves for the reader a journey through a labyrinth. In terms of the focus of this chapter, and the subsequent discussion of Kazua Ishiguro's *When We Were Orphans*, we might highlight some of the following points and commentary. In 'The Girl' the world and consciousness are shown to be implicated one in the other, so one cannot separate place from identity; the one is the absence of the other, which means that they are interrelated in a network of situations, events, and virtualities. Reality itself has a little recognized virtual quality, with its network of absences and lost (yet still palpable) connections with all the moments of the past and the anticipatory future. This reality is impossible to conceive and manage without recourse to narratives and stories, which are the nuclei of our human presence and comprehension of the world. There is a vast internet of situations and events in which place and identity compose and reorient, displace and reanimate that existential presence; it is equally true to say that the world is within the situations and events of this internet, and that there is no outside as far as the capacities of human understanding go. We live in this labyrinth. Piglia has remarked that human beings live in a 'verbal net' and that 'the central quality of narrative is this flow, this apparent fleeing movement toward another story line' (141). Imagination is the stuff of the world, and its most popular form is the story. All of this – the story 'The Girl' and *The Absent City* – has a utopian quality in that it both critiques totalitarianism (i.e., imposition of identity) and offers a liberating vision in which the material and the spiritual are united in narratives that commemorate and look forward to prospective courses. This utopian strain is matched by a dystopic, apocalyptic one. Nothing is certain; disconnections and delusions are equally part of a contemporary imaginary contaminated by totalitarian ideologies, terror, cruelty, and war, and perhaps only a novel with multiple registers can capture both the utopian and the dystopic actualities and possibilities of the contemporary landscape. Propaganda also relies on narratives and dips into the cultural imaginary. 'Culture does not make us more human,' George Steiner contends, reminding us that in the Nazi concentration camps executioners listened to classical music and that 'Buchenwald is located only a few kilometers from Goethe's garden' ('La Culture' 6, 9). Conspiracy and betrayal can infiltrate even narratives of hope; disconnections mark the vast human networks of the city: 'Everybody seemed to be living in parallel worlds, unconnected. "I'm the only connection,"' Junior muses (*Absent City* 17).

The cultural imaginary is itself a city, and we are its inhabitants – not just those who live but, as in Joyce's short story 'The Dead,' all other generations that have not been forgotten and can still be found at least in traces. The imaginary contains presences and absences. Identity and place are hyperlinked, which means that the connection is virtually real, held together by narrative material that must activate the presence; yet this virtuality is equally an absence. Reflecting on the processes of Macedonio's love for Elena, Piglia explains the complex metaphor of the city in the novel: 'The idea of a man in love who walks through a city that belongs to him, but where the city in which he walked with the woman he loved is lost. Because the city is a memory machine. Of course, that lost or absent city also includes other moments of life, not just those associated with a woman' (142). This merger of place and identity, of matter and spirit, leaves the readers of *The Absent City* with much to think about.

When We Were Orphans

Defamiliarizations of place and identity constitute a primary project of Kazua Ishiguro's work. Although these defamiliarizations have historical and political dimensions, I will highlight their aesthetic and philosophical ones. Ishiguro's first two novels, *A Pale View of Hills* (1982) and *An Artist of the Floating World* (1986) were praised for, among other things, a certain Japanese (Oriental) quality of sentiment and compression. (In this context it may be worth noting that Ishiguro's family moved from Japan to England when he was five years old. He speaks, but does not write, Japanese.) A third novel, *The Remains of the Day* (1989), won the Booker Prize and established Ishiguro as an 'English' novelist; hailed as a 'perfect' work by more than a few critics and reviewers, this novel drew comparisons with those of Henry Green, Anthony Powell, and Evelyn Waugh (Kauffmann, 'The Floating World' 43). His fourth novel, *The Unconsoled* (1995), embarked in a completely new direction and disconcerted critics and readers for that reason. Twice as long as any of the previous novels, it mixes the banal with hints of conspiracy, paranoia, and delusion. No one seems quite sure just where the story takes place, or finally what is the point of all its wanderings. Place and identity are defamiliarized, and along with them, characterization, plot, and theme. One brief example will suffice. The story appears to take place in some Central European town, yet its location as well as the notion of place itself is called into question at a number of junctures in the story. At the very beginning of his misadventures, after he checks into his hotel room in an unspecified town, Ryder, the central character, reclines on the bed and suddenly has the impression that he is in the same room where he stayed as a child during his parents' sojourn in England and Wales:

> I was just starting to doze off when something suddenly made me open my eyes again and stare up at the ceiling. I went on scrutinizing the ceiling for some time, then sat up on the bed and looked around, the sense of recognition growing stronger by the second. The room I was now in, I realized, was the very room that had served as my bedroom during the two years my parents and I had lived at my aunt's house on the borders of England and Wales. I looked again around the room, then, lowering myself back down, stared once more at the ceiling. It had been recently re-plastered and repainted, its dimensions had been enlarged, the cornices had been removed, the decorations around the light fitting had been entirely altered. But it was unmistakably the same ceiling I had so often stared up at from my narrow creaking bed of those days.
>
> I rolled over onto my side and looked down at the floor beside the bed. The hotel had provided a dark rug just where my feet would land. I could remember how once the same area of floor had been covered by a worn green mat, where several times a week I would set out in careful formations my plastic soldiers – over one hundred in all – which I had kept in two biscuit tins. (16)

Place and identity are defamiliarized from the beginning to the end of the story, and in ways that puzzled many reviewers, so *The Unconsoled* was judged a curious failure.

This brings us to Ishiguro's fifth novel, *When We Were Orphans*, in which place and identity constitute two of the book's primary concerns in its exploration of human illusion. The word 'orphans' in the enigmatic title refers to the latter of these themes, while the topic of place shows itself in the various section subheadings, which switch back and forth from London to Shanghai. Hong Kong and Macau also figure in the story's plot and the narrator's recollections, which stretch over a half of a century, beginning in the early twentieth century and concluding in 1958. One might argue that the entire narrative, which takes the form of a detective tale, constitutes a search for place and identity. The mystery that the novel's protagonist, Christopher Banks, attempts to solve is the whereabouts of his parents. The father, an executive for Morganbrook and Byatt in 1920s Shanghai, disappears mysteriously when Christopher is a child; the mother is kidnapped sometime afterwards. The two disappearances are unrelated, but this is revealed only toward the end of the novel, whose mood, somewhat like that of *The Unconsoled*, blends the banal with the conspiratorial and the ominous. After his parents' disappearance, Christopher is taken to England for his safekeeping and education; upon his graduation from Oxford, he sets out on a career as a detective. Banks achieves a certain fame in London and England, but his thoughts increasingly turn to the storm brewing in the East and the mystery at the centre of his own life: how and why his parents disappeared, and whether or not they are still alive and can be found. Place and identity are wound together in this mystery; questions of allegiance and belonging criss-cross. Although Banks's family is English, the International Settlement of Shanghai has been his only home; the fates of the family members are determined just as much by this expatriate, somewhat utopian enclave and by events in Asia as they are by anything in England. In true colonial fashion, Shanghai and London become the twin poles of Banks's identity; the former represents a distant home, especially in the narrator's nostalgic recollections, while the latter, although the site of the child's friendships and ambitions, has an ambivalent and shifting quality. Inspecting criminal cases in London turns into a preparation for returning to Shanghai to investigate the mystery at the core of his life, one that impedes him from disengaging himself from the past and finding a sense of belonging in his present circumstances as detective and denizen of London: where are his parents, and who are they really? Who is Banks, and where is his home? Examining descriptions of place in the novel is one path toward the answer to these questions and toward an illumination of Ishiguro's project of destabilization and defamiliarization.

The realist illusion – the neat demarcation between things and consciousness – dissipates in Ishiguro's fiction, more rapidly in some novels (e.g., *The Unconsoled*) than in others (e.g., *The Remains of the Day*). A convention of formalist criticism, the distinction between place and character blurs the fact that, in a novel, language consciousness is all there is. So perhaps the first point about descriptions of place is that there is no zero point of neutrality or objectivity: place is never completely outside a character's consciousness, but rather expresses something of that consciousness (its desires, its perspectives, its attitudes, its memories). The following passages illustrate different points with respect to the conjunction and disjunction of place and identity in the novel. In this first passage, Banks describes the scene of a murder, which he invests with a dark mood and treats as a symbol:

> I had found the walled garden – containing the pond where Charles Emery's body had been discovered – in the lower grounds of the house. Four rectangular steps had brought me down into a rectangular space so perversely sheltered from the sun that even on that bright morning everything around me was in shadow. The walls themselves were covered with ivy, but somehow one could not avoid the impression of having stepped into a roofless prison cell. (37)

It is the *pour-soi*, in Sartrean terms, that imbues this landscape with its atmosphere and significance; any attempted neutral description of the place itself, the *en-soi*, would have a different orientation and would focus on other details. In this passage, through the lens of the *pour-soi*, there is also an aspect of cultural attitudes composing the landscape. The symbolic charge of the description derives from its being the place where a murder has been committed and where a body has been disposed; the body lies hidden, submerged in the dank water of the pond. The landscape thus becomes 'the scene of a crime,' and along with it, a metaphor for a cultural, social attitude that views crime as an evil that must be combated. This evil is something beyond the reach of our comprehension, just as the sun, in the passage, does not penetrate into the recesses of the garden. In his description Banks implicitly expresses cultural-social attitudes such as these, which also constitute his own attitude toward crime and his imaginative capacity to pursue the vagaries of conspiracy. The passage also sketches Banks's sense of identity, for it situates him as someone who must configure 'the scene of the crime' in order to fulfil his professional mission. His identity must pass by way of the signs of place. In fulfilling his professional duty he begins to compose the narrative of who he is, was, and will be, so there is a circularity between subject and object to the hermeneutics of detection in which he engages.

In the next passage, description of place serves to express a nostalgia (i.e., the narrator, in England, looking back on his childhood in distant Shanghai); it expresses a bond between the young Christopher and his Japanese friend, Akira, and their desire to create a calm, transparent world apart from the opaque, confusing world of inscrutable adults and cross-cultural ambiguities:

> Our spot by the canal ... was behind some storehouses belonging to the Jardine Matheson Company. We were never sure if we were actually trespassing; to reach it we would go through a gate that was always left open, and cross a concrete yard past some Chinese workers, who would watch us suspiciously, but never impede us. We would then go round the side of a rickety boathouse and along a length of jetty, before stepping down on to our patch of dark hard earth right on the bank of the canal. It was a space only large enough for the two of us to sit side by side facing the water, but even on the hottest days the storehouses behind us ensured we were in the shade, and each time a boat or junk went past, the waters would lap soothingly at our feet. On the opposite bank were more storehouses, but there was, I remember, almost directly across from us, a gap between two buildings through which we could see a road lined with trees. Akira and I often came to this spot, though we were careful never to tell our parents of it. (117)

What is perhaps most interesting in this passage is its metaphoric, allegoric quality: it is a miniature tableau that captures the significance of the friendship between Christopher and Akira. They seek a world of idealized adventure in a space that circumvents boundaries and frontiers; the storehouses of Jardine Matheson Company, with their cache of opium perhaps, dominate the landscape and signify power and possession, but for the moment, the boys can squeeze their way between buildings and find a clear view. Almost every element of this scene is a sign of something else: the storehouses, their shadows cast on the seated boys, the canal, the junks, the clearing and the trees, the lapping of the waters, and so forth. The boys' daydreams and presentiment compose this place, investing with it unformulated ambitions and a vague awareness of obstacles that loom (as in the metaphysical surrealist Giorgio de Chirico's paintings).

Identity depends upon place in that it depends upon things (photographs and keepsakes, for instance) to engage and manifest itself; it depends on otherness, on friends and family and their shared memories; it can depend on the presence of certain landscapes, such as a lake, mountains, or simply the greenery of the natural world, if these landscapes have in some way become important to the particularity of an identity. It also may depend on significant routines, such as work, and insignificant ones, such as reading the newspaper, walks in a particular neighbourhood, weekly get-togethers, and so forth, all of which give shape and meaning to time. These elements contribute to giving a person a sense of being situated, at home, in a place, and, consequently, a sense of identity. For identity is an em-placement, a being in place. In *When We Were Orphans*, rooms, houses, neighbourhoods, and cities all have a reflective and metaphoric value; they are constructed places, shaped by a person or people, and they reflect, as do mirrors, something that is and that is not part of an identity. Houses externalize identity; depending on the circumstances, they may reveal who we believe we are or, conversely, they may reflect what the world has made us accept. Banks's parent's house in Shanghai and its gardens – a residence provided for them by the British company Morganbrook and Byatt – projects his sense of Englishness and his moral vision of the world. Since Banks can approach these places only through the crooked alleys of memory, they are coloured by a nostalgia or a longing for a being-in-place. In an enclave, surrounded by an alien world he cannot comprehend, the young Christopher wishes to be English, a sentiment that this description of place conveys:

> At the rear of our garden in Shanghai, there was a grass mound with a single maple tree rising out of its summit ...
> From this vantage point, we had a clear view over my garden and of the big white house standing at the end of it. If I close my eyes a moment, I am able to bring back that picture very vividly: the carefully tended 'English' lawn, the afternoon shadows cast by the row of elms separating my garden and Akira's; and the house itself, a huge white edifice with numerous wings, and trellised balconies. I suspect this memory of the house is very much a child's vision, and that in reality, it was nothing so grand. (61)

These impressions of Englishness are heightened by the young Christopher's impressions of visitors: 'usually a house guest would be some young man who brought with him the air of the English lanes and meadows I knew from *The Wind in the Willows*, or else the foggy streets of the Conan Doyle mysteries ... Most of [these Englishmen] ... were probably younger than I am today, and were probably all at sea so far from their home. But to me at the time, they were all of them figures to study closely and emulate' (62). Banks's recollection of his parents' house serves as a mirror of his own youthful ambitions; he, the house, and its guests blend together in an attitude and mood. His final remarks about the age and the status of the visitors, all of them travellers, reveal his awakened awareness that those people whom he identified as essentially English share with him an ambiguity of identity and a strangeness. Like Banks in England (who at Oxford is known as a 'fish out of water'), these travellers and expatriates were also out of place, estranged in one way or another by twists and turns in their life's destiny.

The description of the house of Banks's childhood friend, Akira, is similarly illuminating for its cross-mapping of identity on place and vice versa. Again, memory controls the selection and composition of details, which serve to show an uneasy division between East and West in Akira's parents and their son. Just as the decor of the house conveys an impression of something off-balance or at odds with itself, so too this place emblematizes Akira's character:

> My memory of Akira's house is that, from an architectural standpoint, it was very similar to ours ... But the inside of my friend's house was a quite different affair, and the source of some fascination for me. It was not so much the preponderance of Oriental pictures and ornaments ... but rather his family's eccentric notions regarding the usage of many items of Western furniture. Rugs I would have expected to see on floors were hung on walls; chairs would be at odd heights to tables; lamps would totter under overly large shades. Most remarkable were the pair of 'replica' Japanese rooms ... These were small but uncluttered rooms with Japanese tatami mats fitted over the floors, and paper panels fixed to the walls, so that once inside ... one could not tell one was not in an authentic Japanese house made of wood and paper. (85)

The simulacra of these Japanese rooms in Akira's house function like distorting mirrors, singling out a feature for the viewer and giving it an odd dominance. In the International Settlement of Shanghai, Akira's parents force their child to dress in Japanese clothes and decide to send him back to Japan for schooling, lest he become anglicized or westernized in his habits and self-identity. In a similar vein, the house's interior decoration fends off the Western influences of the Settlement and reasserts a home culture (Japanese) that must be subordinated, even hidden, from the public space of the enclave community. These two elements reside uneasily together in Akira, who never completely resolves a sense of being off-balance, out of place, whether in Shanghai or Japan. The scene, later in the novel, in which Banks rescues Akira the soldier from a crowd of Chinese citizens intent on killing him to avenge the invasion of their city, similarly allegorizes Akira's problematic identity.

Place can be shaped and sculpted to one's ends, and in turn, place can shape and sculpt consciousness: this is the idea conveyed by the Japanese rooms of Akira's English-style house. In the following passage, which describes Banks's stroll outside the International Settlement in Chinese neighbourhoods of Shanghai, the power of place to evoke a mood and merge with identity is highlighted. The atmosphere of the Chinese quarter at night enters Banks's consciousness, temporarily altering it:

> I am still uncertain of my way around the side-streets off Nanking Road, and managed to get a little lost. This was not something I minded so much. The atmosphere in that part of the city is not intimidating, even after dark, and ... I found myself drifting with the night-time crowd in a mood not far from tranquility ... [I]t was a relief to be amidst these pleasure-seekers of every race and class; to have smells of food and incense come wafting towards me as I passed each brightly lit doorway. (196)

In this experience of place a shift from being-here to being-there occurs; consciousness fuses with place in a moment extending back to the recent past and toward the near future. The 'being there' or emplacement that Christopher experiences walking these narrow streets of Shanghai resembles listening to music, for example, and being totally absorbed in the notes' progression and their life, with the result that one's place in the world suddenly becomes much larger.

These moments of durée/expansion are counterpointed by others that emphasize disconnection and disorientation as a result of a break in the link between place and identity. Later in the novel, when Christopher returns to Shanghai after a long absence and visits his parents' former house, he discovers that it has been transformed into a Chinese residence. Like the house, the city also undergoes radical, disorienting changes; Mr Lin, the house's new owner, remarks: '[E]verything has changed and changed again ... There are parts of the city I once knew so well, places I would walk every day, I now go there and I know not which way to turn' (225). Mr Lin's confusion shows a symbiotic exchange between consciousness and place; consciousness gives meaning to place, but place is the imposing material within which consciousness orients itself and fixes its attention. When a familiar place to which a person is deeply attached changes, he or she will be knocked off balance, if only momentarily, for place and identity are in liaison.

These ideas are neither subjectivist nor objectivist. Things exist, we all assume, prior to and without the intervention of human consciousness, but landscape or place depends on human perspective to come into existence, or to take on meaning. Landscape consists of signs, as much as it consists of trees, buildings, mountains, and other such things. Discussing the notion of place as a frame, the Japanese literary and cultural critic Kōjin Karatani argues that 'landscape ... is not simply what is outside. A change in our way of perceiving things was necessary for landscape to emerge, and this change required a kind of reversal' (24). Elsewhere Karatani calls this reversal an inversion of a 'semiotic configuration' (27). Although we commonly think of place or landscape as natural, having an existence independent of human consciousness, place or landscape is situated within a system of signs and depends on a framing mechanism that configures (gives meaning to) the signs of which it is composed. In the following passage, for example, a Chinese lieutenant describes to detective Banks the Shanghai 'warren,' a pocket of extreme poverty within the city:

> The factory workers live there ... You would not believe human beings could live like that. It is like an ant's nest. Those houses, they were intended for the poorest people. Houses with tiny rooms, row after row, back to back ... If you look carefully, you may see the lanes. Little alleys just wide enough to allow the people to get into their houses. At the back, the houses have no windows at all. The rear rooms are black holes, backing on the house behind ... The rooms were made small, because they were for the poor. There was a time when seven or eight people shared such a room. Then as the years went on, families were forced to make partitions, even within these small rooms. And if they still couldn't pay the landlords, they would partition the room further. I remember seeing tiny black closets divided four times, each with a family in it. (276–7)

What makes this a landscape is something more than referents to a specific locale with all its physical features. Clearly, it is a certain social consciousness coupled with a selection of detail that gives meaning to the objects represented, framing them within a larger controlling idea. This description shows, among other things, Ishiguro's westernization of the Chinese lieutenant's perspective, whose focus is on the dehumanizing living conditions of the warren; a social condition that was previously accepted as something normal or natural in the society now stands out in this description as something alienating and objectionable. What renders this description realistic/naturalistic is a configuration of pictorial markers that defamiliarizes and alienates the reader/viewer. The literary critic who said about nineteenth-century fiction that realism is a subject matter and naturalism a style or technique was half right: both realism and naturalism are a code of signs, which is the same thing as saying that they are a style or a manner of framing ideas. Karatani's remarks are again germane here; about nineteenth-century European realism, he comments: 'Both the landscapes and the "ordinary people" ... that realism [in painting] represents were not "out there" from the start, but had to be discovered as landscapes from which we had become alienated' (29). Passages comparable to the lieutenant's description of the Shanghai warren also occur in an early Ishiguro novel, *An Artist of the Floating World* (1986):

> The view below us was framed by two factory plants looming one to our right, the other to our left ... Viewed from the bridge, a stranger may well have assumed that community to be some derelict site half-way to demolition were it not for the many small figures, visible on closer inspection, moving busily around the houses like ants swarming around stones ...
>
> On either side of us were what might have been stalls at some marketplace, closed down for the day, but which in fact constituted individual households, partitioned from the alleyways sometimes only by a cloth curtain ... After a while, I grew increasingly aware of the open-sewer ditches dug on either side of the narrow path we were walking. There were flies hovering all along their length and as I continued ... I had the distinct feeling the space between the ditches was growing more and more narrow, until it was as though we were balancing along a fallen tree trunk ...
>
> Near the entrance of the passage ... I noticed three small boys bowed over something on the ground, prodding it with sticks. As we approached, they spun round with scowls on their faces and although I saw nothing, something in their manner told me that they were torturing some animal. (166–7)

A pictorial technique in which diminution counterpoints monstrosity makes a landscape of this ensemble of referents to people and physical objects. The effect of both descriptions of squalor, the Shanghai warren and the Nishizuru district, is to diminish human size and to show human beings and things in a destabilizing and alienating relation. Place or landscape emerge, are given significance, by way of this pictorial technique, itself guided by an attitude or consciousness that frames the scene as a social critique. Both of these passages, it could be argued, show Ishiguro distancing himself from a late-twentieth-century myth of Asian-ness and other essentialist identities; for the author, it is less the country than the conditions in which human beings live that work to make them who they are. So the important point here about place or landscape is not the relativistic message of a poem such as Wallace Stevens's 'Thirteen Ways of Looking at a Blackbird,' but rather the idea that no landscape is natural; all landscape is a composition of consciousness. Perception frames place, making it a landscape; this landscape reflects back identity. What strikes us as alien in a landscape is just that aspect of identity that is being highlighted or called into question. Place, or landscape, changes in conjunction with a sense of self and identity.

In *When We Were Orphans* place and identity are simultaneously defamiliarized. The International Settlement, the enclave where Christopher's, Akira's, and other expatriate families reside, would seem a perfectly artificial place and identity in that it is a colonial reproduction of a distant home culture: the Englishness of the lawns, gardens, decor, and itinerant guests depend on an illusive perception, as does Christopher's own sense of Englishness. The mixed feelings that he and Akira have for the Settlement reveal their sense of being 'orphans,' metaphorically speaking; dislocated and diffuse, their identity seems to lack something, or to be in search of something. 'I'll tell you an odd thing, Akira,' Christopher says; 'All these years I've lived in England, I've never really felt at home there. The International Settlement. That will always be my home.' Akira shakes his head and replies sceptically: 'Very fragile. Tomorrow, next day ...' And he waves his hand in the air. '[I]t seemed so solid to us,' Christopher concludes (301). A place, like parents, can vanish; the fading of place in the novel is paralleled by the fading of parents.

Futile searches for place and parents serve as metaphors of a general defamiliarization in which the novel engages. Banks's search for the house opposite Yeh Chin's house exemplifies the futility of these pursuits: acting on instinct rather than evidence, Banks is convinced that his parents, kidnapped some twenty years previously, are being held in a residence opposite the house of the famous blind actor, Yeh Chin. The search for parents motivates Banks's return to Shanghai, and finding their whereabouts, he later deduces during his investigations, depends on locating this particular house. The scheme turns capricious and obsessive, and the search leads him into a labyrinth. 'I wondered if I should tell the [driver] the significance of the journey we were making' (265), Banks ponders, in a line that could have come right out of Ishiguro's previous novel, *The Unconsoled*, where each character seems to be part of a completely different story and miscommunication is the rule rather than the exception. Hearing the menace of gunfire in the distance, after skidding through muddy streets and swerving to avoid the crowds scurrying toward safety, Banks and his Chinese driver end up lost, straying from the International Settlement into the dangers of the war zone – the Japanese invasion of Shanghai having begun. The search is futile; the house cannot be found because, for Banks, it resembles more a delusion than a location. Later in the novel, when he does find the house opposite Yeh Chin's, his accomplishment is absurd: his parents – at least his father *and* his mother – were never held there; much less could they have resided there clandestinely for a twenty-year period after their disappearance. Some reviewers of Ishiguro's novel have focused on these kinds of details as evidence of Banks's unreliability as a narrator, or of his mental instability. There may be a more comprehensive explanation, however: Banks's search for place and parents has an allegorical significance. In a postmodern world, place and identity have become labyrinthine, hard to fix and define. Another way of saying this is that relations, not essentialist identities, map where we are and who we are; place and identity have become obsolete markers because both have become spread out, diffuse. Jean Baudrillard uses the term 'hyperreality' to designate this contemporary world of dislocations and simulacra.

The war zone, eventually extending into the neighbourhood of the house for which Banks is searching, exemplifies another defamiliarization. The locale has been reduced to rubble by bombings and intense fighting between Japanese and Chinese. Although the battle lines are sharply drawn, there is another sense in which the no man's land reveals a universal predicament. Nationality is stripped away, and being in the world is reduced to a certain elemental struggle. In the following passage, a recognition of difference – language differences – ironically triggers Bank's insight into an underlying 'universal' human condition; that condition becomes perceptible only because the normalcy of life is radically inverted, defamiliarized, by war:

> We sat in the dark for some time ... Then suddenly the gunfire started again ... It ended abruptly; then after another moment of quiet, a strange noise rose through the walls. It was a long, thin sound, like an animal's call in the wild, but ended in a full-throated cry. Next came shrieking and sobbing, and then the wounded man began to shout out actual phrases. He sounded remarkably like the dying Japanese soldier I had listened to earlier, and in my exhausted state, I assumed this must be the same man; I was on the point of remarking to Akira what a singularly unfortunate time this individual was having, when I realized he was shouting in Mandarin, not Japanese. The realisation that these were two different men rather chilled me. So identical was their pitiful whimpers, the way their screams gave way to desperate entreaties, then returned to screams that the notion came to me this was what each of us would go through on our way to death – these terrible noises were as universal as the crying of new-born babies. (304)

The war works other inversions, where place is reduced to a chaos of rubble and human beings are turned into patches of stale blood and piles of intestines littering the path that Christopher and Akira meander. '[A]ll the ghastliness that had been hidden by the darkness was not visible to us, taking a profound toll on our spirits,' Christopher recounts (311). Through these defamiliarizations of place and human presence within it, Ishiguro renders identity as situational and relational.

Banks fails to locate his parents. The information that he receives about them after their departure from Shanghai is tinged with uncertainty, since it comes by way of his Uncle Philip, who has betrayed them. Twenty years later, in 1958, when he receives news of the whereabouts of his mother, now alias Diana Roberts, who is being cared for at a nursing home in Hong Kong, she has lost her capacity to recognize him or remember her past. His father, Christopher learns, was not kidnapped but fled with a mistress and has been dead for several years. Sarah Hemmings, the woman with whom Banks planned to elope to Macau, has also died. So the scope of his life's connections narrow to his adopted daughter, Jennifer, and his memories. If the novel, as some reviewers contend, calls into question the reliability of Christopher as narrator, certainly the narrowing of perspectives also calls into question facts, places, and identities. It would be an exaggeration to claim that the novel conceives of identity as nomadic, but its title metaphorically suggests the difficulty of locating identity and of assigning it an autonomy. It also suggests that place and identity are discontinuities rather than persistent unities. Banks's commentary on the final letter he receives from Sarah attempts to draw out the meaning of the search that both she and he have engaged in:

> Was her life ... really what she set off to find that day she stepped out on to the jetty in Shanghai? I somehow doubt it. My feeling is that she is thinking of herself as much of me when she talks of a sense of mission, and the futility of attempting to evade it. Perhaps there are those who are able to go about their lives unfettered by such concerns. But for those like us, our fate is to face the world as orphans, chasing through long years the shadows of vanished parents. (367)

The tone seems a bit theatrical, overreaching itself in its effort to make proper sense of things. Yet what is interesting here is a kind of mirroring of situations and searches, and the nostalgia for a receding origin, itself more of a simulacrum than a reality. First, Sarah's search mirrors Christopher's. Second, similar words and phrases describe the identity (i.e., lost parents) that Banks seeks and the city or place where he seeks it (them). The phrase 'shadows of vanished parents' compares with the following lines: 'Shanghai today is a ghostly shadow of the city it once was'; and again Banks remarks, upon having returned to Hong Kong: 'Shanghai of today is likely to prove no less painful a parody of the old city than did Hong Kong' (352). Identity and place possess a certain interchangeability; the search for parents and the search for place conflate, and multiply in a net of relationships.

It is worth asking to what extent Banks succeeds or fails in his 'mission,' how this can be measured, and what questions the book poses to its readers. A reference to detective fiction may be helpful, since the novel can be read as an attempted innovative extension of the genre, like Umberto Eco's *The Name of the Rose* (*Il Nome della rosa*). From his childhood, Christopher's model has been Sherlock Holmes, that representative of Englishness and the powers of ratiocination. For Holmes, the clues that he must decipher exist apart from him, in an objective world; anyone can read them, if they have the perspicuity. Conversely, Banks cannot rely on such neat divisions; he must search the winding, shifting paths of his memory, where boundaries between 'inside' and 'outside' blur. Furthermore, he depends on reports from others for key information about the whereabouts and activities of his parents after their mysterious departures in Shanghai. Whereas Holmes confidently reads, deciphers, the text of the world, Banks reads the text of a text of a text – and so on. Holmes's clues are usually material (a footprint, a map, a piece of clothing), whereas Banks's clues are immaterial. He works with memory, desire, and second-hand narratives coloured by the tellers' motives and self-interest. Unlike Holmes, Banks fails, and perhaps he fails in part because there is no Watson (who functions in the Conan Doyle tales as a kind of reality check) to keep everything straight. As both narrator and character in the story he is telling, Banks has a divided mission: it is unclear whether his underlying goal is to remember (and commemorate) his parents or to find them, for the latter would involve revising his childhood image of them. Through remembering the place of his mother's disappearance he will re-establish the relation between his parents, himself, and Shanghai; although he does not find his parents, through memory he can reconstruct the chain of relation with them and a place of belonging. Indeed, perhaps the most incongruous aspect of detective Banks's behaviour is his insistence on returning to a particular neighborhood and house in Shanghai more than twenty years after his parents' disappearance. He is convinced that his parents are still there, as if time is at a standstill. The location of Yeh Chin's house, and the finding of his parents, are somehow related to saving the world from impending catastrophe, but how this is so is never clarified. A vague presentiment of conspiracy and a disjunction of logic mark the narrative.

Whereas the narrative in a Sherlock Holmes tale depends, then, on certainties (i.e., the capacity of Holmes, the power of reason, the rightness of his mission), *When We Were Orphans*, like its precursor, *The Unconsoled*, depends on uncertainties. It is criss-crossed by missed connections, miscommunication, and mistaken identities. Uncle Philip, who turns out to be the informer Yellow Snake, is not who Christopher thought he was, nor is Christopher's father or mother. Christopher mistakes his own identity: wanting above all to be English, he has his Englishness undermined by sentiment – he feels more at home in Shanghai than in London – and the facts of his personal history (e.g., his comfortable residence and his Oxford education have been financed by Chinese links in the opium trade). In the final paragraph of his recollections, he engages in a kind of rebuilding of identity and place of belonging:

> [D]rifting through my days here in London, I believe I can indeed own up to a certain contentment. I enjoy my walks in the parks, I visit the galleries; and increasingly of late, I have come to take a foolish pride in sifting through old newspaper reports of my cases in the Reading Room at the British Museum. This city, in other words, has come to be my home ...

Nevertheless, there are those times when a sort of emptiness fills my hours. (368)

In this passage, place and identity are composed in part of certain performances (i.e., walks in the park, visits to the gallery, reading in the library), which through repetition lend an aura of stability and solidity. These performances constitute the reality with which Christopher makes his separate peace and outside of which an indefinable anxiety reigns.

When We Were Orphans presents a process of incongruity and defamiliarization, a stripping away of certainties; the process works subtly, not by sudden inversions but rather by a slow removal of the foundation of assumptions on which Banks depends for his sense of identity and place. This epistemological aspect of the novel shows a postmodernist orientation, moving it away from the rationalist, realist orientation of the detective story as a genre. The novel focuses on interpretation, which, with a postmodern twist, becomes a question not of interpreting the world (à la Sherlock Holmes) but of interpreting Banks's and others' interpretation of virtualities. The text, not the world, becomes the primary focus. The story can also be read as a veiled narrative of migration: the detective's search for the truth and the whereabouts of his parents becomes an homology of his reflection on his own identity and sense of belonging.[4] That is the post-colonial twist. Philosophically speaking, the novel illustrates a fundamental idea of twentieth-century existentialism: that knowledge of ourselves and the world is more of a negation, a not-knowing, than an affirmation and a certitude. 'It is impossible to count on anything whatsoever in this world,' Karl Jaspers writes (*Introduction* 22). We walk in uncertainties: 'When we feel sure, that is just the moment when we begin to go astray' (81).

Locale and Identity

'What we call "the world," "reality," "normal life," is situated in a thin layer, easily perturbed,' remarks philosopher Roger-Pol Droit (*101 Expériences* 58). Exploring these perturbations of the everyday has become one of the literary provinces of Ricardo Piglia and Kazua Ishiguro. In an interview with Pico Iyer, Ishiguro has commented that after winning the Booker Prize it became possible for him (for the first time) to 'produce something ... strange and weird' (Iyer, 'The butler didn't do it' 22). He went on to do just that in *The Unconsoled*. *When We*

Were Orphans does not so much return to a familiar terrain as blend the earlier Oriental elements of *An Artist of the Floating World* with the miscommunications and misconnections of the later fiction. The novel depends on perturbations and defamiliarizations to raise questions about the nature of place and identity. In a sense these questions are as old as the fragments of Presocratic philosophy with which this chapter began, but they have been given a postmodern and post-colonial highlighting by late-twentieth-century phenomena such as global emigration/immigration and cyber virtuality that call into question local identities.

In general, what gives people a sense of place and identity? We could categorize this response as some combination of five things: possessions, performances, presences, relationships, and beliefs. Possessions may be something substantial, such as a house, or something quite insubstantial yet important, such as photographs, glass cups, keepsakes, and other souvenirs of the past and links with previous generations. Performances we have already discussed; these take the form of innumerable activities, shared or unshared, including meetings and dinners with friends, songs that are sung together, memories that are shared in conversations, and so forth. These performances may become rituals, which solidify the bond of place and identity. Presences may be of little or, conversely, of great importance; in a place where mountains, a lake, the ocean, or some other geographic feature dominates, this presence may be one of the most important defining elements that people incorporate into their sense of identity. Relationships may be part of all of the above, or we may think of them as a separate category. Certainly Christopher's relationship with Jennifer, his adopted child, turns out to be the most solid and anchoring element in his life. Beliefs draw possessions, performances, presences, and relationships into a unity; place and identity are based finally on beliefs, as neatly illustrated in a passage from Jorge Luis Borges's short fiction, 'Ulrica': 'What does it mean to be a Colombian?' one character inquires. 'I don't know,' responds the other. 'It is an act of faith' (*El libro de arena* 16).

A certain inter-geography defines a locale in relation to all other locales. 'If one does not expect it,' Heraclitus has remarked, 'one will not find the unexpected; it is not to be tracked and no path leads to it' (quoted in Hussey, *The Presocratics* 39). With this in mind, we might say that a place must also be defined negatively, in contrast with and in relation to other places. It is the unexpected, that which surprises and sticks in the mind and will be remembered, that defines a locale; for the individual, a place is composed of just those elements that one cannot find in other places, but which are in some way related, negatively as well as positively, to one's identity, to what an individual is capable of perceiving and experiencing. So there is an exchange of sorts that one encounters in any particular place between the routine, the habitual, and the expected, on the one hand, and the unusual and unexpected, on the other hand.

From a global and post-colonial perspective, place has become a labyrinth, defamiliarizing us with (a) its interplay of simulacra – all modern cities tend to resemble one another and reproduce certain urban characteristics such as skyscrapers, subways, and shopping malls – and (b) its shifting human presence in this era of emigration/immigration of peoples throughout the world. To be an 'orphan,' as in the title of Ishiguro's novel, is to lack something, to have a sense of absence within one's being; the postmodern orphan has neither an easily traceable identity nor an easily recognizable homeland and network of allegiances. The gap between our world and our parent's world defamiliarizes us; any attempt to establish identity as a unique root, as a vertical inheritance, that continues in us and that we then transmit to our children becomes hypothetical. It is likely that we share more with those who are our contemporaries than with those with whom we share a vertical, familial link (Maalouf, *Les Identités meurtrières*). Christopher Banks's final thoughts turn to his own sense of being in the world, and his uncertainties: on the one hand, London, where he lives alone, frequenting the British Museum and rereading newspaper accounts of old cases he solved, has become his home; on the other hand, he feels a certain emptiness, like an exile or an orphan, which reveals his lack of belonging firmly anywhere (368).

In sum, we find all of these aspects of locale and identity in Kazua Ishiguro's works. Place is inverted in a fundamental sense in that it tends toward the expression of a mood. This is the case not only in *When We Were Orphans* but in other works as well: *A Pale View of Hills, An Artist of the Floating World, The Remains of the Day,* and *The Unconsoled.* Ishiguro may be, as he is sometimes called, the 'most English' of contemporary British novelists, but he is also the most oriental. He defamiliarizes conventional conceptions of place and identity, pushing them toward the indefinable; a certain oriental composition of mood is all that remains. Where is place? What is identity? When you think about them long enough, you may find that they begin to float away.

5. At the End of East/West: Myth in Salman Rushdie's *The Moor's Last Sigh*

> Myths do not die; they sleep. When they awaken, they travel, passing from one epoch to another, crossing oceans and continents, taking their abode in the most secret thoughts of humankind.
>
> Pietro Citati

Toward the end of Part I of *The Moor's Last Sigh*, Flory Zogoiby, the wife of Solomon Castile and mother of Abraham Zogoiby, sits in a 'sunset's vermilion afterglow,' rapt in a mixture of reverie and contemplation. She is admiring a magnificent collection of Cantonese tiles that decorate the walls, floor, and ceiling of a synagogue in Cochin, site of the first European (Portuguese) settlement in India in 1500. How strange to find these Chinese tiles there, she muses, which sometime during the eleventh century made their way from southern China to India. In her service to the synagogue Flory has cleaned and buffed them many times and has enjoyed imaginatively entering 'their myriad worlds ... contained within the uniformity of twelve-by-twelve' squares. She is 'enthralled' by the tiles, but in a moment of anguish, her son's discovery that they, the Zogoibys, are a mixture of both Moslem and Jew – as her son, Abraham, puts it, 'myself, born of the fat old Moor of Granada's last sighs in the arms of his thieving mistress – Boabdil's bastard Jew' (83) – in this anguish the Cantonese tiles 'unvei[l] a secret' (84). The narrator of the novel, Moraes Zogoiby, alias the Moor, describes Flory's revelation in this way:

> Scene after blue scene passed before her eyes. There were tumultuous marketplaces and crenellated fortress-palaces and fields under cultivation and

thieves in jail, there were high, toothy mountains and great fish in the sea. Pleasure gardens were laid out in blue, and blue-bloody battles were grimly fought; blue horsemen pranced beneath lamplit windows and blue-masked ladies swooned in arbours. O, and intrigue of courtiers and dreams of peasant and pigtailed tallymen at their abacuses and poets in their cups ... in Flory Zogoiby's mind's eye, marched the ceramic encyclopaedia of the material world that was also a bestiary, a travelogue, a synthesis and a song, and for the first time in all her years of caretaking Flory saw what was missing from the hyperabundant cavalcade. (84)

For the devout Flory, an unexpected conclusion hits with force: 'There is no world but the world,' she murmurs. 'There is no spiritual life,' she whispers shockingly; the material world consists of just this infinite and inexhaustibly imaginable cornucopia.

In this excerpt we find some of the essentials of Rushdie's art and of Rushdie the (re)orientalist. (I use the term here, in lower case, not in a reductive, ideological sense but rather in a neutral sense to denote any artist who treats materials with origins in Middle Eastern and Asian cultures and societies.) Rushdie, or specifically here his narrator, Moraes, is above all a storyteller; the latter spins his threads of stories as does his Indian creator with the precarious sword of Damocles dangling above his head. The Moor tells his tale as a dying captive in Vasco Miranda's phantasmagoric 'Little Alhambra,' a castle-fortress in Benengeli, Spain. 'May you never find what you seek,' the cabbie who drives the Moor to Miranda's castle shouts to him. 'May you stay lost in this infernal maze, in this village of the damned, for a thousand nights and a night' (389). As in *Alf Layla wa Layla* the Moor, like Shahrazad, must tell stories until there are no more to tell; or to rephrase this in existentialist, postmodern terms, like Samuel Beckett's Malone in *Malone Dies*, he must keep talking or writing because that is the plight of man the language-bound, talking animal. For Rushdie, though, man is also the mythmaking animal, and myth, as an extension of humankind's imagination, is about possibility. Myth and utopia overlap, or perhaps it would be more accurate to say that myth, when it does not itself overtly express a utopian possibility (e.g., the Age of Gold in Greek and Roman myth), is sufficiently accommodating and malleable, and therefore capable of being translated and transformed by an illuminating, utopian dynamic. This chapter will be about, among other things, that dynamic as well as being a critique of its antithesis: ideological fundamentalism, or the non-dynamic and the frozen.

Flory Zogoiby's encounter with the Cantonese tiles, which highlights Rushdie's mythopoeic prowess, also puts in relief the theme of cultural hybridity and illustrates its complementary compositional style of mixed prose registers, a theme and style by which the author has made his mark as a post-colonial and postmodernist writer. These Chinese tiles decorate a synagogue in India, whose caretaker is proud of tracing her heritage back to the fifteenth-century Portuguese navigator, Vasco da Gama. In terms of the passage's prose registers, elegant, poetic language mixes with slang: 'blue horsemen pranc[ing] beneath lamp-lit windows' is juxtaposed with phrases like '[h]ocus-pocus' and '[m]umbo-jumbo' (84). Rushdie's India, his Orient, is no less an imaginative fabrication than the Orient of earlier orientalists; here, however, the Orient is being reinterpreted and reconceived along lines that historicize it differently. The cross-cultural, multicultural nature of historical events is being imaginatively highlighted. The novel's narrator points out that Cabral Island, home of the novel's da Gama family, takes its name from Pedro Álvares Cabral, the Portuguese navigator who founded Cochin; later Vasco da Gama established there the first Portuguese trading post. When Portuguese rule began to flag, the Dutch took over. The city became prosperous. Through its harbour goods such as pepper, cardamom, and other spices and drugs as well as coir, coconut, and copra were shipped. 'All of the city's racial and religious groups, including its Hindu majority and Muslim, Syrian Christian, and Jewish minorities, shared in the ... prosperity.'[1] These were Cochin's heydays. After 163 years of Portuguese rule and 132 years of Dutch rule, the British took over the colony from 1795 to 1947. In its own manner Rushdie's novel is faithful to the history of Cochin and adjacent Mattancheri, with its Jewtown and renowned synagogue; these were indeed multicultural places, and Rushdie's India is also a multicultural place – and a fantastic one. The synagogue and the tiles have a factual basis, which Rushdie then transforms into stories. Legends spring up about the tiles' magical powers, Moraes recounts: 'if you explored for long enough,' it was claimed, 'you'd find your own story in one of the blue-and-white squares, because the pictures on the tiles could change, were changing, generation by generation, to tell the story of the Cochin Jews' (75–6). The tiles become, then, a kind of pictorial version of the *Arabian Nights* and other narrative treasure hordes; they are, we could say, a metaphor for the literary, cultural imaginary. A bit like Elena the writing machine of *The Absent City*, they constitute a metaphor for a process of translation and transformation – for the reorientation of history and story in which

Rushdie engages in the novel. When, as a boy, Abraham Zogoiby scans the Cantonese tiles, he begins to read the story of the father who has deserted him and his mother. He sees his father in a 'cerulean scene of Dionysiac willow-pattern merrymaking amid slain dragons and grumbling volcanoes'; later, the father changes into Sinbad and has other adventures in the course of his odyssey (76–7). Finally, as Abraham turns into a less believing adolescent, the father disappears forever into the tiles' ethereal blue.

Mythmaking

The vignette of the Cantonese tiles is one among numerous tales in miniature that illustrate the creative, mythmaking process of *The Moor's Last Sigh* as a whole. 'In the end, stories are what's left of us, we are no more than the few tales that persist,' muses the dying Moor. Rushdie's novel is a veritable treasury of stories that retell, reinvent, and improvise all manner of fairy tale, legend, myth, and historical allegory. To analyse how the elements of this narrative network interact and carry forward the novel's aesthetic and ideological project is the primary task of this chapter. In the process we will have recourse to discussions of myth and utopia in the writings of Walter Benjamin, Ernst Bloch, Paul Ricoeur, and Emmanuel Lévinas, as well as other contemporary scholars such as Peter Munz, Laurence Coupe, and Don Cupitt. Hans-Georg Gadamer has said that a book as a written text is part of a dialogue, and in this sense it seeks to answer a question or questions. To what question or questions, we might ask, does Rushdie's novel respond? Michelet has written that '[c]haque époque rêve la suivante' ('Each age dreams the next') (Abensour, 'Walter Benjamin' 23); or, in other words, the present (and the past) are pregnant with the future. We might say then that among the questions that Rushdie's novel implicitly poses would certainly be these: First, how did the world in which we live today – a world of intensifying fundamentalist conflict and violence – emerge from or grow out of the past? Second, to again paraphrase Michelet, what future world is the present one in the process of dreaming? And third, to what degree might narrative/story be not only a means to record history (the past) and entertain the contemporary reader (the present), but also a tool of critique and of anticipatory and emancipatory power? Can narratives also cure and lead the way into a future that overcomes the conflicts and violence that have marked the end of the twentieth and beginning of the twenty-first century?

Rushdie's responses to these questions demand analysis and interpretation, but certainly one thing that distinguishes them is that he translates and transforms all manner of story nuclei and in so doing seeks to take ideas *to the superlative*. I recall a phrase from a work of the Lithuanian-French philosopher Emmanuel Lévinas, *De Dieu qui vient à l'idée*: 'a novel idea does not take shape in its first effervescence, but rather, emerges from a carrying of it to the superlative form' (quoted in Calvora, 'Levinas' 130). Rushdie is a re-orientalist of the literary and cultural imaginary, and what he attempts in this novel is to reinterpret and reconceive the world – through the hermeneutic of his stories, to give the East (and, in turn, the West) another possible history and identity. Rushdie's project in this novel is simultaneously historical (to comment on the past), critical (to enter into the intellectual debate of the contemporary moment), and utopian (to anticipate and to emancipate the future). 'In my family we've always found the world's air hard to breathe; we arrive hoping for something better,' Moraes Zogoiby explains. Rushdie also seeks something other: an inversion, a re-vision of the world, in which the many are not conquered by the one and the power of the imagination, as it was for the Romantic poets, occupies a prominent place. Reinterpreting history and conceiving of new possibilities of the present and future, the imagination has a hermeneutic and a vatic capacity, and in both roles it stands in opposition to the trend toward instrumentalization of the modern world. '[T]he first danger in our present culture,' explains philosopher Paul Ricoeur, is a 'reduction of language to communication at the lowest level ... We have only one model of language – the language of science and technology' (*Ricoeur Reader* 448). It is against this 'instrumentalization of language,' a reduction of language's basic polysemy to the rule of one-word one-meaning, that poets, by the very nature of poetry, as well as imaginative, mythopoeic writers such as Rushdie struggle. Myth is a kind of narrative polysemy that rather than narrowing a story toward a single meaning, enlarges it, keeping it indefinitely open, indefinitely capable of new interpretations and rewritings. Myth infuses story with hidden, as yet unrealized meaningfulness, which takes presence only later, under the right circumstances, with the right readers, if at all.

This idea coincides with the concept of 'radical typology,' a term that I borrow from Laurence Coupe, who in turn has borrowed it from Peter Munz and other scholars. Radical typology claims for myth a transformative quality and an open-endedness as well as a capacity to endure. It is important to think of myth as narrative rather than as a static collection of symbols and symbolic relationships. 'Every myth we know has both a past and a future,' Munz states (*What the Golden Bough Breaks* ix). Elaborating on this aspect of myth and differentiating 'orthodox typology' from 'radical typology,' Coupe explains:

> All myths presuppose a previous narrative, and in true form the model of future narratives. Strictly speaking, the pattern of promise and fulfillment need never end; no sooner has one narrative promise been fulfilled than the fulfillment becomes in turn the promise of further myth-making. Thus myths remake other myths, and there is no reason why they should not continue to do so, the mythopoeic urge being infinite. This understanding is what we are calling radical typology. Where orthodox typology [an example of which would be viewing Christ as the fulfilment of the type that Moses incarnates] works in terms of closure, radical typology works in terms of disclosure. (*Myth* 108)

Orthodox typology is essentially allegorical in its functioning, the word 'allegory' deriving from the Greek, *allos*, or 'other'; that is to say, '[a]llegorical tales are those which in effect announce, or are made to announce, their own intention: to say *this* in terms of *that*. Thus the "other" is always subsumed under the "same"' (ibid. 105). No matter how many levels of meaning an allegory might feature, it is still limited and fairly static in comparison with radical typology, which possesses the power of story or narrative. Although *The Moor's Last Sigh* relies on allusion and allegory, and often uses them brilliantly, it would be reductive to read the novel as an allegorization of the author's own personal and political predicament or as a *roman à clef* in terms of the history and politics of twentieth-century India (e.g., reviewers cite the character Raman Fielding as a thinly disguised caricature of the Hindu nationalist leader Bal Thackeray).[2] Rushdie likes to get in his jabs, that's for sure, but he is not primarily a political satirist. He is more interested in the capacity of narrative to destabilize and break apart a stagnancy of assumptions and a tyranny of orthodoxy; he uses myth to reinterpret and rewrite East-West histories and stories.

Myth and Utopia

Given the array of diverse and contradictory approaches to myth and utopia, in the following paragraphs I want to sketch the tradition upon which I draw in my analysis of narrative forms, networking, intertextuality, translation, and transformation in Rushdie's novel. I will begin with Walter Benjamin, who often assigns a negative value to myth, considering it as a masking device – in other words, as something that fosters and perpetuates an illusion. In contrast, utopia has a potentially positive value, but to divulge this positive value requires an interpretive operation. Utopia has a dualistic structure: it is partly myth, which tends to be regressive in its import, and partly emancipatory possibility. Through a hermeneutic, the reader/analyst separates the two and reorients the material, drawing out its message of prospective emancipation. Utopia moves toward the new, yet takes a detour by way of the old or the ancient, or the mythic, narrative envelope in which it is often contained. The hermeneutic consists of an awakening from a 'dream' (in Michelet's phrase): first, exposing the myth within the dream, and second, liberating the utopian impulse. As Menninghaus observes, Benjamin's work is concerned with the 'dialectic of breaking apart *and* rescuing myth' (quoted in Gilloch, *Myth and Metropolis* 13). With the rescue operation, myth transforms and releases its positive messages.

In the writings of Ernst Bloch, whose masterwork is *Das Prinzip Hoffnung* (*The Principle of Hope*), the need to establish a new relation with the past forms an important theme. Jean-Marie Vincent describes that new relation as one in which the 'unvoiced' is liberated:

> Bloch does not draw the conclusion that one must erase the past and turn resolutely toward the future. Quite the contrary, he thinks that it is necessary to establish new critical relations – non-linear and more complex – with the past, present, and future. From the past, it is above all important to retain the unvoiced, which exists in traces and in what was rejected, deformed by the victors and the powerful, themselves desirous to throw a veil of oblivion over that which troubles them. Consequently the present is not something smooth and non-contentious, it is made of conflicts, past contradictions, and confrontations having to do with the process of memory and recording of history. ('Ernst Bloch' 29)

Again, a hermeneutic of history and myths becomes necessary if the individual and society are to tear the veil of illusion and throw off the regressive aspect of myths (e.g., a tendency toward scapegoating and victimization, at least as interpreted by René Girard). Something more is necessary, however. Bloch believes that we must cultivate an anticipatory consciousness, which is at once subversive and prospectively oriented (looking for the 'not yet' known and seeking to effectuate the 'not yet' constructed). Humanity and the world are incomplete, and our utopian charge is to engage in the development of the human and the construction of an emancipated world.

Emmanuel Lévinas adds some interesting twists to the ordinary notion of utopia, considering it not a land or a place, but rather an eccentricity of the human spirit, 'hors de tout enracinement et de toute domiciliation' ('outside of all rootedness and all residing') (Célan, quoted in Calvora, 'Levinas' 131). Like Bloch, he emphasizes the notions of consciousness, incompleteness, process, and becoming; he adds the notion of the superlative, of going beyond limitations. For him, utopia is nowhere where there are endings or limits; that which is human cannot rest enclosed in its place, for it seeks to go beyond its situation toward a something-missing. Benjamin, Bloch, and Lévinas all enact reorientations of myth and utopia. In regard to myth, perhaps the central point to draw from these reorientations is that myths contain mixed messages and therefore the reader/writer must engage in a double operation. Benjamin, for instance, focuses on the necessity of the hermeneutic to expose the illusion within the myth, while Rushdie depends on narrative translations and transpositions to turn the legend or myth in the direction of anticipatory identity and emancipatory possibility.

Myth has multiple functions in Rushdie's novel, three of which are patterning, the imagining of possibilities, and re-territorializing. Mythmaking is 'a primal and universal function of the human mind as it seeks a more-or-less unified vision of the cosmic order, the social order, and the meaning of the individual's life,' mythologist Don Cupitt contends. 'The individual finds meaning in his life by making of [it] a story set within a larger social and cosmic order' (*The World to Come* 29). Certainly we find this argument for the power of narrative in Rushdie's novel: Moraes Zogoiby gives meaning to, or patterns, his individual and family experiences through the numerous mythic and other allusive parallels, often ironic, that he constructs about their lives. This patterning becomes something more dynamic when Rushdie uses the narrative capacity of myth to reinterpret myth itself and conceive of other possibilities. 'Every telling of a myth is a part of that myth,' mythologist and feminist fiction-writer Marina Warner insists; 'there is no Ur-version, no authentic prototype, no true account' (*Managing Monsters* 8). She continues: 'Myth conveys values and expectations which are always evolving, in the process of being formed, but ... never set so hard they cannot be changed again' (14). Related to this liberating function of myth is mythmaking as re-territorialization. In 'Myth as the Bearer of Possible Worlds,' Paul Ricoeur argues that there are essentially 'two uses of the concept of myth': first, as 'creative symbol,' and second, as 'reductive ideology' (487). In the latter use, myth 'serves as an *alienation* of [a] symbolic structure; ... it becomes reified and is misconstrued as an actual materialistic explanation of the world' (487). Reductive ideology of this sort would include European or American imperialism and contemporary fundamentalisms, no matter the region or religious persuasion. In other texts, such as *Ideology and Utopia*, Ricoeur makes a distinction between ideology, which he compares to a frozen picture, and utopia, which takes the form of a narrative and a process. Although ideologies often have utopian aspects – and utopias have ideological qualities – the former tends toward a closed view of reality, whereas the latter tends toward openness. In this distinction we see a refinement, using different terminology, of the basic distinction that Benjamin established between myth as distortion/delusion and myth as potentiality.

In *The Moor's Last Sigh* Rushdie seeks to invert certain myths that constitute reductive ideologies, such as the founder myths of European imperialism embodied in certain features of epic accounts like Luis Vaz de Camões's *Os Lusíadas*, where the Portuguese are elevated to a superior identity vis-à-vis the Moors, who conversely are demeaned and diminished, and where lands of Asia (the 'Orient') are taken into Portuguese and Christian possession. Through telling a radically different, inverted epic tale whose theme is not ethnic identity and exclusion, but rather multicultural identity and inclusion, Rushdie reinterprets imperial history and re-territorializes the post-colonial world. He writes a novel that is another version of 'the empire writing back,' a counter *Os Lusíadas*, in the respects just mentioned. In the Portuguese epic, Europeans circumnavigate Africa and 'discover' the Indian subcontinent; in Rushdie's serious and mocking ironic epic of the spice trade and the 'sub-condiment,' India goes to Europe. A related function of Rushdie's hermeneutic reinterpretation of myth (à la Benjamin and Ricoeur) and his mythmaking in *The Moor's Last Sigh* is a post-colonial recuperation in which stories of the West are shown, through recomposition and reorientation, to be mixed up with stories of the East. Rushdie reorients the literary, cultural imaginary, restoring and replacing that which has been displaced through centuries of distortion, neglect, and hierarchical slanting. Through reinterpreting and rewriting narratives – that is, histories and myths – Rushdie reimagines the cultural imaginary and the world. Because he treats both history and myth as narratives, as stories open to interpretation and rewriting, he eludes static dichotomies and can, on the one hand, show fully the violence of the past and present as well as, on the other hand, avoid falling prey to a deterministic vision of the human predicament. At the end of his family saga, Moraes is exhausted and disillusioned, yet the manner in which the history has been interpreted and told raises the possibility that the future need not be the same as the present. A utopian, emancipatory hope is part of his narrative. Although the final chapters may be interpreted as apocalyptic in their vision of destruction and catastrophe, the novel's broad message is a positive one, emphasizing the role of resistance, identity making, and possibility seeking in the interpretive, mythopoeic process. All narratives, including human societies' histories, demand reinterpretation and recomposition. Every story remains incomplete, because the present alters the past, and the future becomes with each new moment potentially different. Stories must be continually rewritten because every end is arbitrary, and there is always some new beginning that may be enacted or at least envisioned.

Paradigms of Myth, Reoriented

What, then, are the main mythic paradigms or narrative superstructures within which the novel unfolds? There are primarily three: the vision, the fall and subsequent wandering in quest of redemption, and the labyrinth. *The Moor's Last Sigh* is Rushdie's Xanadu; in terms of myth, one can draw a connection between the novel and the dramatic situation and mythic components of 'Kubla Khan,' Samuel Coleridge's celebrated poem whose images are drawn in part from accounts of the life of the first emperor of the Yüan, or Mongol, dynasty in China, and his residence of K'ai-p'ing, or Shang-tu, in southeastern Mongolia.[3] Kenneth Burke has argued that 'Kubla Khan,' which he calls a 'protosurrealist' poem, is a narrative statement of romantic principles of creativity ('Kubla Khan' 221). Its tripartite structure moves from beatific vision (thesis), to a recognition of the sinister and turbulent (antithesis), to a fusion of these two components (synthesis, as in the phrases 'sunny dome,' 'caves of ice,' and 'holy dread') (201). The poem progresses through a series of visions, from 'stately pleasure dome' to 'romantic chasm' to the 'damsel with a dulcimer.' These visions tell a story, one mythic correlative of which is the narrative of innocence and experience, or the myth of the fall, the quest, and an imagined paradise regained. Like 'Kubla Khan,' *The Moor's Last Sigh* presents a vision, combining realistic and fantastic elements; its dramatic situation recalls, ironically, Xanadu: Moraes, or the Moor, a prisoner in an Andalusian castle, spills out his life's story to a young Japanese damsel in distress, Aoi Uë, who is likewise a prisoner of Vasco Miranda. The novel's narrative progresses through an ironic version of 'Kubla Khan's' series of visions, which imply a movement from innocence to experience, or from a fall to an imaginative recovery. In terms of radical typology, 'Kubla Khan' could thus be called an 'anti-type' (i.e., fulfilment)[4] of the myth of the fall, or paradise lost, as is the specific legend from which all the legends of Moraes's family history derive, a story surrounding the final defeat of the Moors in Spain and the end of their seven-hundred-year reign in the Iberian Peninsula. The legend of the last Sultan, Boabdil, and the Moor's defeat in Spain in 1492 moves narratively from the lovely gardens of the Alhambra to the bitterness of the expulsion from Granada to wandering and exile in Fez, Morocco. The paradigmatic myth of innocence–fall–imagined recovery structures many stories, both Eastern and Western; it underlies the narrative of human maturation – that is, the individual's development from child to adult, including the tests and trails of various sorts undergone along the way – and an ironic version of this myth structures *The Moor's Last Sigh*. Other paradigms and variations of this narrative pattern that inform the novel are the myth of a return to origins (which we see, by the way, in Moraes's telling of his family history); the artist's vision, a myth popular with romantics from Wordsworth and Coleridge to W.B. Yeats; and the myth of the apocalypse, in the sense both of a world coming to an end and of a re-visioning of a new world. Throughout Moraes's complex tale there is a fundamental struggle between Eros and Thanatos. In addition to the myths of the sacred vision and the fall-redemption, another important mythic-thematic structure informs the novel: that of the man in the labyrinth, as in the Greek tale of Theseus, Ariadne, and the Minotaur. The Moor – and the reader as well, because the novel has an aspect of detective fiction in which the author/text and reader play a game – must find his way through the twists and turns of clues and events. In the Greek myth, the monster is slain and the hero, in the end, emerges victorious; here, however, the monster changes form and, in the end, we remain in the labyrinth – the labyrinth of interpretations and possibilities.

But what is the name of the game? Myth and legend pervade *The Moor's Last Sigh*, yet it uses mythic paradigms postmodernistically, drawing the reader into the maze; it recomposes these myths and reorients them in new directions. I suspect that many readers will find Rushdie's performance both daunting and confusing; like Joyce's *Ulysses,* this is an epic-like novel that many more readers will begin than finish. To respond to my own question, however, I must draw one more parallel with Coleridge's 'Kubla Khan.' At a fundamental level, the poem ponders (post-colonial, postmodern) identity; just as, at the dawn of Western philosophy, Presocratic philosophers such as Anaximander, Pythagoras, and Heraclitus meditated on the basic matter of the world, on transformation, on oppositions and arrangement – the Greek word 'kosmos' means harmonious arrangement – so too 'Kubla Khan' ponders these basic concepts of being as the creative principle of poetry and the universe. The final game in *The Moor's Last Sigh* is an identity game, a poetic and zany spectacle of the enigma 'Who (or what) are we?' In treating this question Rushdie draws on Eastern and Western sources, Indian as well as classical Greek and Roman myth. With the disruptions and displacements at the end of the twentieth and beginning of the twenty-first century we return in some ways to fundamental questions and conceptions first articulated in the West by the Presocratic philosophers and before that, in different form, in East Asian religion and myth. More than fifty years ago, Northrop Frye in *Anatomy of Criticism* viewed all literature as part of a great cycle, beginning with myth and concluding in the ironic mode, which itself turns back to myth. That is what we have in Rushdie's novel.[5] In an interview following the publication of his book on the great myths of the world, *La Lumière de la nuit: Les grands mythes dans l'histoire du monde,* Italian writer and mythologist Pietro Citati remarked: 'Myths do not die; they sleep. When they awaken, they travel, passing from one era to another, crossing oceans and continents, taking their abode in the most secret thoughts of humankind' (quoted in Rondeau, 'Citati, premier rayon' 78). Rushdie and Citati would agree completely on this point; the 'travelling' through time and space in which myths, legends, and stories engage is not merely a form of displacement (à la Northrop Frye), but a form of translation and transformation. Great writers recompose and reorient these narrative nuclei, because in doing so they go to the heart of the literary and cultural imaginary of humanity; it is there that fundamental questions of identity can be addressed, but addressed indirectly, obliquely, in the form of stories.

The Moor's Last Sigh is a narrative in an ironic mode, with a hero confronting a certain 'bondage, frustration,' and 'absurdity' (Frye, *Anatomy of Criticism* 33–4); at the same time, it is a narrative that plays postmodernistically with myth, making it and mocking it in almost the same phrase. Scenes transform mercurially, and the tone flip-flops between poles of epic seriousness and postmodern slapstick. Even those ideas that Rushdie defends throughout the novel – such as the idea of hybridity and cultural plurality – are approached with an attitude that ranges from the dignified to the street-corner matter-of-fact. Thus, the premarital love between Abraham, the Moorish Jew, and Aurora, the Catholic, is implicitly likened to that of Romeo and Juliet. Moraes describes the scene in Aurora's fabulist painting 'The Scandal' in this manner: 'Warring Lobo and Menezes clans can be spotted on the mountains ... : the Menezes people all have serpents' heads and tails and the Lobos ... are wolves ... [I]n the foreground are the streets and waterways of Cochin, and they teem with scandalised congregations: fish-Catholics, dog-Anglicans, and the Jews all painted Delft blue, like figures in Chinese tiles' (103). Abraham and Aurora rest 'asleep on a peaceful island at the centre of the storm' (103). Their zoomorphic bodies feature feathers, wings, and heads of eagles. 'We soared above it,' Abraham recounts to his son, recalling the phoenix and other Greek myths of metamorphoses; 'we defied the lot of them, and we endured' (103). Explaining the difference between their struggles of cultural identity and his, Moraes writes, 'I ... was raised neither as Catholic nor as Jew. I was both, and nothing: a jewholic-anonymous, a catchjew nut, a stewpot, a mongrel cur ... Yessir: a real Bombay mix' (104). He gaily declares his cultural impurity: 'I like the sound of the word. *Baas*, a smell, a stinky-poo. *Turd*, no translation required. Ergo, *Bastard*, a smelly shit; like, for example, me' (104). There is something irreverent and mad-cap in Moraes's recounting of his family history; the mockery and irony do not dispel myth, but rather displace and reorient it. In its own topsy-turvy fashion, the novel puts forward a vision of a pluralistic society that, with reference to the multicultural societies of colonial-Dutch Cochin and Moorish Spain, has a historical reality as well as an immediate contemporary necessity. In this sense the novel is the history of civilization, with its periods of violence and war as well as its realized harmonies of complex cultural order. Rushdie is both a reinterpreter of history and a maker of myth based on this history; this is a hermeneutical as well as translational and transformative task. Regressive ideologies are separated out, and utopian, emancipatory narratives are composed.

Networks of Stories

The Moor's Last Sigh features numerous interlinked narratives that mix fairy tale, legend, myth, fantasy, and allegory of a historical, a literary, and an autobiographical nature. Rushdie constructs a rhizome-like network that defies categorization because everything becomes mixed up and hypertextually intersects with everything else. Within the overall narrative structure there are, for example. (1) fairy tales, (2) family legends, (3) Hindu and other religious mythology, (4) cartoon and pop culture, (5) the surreal and the fantastic, (6) literary fantasy, (7) allusions to Indian history in the context of European and contemporary history, (8) *The Lusiads*, the *Reconquista*, and tales of Moors and Jews in Spain, (9) Xanadu, or the artist's dreamlike vision, and (10) religious fundamentalist ideologies and autobiographical elements. I will consider only a few examples of these diverse yet hybridized categories, focusing on Xanadu, the artist's dream-like vision, whose primary avatar is Moraes's mother, Aurora, the novel's dominant figure.

Rushdie interweaves in his narratives many fairy-tale elements, including a basic struggle between good and evil: there are castles, damsels, witches, monsters of a sort, magic spells, and a treasure, but none of these without specific ties to historical milieux. Flory Zogoiby's chest of keepsakes, for example, contains a silver dagger and a 'tattered crown' four-and-a-half centuries old, made not of precious metals but of cloth, 'a dark green turban.' What is this crown? Nothing other than, or so the legend has it, '*the last crown to fall from the head of the last prince of al-Andalus; ... the last crown of Granada, as worn by Abu Abdallah, last of the Nasrids, known as "Boabdil"*' (78). Rushdie reorients this common fairy-tale component – in the manner of the *Arabian Nights* – and places it within a specific historical context: the fall of Granada and the *Reconquista*. As befits the nature of Rushdie's art, where treasure is not something equated with administrative power, but rather with imaginative potential, the final object in Flory's trunk is a manuscript of parchment pages that tells Boabdil's sad story, how he sighed and wept as he looked back on the sight of Granada and contemplated the end of Moorish rule in Spain. The sighs of Boabdil transform into the mixture of asthma and *saudade* (that special variant of Iberian nostalgia) that touch the male descendants of the da Gama–Zogoiby family lines: '*These wheezing sighs not only mine, but his. These eyes hot with his ancient grief,*' Abraham reflects; '*Boabdil, I too am thy mother's son*' (80). Moraes also has respiratory problems, as do Francisco da Gama, Aires da Gama, and Abraham Zogoiby, so the sighs and sadness of Boabdil are passed on (narratively) through the generations; the Moor's last sigh is not only Boabdil's upon saying farewell to Granada, but Moraes's last words as he reclines in the graveyard overlooking the Alhambra. Thus, we see here that Rushdie basically uses fairy-tale elements to combine with historical and other imaginative elements in the novel. This is a kind of magic realism, but not of the same kind that we find in South American writers such as Borges and Márquez. In any case, Rushdie and Borges are similar at least in the respect that both artists place fantastic elements within historical milieux, and both compose labyrinths of stories within stories.

Family legends constitute a second category of mythmaking, with all narrative elements relating to or growing out of them. The story of Flory Zogoiby's treasure chest is both legend and an oriental *Arabian Nights*-like tale; many elements in the novel, whose overall organization is like a rhizome, function this way as a story within a story branching out to still other stories. Francisco da Gama, the family patriarch, brings his bride, Epifania Menezes, to a lovely mansion with Edenic gardens on Cabral Island. Almost immediately restless, Francisco hires a Frenchman, who builds two houses within the gardens, one modernist, 'with furniture looking like something made for a ... geometry class,' and the other in Japanese style, 'a paper house of cards' (15–16). Francisco enjoys going back and forth between them: 'moving East' or 'going West,' he commands and gives orders to the household domestics (16). This division of houses prefigures a division in the family, with the two sons Camoens and Aires holding divergent views on all things, including business affairs and the British empire. All the members listed in the Da Gama–Zogoiby family tree have some legend through which they are immortalized. The branching of the tree, one branch proceeding from Camoens and the other from Aires, is the source of 'the legends of the battling da Gamas.' 'I tell them as they come down to me, polished and fantasticated by many re-tellings,' Moraes recounts. 'There are old ghosts, distant shadows, and I tell their tales to be done with them ... From Cochin harbour to Bombay harbour, from Malabar Coast to Malabar Hill: the story of our comings-together, tearings-apart, our rises, falls, our *tiltoings ups and down*' (11–12). The stories are often sad. A harried Francisco commits suicide, diving into the sea at Cabral Island and swimming away: 'perhaps he was trying to find some air beyond the island's enchanted rim,' Moraes sardonically speculates (24). His two sons Aires and Camoens do not fare better. Gay Aires is celebrated in family legend for his 'secret wildness' and his 'gowned adventure'; he costumes himself in his wife's wedding garments and goes to the harbour to tryst with a sailor nicknamed Prince Henry the Navigator (14). Camoens, following in his father Francisco's footsteps, commits suicide; unable to live without his wife, he dives into the harbour and is carried away by the tide, or so eyewitness Snow White reports (67). All family members have some personal trait or idiosyncrasy that provides the gist of legends, such as Moraes's oversized hand and Aurora's Ganpati dance. These legends often tie in with other networks of fantasy and allegory. For example, the two branches of the da Gama family engage in a dirty war for control of the family's spice enterprise, a war that culminates in an act of arson and various atrocities that clearly allude to the excesses of religious fundamentalism, one of whose real-life victims is Rushdie himself. The legendary fire in the da Gama spice fields results in several deaths: an overseer and his family are tied to a tree with barbed wire and burned like heretics, while three brothers who support the other side of the family are nailed to trees in the fashion of a crucifixion (40). 'What sort of family is this? Is this *normal*? Is this what we are all like?' a dejected Moraes ponders. And then concludes, with a broad generalization meant to apply to humanity: 'We are like this; not always, but potentially. This, too, is what we are' (40). The family quarrel and the fire in the spice fields are thus turned in the direction of an allegorical comment on the dark side of humanity and civilization.

A third category of imaginative material integrates Hindu, biblical, and other religious and mythological stories into the novel's larger narrative network. Aurora Zogoiby's controversial painting 'The Kissing of Abbas Ali Baig' takes an innocuous incident at a cricket match and turns it into an erotic statement: 'a tangle of womanly limbs and the cricketer's pads and whites that recalled the eroticism of the Tantric carvings at the Chandela temples of Khajuraho' (229). Hindu mythology informs Aurora's 'Ganpati' dance and the characterization of another dominant female, Uma Sarasvati, Moraes's *femme fatale* lover. The word 'Ganpati' is a variant of 'Ganapati,' itself another name for the Hindu elephant god Ganesha. A patron of letters and learning, Ganesha is the legendary scribe who wrote down the *Mahabharata*, the epic of the Bharata Dynasty, from Vyasa's dictation.[6] It is appropriate, then, that Aurora, whose name alludes to the East and to the Roman goddess of the Dawn, should be linked with the Hindu god Ganesha, who is the first god invoked at the beginning of worship, or of a new enterprise, and whose image is often seen at the entrance of temples or houses.[7] Aurora, as we will discuss later, represents the East (the Orient) as the place and power of stories and superlatives of imagination and fantasy. Uma Sarasvati is similarly mythically potent; her name incorporates the power of two goddesses, the supreme Hindu goddess Shakti, who in popular worship also goes by the names Uma, Parvati, and Ambika, and the goddess Sarasvati. 'I am the goddess who knows your secret heart,' she tells Moraes, and she becomes a force for both his destruction and creative expression (248). In Hindu mythology, Sarasvati is the goddess of learning and the arts; she is the patroness of art, music, and letters, and is given legendary credit for having invented the Sanskrit language and the Devanagari script in which it is written. In paintings and sculpture, she is represented holding a lute and a manuscript or book.[8] So much mythological and psychoanalytic narrative – Hindu, Greco-Roman, Germanic, Freudian – winds about in Uma: 'Like a goddess from the machine she came upon us, speaking to our inmost selves,' Moraes remarks (244). Her relationship with him is one of the principal vehicles in the novel for Rushdie's probing of the connection between love and betrayal. He does not attempt to explain such behaviour; rather, he places the characters of his story in a network of other, ancient stories of betrayal and tragedy. Like Tristan and Iseult, Moraes and Uma prepare to die together, to immortalize their love; at the last moment, however, he refuses the poison tablet. Who betrays whom? Later Moraes learns that it is she who has betrayed him. Betrayal is also the theme of the relationship between Moraes and his father and mother. Who betrays whom? Like a detective story, the novel does not reveal the answer or the solution until the final pages, and then its solution is open to interpretation. The biblical story of Abraham and Issac provides another framework that the Moor draws upon to interpret both his mother's and father's treatment of him. Both attempt to sacrifice him to achieve their ends: 'O Abraham! How readily you sacrificed your son on the altar of your wrath!' Moraes exclaims. 'Whom did you hire to blow the poisoned dart?' (225, 418) – the dart, that is, that kills Aurora, his mother. In the prison Under World of Bombay Central, Moraes reflects that any mother who would sentence a son to such a Hell can only be a monster: 'O, an age of monsters has come upon us. Kalyug, when cross-eyed red-tongued Kali, our mad dam, moves among us wreaking havoc. – And remember, O Beowulf, that Grendel's mother was more fearsome than Grendel himself ... Ah, Aurora, how easily you turned to infanticide' (288). The allusion to the age of monsters refers to the tale of the woman on a frozen tundra, fleeing wolves that chase her; to placate them she tosses out one child after another. 'Everyone thought it ghastly a hundred years ago,' a character in Paul Bowles's novel *Let It Come Down* (1952) comments; '[b]ut today it's much more terrible. Much. Because then it was remote and unlikely, and now it's entered into the realm of the possible' (222). Moraes is eventually released from this underworld, but enters another one – this time a tower prison – in Vasco Miranda's Little Alhambra.

The modernist takes himself seriously – or so the cliché goes – whereas the postmodernist is willing to make fun of his own serious intentions. Rushdie places himself in the latter category, which is another way of saying that the author never lets the reader forget that he is playing a linguistic, cultural game. Moraes's mother, Aurora, probably epitomizes this (postmodernist) esprit better than any other character in the novel, with the hero-turned-villain Vasco Miranda placing second. Lambajan Chandiwala, the security guard of *Elephanta*, the da Gama–Zogoiby family residence, is one of Aurora's hybrid – biblical, mythological, literary, pop – creations. Moraes remembers him in this way: 'that simple Peter at the doors of an earthly Paradise, who became my personal cut-price Virgil, leading me down to Hell – the great city of Hell, Pandaemonium, that dark-side, through-the-looking-glass evil twin of my own golden city: not Proper, but Improper Bombay' (126). The name 'Lambajan Chandiwala' is a kind of Joycean invention that translates as 'Long John Silverfellow': 'lamba, long; jan, sounds like John; chandi, silver' (126). To make him a perfect pirate, Aurora insists that he be equipped with a 'green clipped-winged' parrot that 'squawk[s] obscenities on his shoulder' (126). Part of the fun of Lambajan is that he is pretty harmless – 'hairy-faced' like his namesake, but toothless and gentle, with a gift for mythmaking, especially the spinning of elephant stories: 'Why do you think-so god Ganesha is so popular in Bombay City?' he rhetorically inquires, a bit awkwardly, and then explains that, long ago, elephants sat on thrones and argued philosophy; after the elephants' fall from rule, when men first arrived on Elephanta Island, they found statues of mammoths and destroyed them out of fear. 'Yes, men wiped away the memory of the great elephants but still not all of us have forgotten,' Lambajan concludes (127–8). The world bristles with stories – what is the world *but* its stories? Moraes asks – and the author continuously turns all into legend and shows how all legends have a reality. He is a postmodern (re)orientalist who comprehends that the greatest storyteller herself, Shahrazad, knew that she was playing a game and that she had no choice but to keep playing this game.[9] From the Lone Ranger and Tonto to Walt Disney cartoon characters, to the tales of Hans Christian Andersen, Rushdie finds ways of making connections and inventing new stories based on old ones. Thus, the lost needle in Vasco Miranda's stomach – left there after a 'botched appendix operation' – is an inventive variation of an element in Andersen's 'The Snow Queen.' Like Kay, who escapes the villainous queen but carries as a wound 'a splinter of ice in his veins,' Vasco knows that the lost needle will someday enter his heart and kill him. The fateful needle transforms his character: 'This was the secret of his hyperactive personality – he slept no more than three hours a night, and when awake, was incapable of sitting still for even three minutes' (154). 'Until the day of the needle I have much to do,' Vasco tells Moraes; '[L]ive until you die, that is my creed' (154–5). This is a creed with which Moraes can readily identify, for he too is '*short of time.*'

Pop culture, the surreal, and literary fantasy are three other categories of imaginative material in the novel. We find allusions, for example, to Othello, morality plays, *Gulliver's Travels*, and the *Arabian Nights*. The boundaries between categories blur, with pop culture blending into fairy tale blending into the fantastic, or at least that is the case with the Moor's own sense of the shortness of time, caused not by a lost needle or a splinter of ice in his veins, but rather by an accelerated growth rate of incredible proportions. 'I have aged twice as rapidly as the old earth and everything and everyone thereupon,' he relates (144). Moraes gestates a mere four-and-a-half months in his mother's womb; at the age of seven, he has the size and desires of a fourteen year old, and at thirty-six, he feels seventy-two. From the beginning, he is, as he puts it, not pre- but 'post-mature' (144). Another of the Moor's surreal idiosyncrasies is his deformed right hand, which resembles a 'club'; through Lambajan Chandiwala's mentoring, he becomes deft at boxing and uses his physical prowess to his advantage (146). Is he the hero of a mock postcolonial epic or a character in a daffy cartoon? Moraes defies facile categorization. His narrative mixes the serious with the comic in a postmodern game. Consider Moraes's name, which at once alludes to his family's Afro-Iberian heritage – Portuguese, Spanish, Arabic, and Jewish – as well as to popular nursery rhymes and those masters of slapstick, the Three Stooges. His sisters are named 'Ina, Minnie, Mynah,' and he is Moe – Moraes or the Moor (142). The children's nursery, conceived and painted by Vasco Miranda as a universe of cartoon pop culture, provides much of the primordial matter for Moraes's imagination and self-identity. The nursery walls, full of 'trompe-l'oeil windows' in various styles – 'Mughal-palatial, Andalusian Moorish, Manueline Portuguese, roseate Gothic' – are described as 'magic casements' that 'open on the world of make believe' (151). A cursory list of the figures depicted there includes Mickey Mouse, Donald Duck, Huey-Dewey-Louie, Goofy, Pluto, Heckle'n'Jeckle, Chip'n'Dale, Porky the Pig, Bugs

Bunny, Elmer Fudd, Batman and Robin, Superman, Wonder Woman, Lois Lane, Green Arrow, Phantom, Flash, the Lone Ranger, and Tonto (151–2). About Vasco Miranda's hybrid marvels, Moraes remarks, gaily piling literary allusion on literary allusion: 'He gave us story-oceans and abracadabras, Panchatantra fables and new lamps for old. Most important of all, however, was the notion he implanted in all of us through the pictures on our walls: the notion ... of the secret identity' (152). This notion of something hidden is central to fairy tale, myth, legend, and fantasy of all sort: things are never quite what they seem is the essential message of magic and magicians. Borges defines magic as a 'unique causality': 'We rub a lamp, and a genie appears. That genie is a slave who is also omnipotent and who will fulfill our wishes. It can happen at any moment' (*Seven Nights* 51).

In *The Moor's Last Sigh* the magical and the fantastic are the product of narrative movement (e.g., the legend of Flory Zogoiby's chest and the stories spanning the Cantonese tiles) and inventive characterization. Aurora, Vasco Miranda, Lambajan Chandiwala, the Moor – each has a secret identity that expresses itself through different artistic media. For Aurora, her paintings take an increasingly dreamlike, fantastic quality as her career develops and as her relationship with her husband and son grows more estranged. Jilted by Aurora and Abraham, Vasco Miranda goes into exile in Spain and sets up his 'Little Alhambra,' a postmodern kitsch version of the great Moorish palace in whose Generalife-like gardens he strolls costumed as a half-mocking, half-nostalgic 'old-time Sultan' (398). As for Moraes, his multifaceted identity has the quality of a glass chandelier in a ballroom of dancers, and his confession – that is, this text of his 'last sigh' – casts its light in all directions. He and it comprise a variety of male and female personages, all of whom are counterparts and secret sharers in this tale of many tales: Aurora; his sisters; his father, grandfathers, and great-grandfathers; Uma Sarasvati, Aoi Uë, and Vasco Miranda, to mention the principals. Masks, disguises, deceptions, betrayals, even the aesthetic concepts of 'Moonstan' and 'Palimpstine,' project a sense of the world as one of secret identities and hidden correspondences. The Lone Ranger and Tonto, Clark Kent and Superman, Bruce Wayne and Batman, Vasco Miranda (the Moor's dark self and final adversary) and Moraes: all lead a double life, a life in a labyrinth, one of whose final twisting paths is exile, which Moraes calls a 'surreal foreignness.' 'The place, language, people and customs I knew had all been removed from me by the simple act of boarding this flying vehicle; and these, for most of us, are the four anchors of the soul,' he laments upon leaving India. 'I felt as if all the roots of my self had been torn up like those of the flying trees from Abraham's atrium ... I was alone in a mystery' (383). Moraes's plight is Rushdie's plight. Fantasy is sometimes a subversion and a line of escape, but it is also a critique and a scream in a prison cell, a cry from 'Pandaemonium' (5). In the end a 'banished,' sick, debilitated Moor chooses, like Rip Van Winkle, to go to sleep, to give himself over to the final metamorphosis; he becomes his fiction, the final page in the da Gama–Zogoiby family saga.

History and Myth

Page by page, myth, legend, and fantasy of diverse sorts abound in *The Moor's Last Sigh*, but at the base of all this imaginative material is a historical network, which the author treats less as an unalterable reality than as a malleable narrative, not totally unlike other narratives, open to varying interpretations. (As an aside, it might be noted here that we find support for this linkage of narrative structures in Paul Ricoeur's three-volume treatise *Temps et récits*, where history and fiction are shown to share narrative structures as well as basic processes, when written and read, of pre-configuration, configuration, and reconfiguration.) The novel establishes links between the da Gama–Zogoiby family history and Portuguese, Spanish, and English imperial history, pulling the narrative away from the pole of fantasy and drawing it toward the pole of social and political commentary, giving it a potential significance as a postcolonial story of East and West reinterpreted and imperial history given a different, less noble highlighting. '[A]ll this from a pepperpot!' Moraes exclaims, of the navigations and colonizations that define the Age of Discovery in modern European history:

> Pepper it was that brought Vasco da Gama's tall ships across the ocean, from Lisbon's Tower of Belém to the Malabar Coast ... English and French sailed in the wake of that first-arrived Portugee, so that in the period called Discovery-of-India – but how could we be discovered when we were not covered before? – we were 'not so much sub-continent as sub-condiment,' as my distinguished mother had it. 'From the beginning, what the world wanted from bloody mother India was daylight clear ... They came for the hot stuff ...' (4–5)

Here, both playfully and seriously, Moraes is reinterpreting and reorienting the history of Portuguese exploration and empire in Asia; the da

Gama–Zogoiby family saga takes its meaning in part through this recasting of the story of the Portuguese presence in India. Not unlike a parody, the novel toys with *The Lusiades*. In the latter, the great epic of Portugal, Vasco da Gama's voyage to India and the subsequent beginning of European colonization of the Far East is celebrated in conjunction with the battle against Moorish reign in the Iberian Peninsula and throughout the sea routes of the Eastern world. But all for pepper, Moraes sarcastically adds.

In *The Moor's Last Sigh*, a mock epic and a post-colonial rewriting of the Portuguese founding myth, Moraes, the Indian of Portuguese, Jewish, Islamic heritage, journeys in a westerly direction, this time to the Iberian Peninsula, and in the course of his story East and West are shuffled around and the notion of History treated mischievously. In Moraes's cartography, Bombay becomes the point of many virtual intersections:

> [It] was central, had been so from the moment of its creation: the bastard child of a Portuguese-English wedding, and yet the most Indian of all Indian cities. In Bombay all Indias met and merged. In Bombay, too, all-India met what-was-not-India, what came across the black water to flow into our veins. Everything north of Bombay was North India, everything south of it was the South. To the east lay India's East and to the west, the world's West. Bombay was central; all rivers flowed into its human sea. It was an ocean of stories; we were all its narrators, and everybody talked at once. (350)

Rushdie as re-orientalist views the world from a vantage point whose centre is neither Lisbon nor London nor Paris, but Bombay; furthermore, it is not so much History as a unified, definitive series of events and personages that interests him, but rather the world as an 'ocean of stories' whose historians are Shahrazad-like raconteurs, the Oriental storyteller par excellence. The novel, then, is less about a decentring in the spirit of a critique from the margins, than about an assertion of the potential of the imagination, of the capacity of stories, to discern and envision realities.

The historical reinterpretations, reorientations, and various fantastic aspects of Moraes's narration are part of an approach of '*unnaturalism*,' which, he claims, is the 'only real ism of these back-to-front and jabberwocky days' (5). This approach, which we could label postmodern myth and fantasy, and in Rushdie's case a taking of ideas 'to the superlative,' responds to at least three dangers of the twentieth-first-century world: first, fundamentalist ideologies; second, a sense of hopelessness in the face of seemingly insurmountable problems; and third, the struggle to safeguard for language its poetic potential. The imaginative and the fantastic do not do away with concepts like reality and history, but perhaps what Rushdie suggests is that history and reality are what one must reconcile oneself with when one has no other stories to imagine and to tell. One 'tumble[s] toward history' when the high-wire act of the imagination no longer moves precariously forward into its unknown: at any moment Shahrazad may fall from the realm of intrigue and make-believe and become the king's next victim. To imagine and to make stories is a means of survival. It is also, of course, a resistance to power: in a totalitarian society, language and stories are imposed; in a society that moves toward emancipation, people have their own language and compose their own stories.

Epics, Legends, and Mock-heroic Elements

Legends, such as those drawn from the history of the Moorish rule in the Iberian peninsula, provide stories against which Moraes's narrative plays and juxtaposes itself. Legends surrounding the life of Rodrigo Díaz, or El Cid – the Castilian military leader and national hero whose popular name derives from Spanish Arabic as-sid, 'lord' – and his wife, Ximena, become a comfort to the cancer-stricken Isabella Ximena da Gama; on her deathbed she asks her husband, Camoens – his name a variation of that of Luis Vaz de Camões, author of the Portuguese epic *Os Lusíadas* – to remember 'the story of El Cid Campeador in Spain' (52). According to one of the legends, after the Cid is mortally wounded in battle, in his last breath he orders his wife Ximena to strap his body to a horse and then send it into battle so as to lead the enemy forces to believe that he is still alive and continues to fight. Isabella, who is engaged in a bitter family quarrel with her sister-in-law Carmen Lobo, suggests something similar: '*Then tie my body to a bloody rickshaw or whatever damn mode of transport you can find, camel-cart, donkey-cart bullock-cart bike ... Because the enemy is close and in this sad story Ximena is the Cid*' (51–2). Rushdie uses this pastiche of legend to underscore, in a mock-epic fashion, the heated conflict between the two branches of the family; he alters the legend to suit his purposes, one of which is to underscore the recurrent nature of story. Underlying this legend of El Cid is, of course, an episode in the *Odyssey*.

The novel's principal narrative interweaves the da Gama–Zogoiby family history, contemporary events in post-colonial India, and the history and legends of the *Reconquista*; from these criss-crossing threads the themes of ethnic and religious intolerance, internecine war, alienation, and exile take shape. Myth, although always open to new interpretations and new recompositions, insists that there is something universal and perennial in the human condition. To the questions, What is this human condition? and What does it mean to be civilized? Moraes's response is sometimes as bleak at that of Marlow in *Heart of Darkness*: 'Civilization is the sleight of hand that conceals our natures from ourselves' (365). Technology changes rapidly; human beings much less so. From the fire in the spice fields, with its crucifixions and Inquisitional *autodafé*, to personal betrayals, to the horrors of the Bombay underworld, all along the course of his story Moraes has puzzled over and been the victim of the irrational aspects of human nature, and all along the way the violent eruptions within the da Gama–Zogoiby family story have been running in parallel with the larger eruptions in twentieth-century Indian colonial history, stretching from the country's independence to partition, persistent religious feuds, and the Emergency. In the final sections of the novel, fundamentalist feuding reaches a climax with the destruction of the Ayodhya mosque and the series of bombings that it sparks in Bombay.[10] There is not much sense in it all, Moraes points out; it was a Muslim worshipper at the Babri mosque who first claimed to see a vision of Lord Ram, and Muslim and Hindu have shared the site in the past: 'What could be a finer image of religious tolerance and plurality than that?' he inquires (363). Still, the violence of the moment overwhelms everyone, including Moraes: 'Hindu and Muslim, knife and pistol, killing, burning, looting, and raising into the smoky air their clenched and bloody fists. Both their houses are damned by their deeds,' he concludes; 'both sides sacrifice the right to any shred of virtue; they are each other's plagues' (365). In a grand sweep of allusion and invented narrative parallelism the novel links religious intolerance, artistic freedom, the *fatwa* against Rushdie, the *Reconquista*, and Zionism; thus, when Aurora's paintings are stolen from the Zogoiby Bequest – an allusion to the theft and destruction of images in India's temples and monuments – Raman Fielding, the family's most dangerous enemy, comments approvingly: 'When such alien artifacts disappear from India's holy soil, let no man mourn ... If the new nation is to be born, there is much invader-history that may have to be erased' (364). Just as the Muslims and Jews were banished from Catholic Spain, so too, according to the fundamentalist argument, the Portuguese-Muslim-Jewish heritage that the da Gama–Zogoiby family line represents must be purged from Indian society.

Moraes dips his own hands in the communal blood when he takes revenge on Fielding, pummelling him to death with a frog-shaped telephone; the Moor likens this murder to Lord Ram slaying Ravan and Achilles slaying Hector. In a mock-epic stylistic flourish he notes: 'After Ram killed Ravan he chivalrously arranged a lavish funeral for his fallen foe. Achilles, much the less gallant of these high heroes, tied Hector's corpse to his "chariot-tail" and dragged him thrice round dead Patroculus's grave ... [N]ot living in heroic times, I neither honoured nor desecrated my victim's body' (368). Having no choice but to flee, Moraes does so with much historical and legendary allegory:

> Just as the fanatical 'Catholic King' had besieged Granada and awaited the Alhambra's fall, so now barbarism was standing at our gates. O Bombay! ... *Star of the East with her face to the West!* Like Granada ... you were the glory of your time. But a darker time came upon you, and just as Boabdil, the last Nasrid Sultan, was too weak to defend his great treasure, so we, too, were proved wanting. For the barbarians were not only at our gates but within our skins. We were our own wooden horses ... We were both the bombers and the bombs ... And now can only weep, at the last, for what we were too enfeebled, too corrupt ... to defend. (372–3)

In the final lines of this passage, Rushdie rewrites the legendary words of Ayxa to Boabdil upon the flight from Granada: '*Well may you weep like a woman for what you could not defend like a man*' (80). Although the tone of the passage signals a serious rather than mocking or parodic commentary, even the best of readers must wonder whether Rushdie – after so much inversion, mixing of registers and messages, and linguistic shenanigans – can possibly pull off a moral statement at this point in the narrative. The author's recasting, five hundred years later, of an episode of the Boabdil legend into a commentary on fundamentalist violence in India (and the world) would seem to attempt to do just that. Identity conceived within a narrow political, religious, or ethnic framework, Rushdie is saying, can only be destructive in a world where religions and ethnic groups must mix and coexist. Essentialist identity was *never* anything but an ideology – that would seem to be the whole point of Rushdie's return to the history of the Arabs and Jews expelled from fifteenth- and sixteenth-century Spain – although the blood it sheds through conflicts it engenders continues to flow somewhere on every continent of the globe.

Significances of the Story Networks and of Aurora as Symbol

The Moor's Last Sigh both critiques and envisions. In the former capacity, we find some of the following manoeuvres. First, the text attacks religious fundamentalism. In the expulsion of Arabs and Jews, the *Reconquista* represents a victory of the one over the many; conversely, Aurora's art and Moraes's narrative seek a reversal, a re-vision of cultural plurality. They imagine a future that develops from an aspect of the past that has been occluded or erased. Second, the text suggests a related point that widens to include a commentary on civilization: today's fundamentalist extremism is nothing new; ethnic and religious intolerance and extremism have long been a part of the human condition. The feud within the da Gama–Zogoiby family – and the myths that referentially narrate it – is a metaphor for violence and eruptions throughout the course of human history; the *Reconquista* and legends surrounding it illustrate that 'fundamentalism' is neither Islamic by nature, nor is it a particularly new phenomenon. Thus, the link between Hindu and Muslim fundamentalism today and Christian fundamentalism five hundred years ago is a means to broaden Rushdie's commentary and to oppose an Orientalism (i.e., a prejudice) in which Western analysts of contemporary events in the Middle East and Asia sometimes indulge. Third, the text re-orientalizes the history and legends of the *Reconquista* by looking at it from Arabic and Jewish perspectives, somewhat as Lebanese French writer Amin Maalouf does in *Les Croisades vues par les Arabes* and *Léon l'Africain*. From a Western perspective, the *Reconquista* is the recovery of an occupied Christian territory; from an Eastern perspective, it is a story of loss and exile. Yet there is more than this implied relativism of perspectives: the text goes further to suggest that Western civilizations have always drawn upon the genius of Eastern civilizations, and in this sense the text re-orientalizes the history of civilizations. Fourth, with an oriental storytelling flair, Rushdie turns Bombay into a *tout-monde*, a wild and crazy meeting place of languages and cultures. Moraes the storyteller inhabits a kind of Xanadu, a vision of the literary, cultural imaginary of an intersecting East and West. Whereas belated Orientalists of the nineteenth century turned to the East to fill an absence, to engage their desire for an otherness, Rushdie the re-orientalist turns to the cultural imaginary as a source of self-invention and as an inspiration for an emancipatory vision of the world. With its allusions, allegory, and mythic structures, his Orient as imaginary subsumes, holds all the world in its extensions and narrative peregrinations. East and West come to an end in the interrelationships and cross-cultural mixings of the cultural imaginary, for Rushdie shows that each has something of the elements of the other. Locale takes on a virtuality that subsumes old notions of rootedness and emplacement.

Aurora's artistry represents in an exemplary fashion the novel's imaginative, re-orientalizing project; this category of the novel's imaginary material I have referred to as 'Xanadu, or the artist's dreamlike vision.' Aurora is above all an artist of life; her acts are symbolically part of her art, just as her art is itself a symbolic act. Her Ganpati dance is at once a rebellious mock gesture and an appropriation of the sacred:

> [S]ky-high above crowds and gods, year after year – for forty-one years in all – fearless upon precipitous ramparts of our Malabar Hill bungalow, which in a spirit of ironic mischief she had insisted on naming *Elephanta*, there twirled the almost-divine figure of our very own Aurora Bombayalis, plumed in a series of dazzle-hued mirrorwork outfits, outdoing in finery even the festival sky with its hanging gardens of powdered colour. Her white hair flying out around her in long loose exclamations (O prophetically premature white hair of my ancestors!) ... [S]peaking incomprehensible volumes with her hands, the great painter danced her defiance, she danced her contempt for the perversity of humankind. (123–4)

Aurora Bombayalis – like the inspired poet of 'flashing eyes' and 'floating hair' in the third stanza of 'Kubla Khan' – becomes semi-divine, an aurora borealis, the goddess of the dawn. And just as in Coleridge's poem, whose figure in reverie seeks to synthesize antinomies, Aurora's dance poses a question that intersects with the novel's two tendencies (its critique of ideology and its quest for an emancipatory vision): which is greater, 'human perversity' or 'human heroism'? (124). 'Whatever today's excess, tomorrow's will exceed-o it,' Aurora exclaims (124). The narrative network of the novel concerns this battle between evil and good, between a tyranny that enforces a narrowing of human vision and a struggle to keep it open. Aurora the artist, who would seem to personify Rushdie's convictions, gives expression to her own vision through a mixture of superlative strategies: silent refusals, defiant acts, imaginative interventions, and a fantastic visionary art. Her acts, no less than her art, are symbolic. Upon learning that her husband has promised his mother,

Flory, to raise a first child according to the strictures of Jewish religious doctrine, she refuses to have sexual relations with him and thus to bear a child. Similarly, although she becomes a heroine of the Indian nationalist movement, she defies the Hindu fundamentalists who try to co-opt her rebellious acts to their own narrow purposes. An urban pirate flying her Jolly Roger over Elephanta Island, she is a fictional flowering of the artist *engagée*. 'In Bombay you live crushed in this crazy crowd ... your own story has to shove its way through the throngs,' Moraes writes, commenting on his mother's depiction of a swarming humanity in her celebrated painting 'The Last Supper.' Here, as elsewhere, there is an allegorical element at play, for Rushdie is also commenting autobiographically on his life and writing.

Aurora's accidental maiming then healing of a sailor on strike is an illustration of her capacity to redeem life through art. After accidentally backing her car over his leg, Aurora not only makes retribution, but heals and transforms the wounded man. 'She brought him home and changed his life,' Moraes explains. 'She had diminished him, subtracted a leg and therefore his future in the navy; and now she sought fiercely to enlarge him again, providing him with a new uniform, a new job, a new leg, a new identity and a grumpy parrot to go with it all' (135). The wounded sailor metamorphoses into Lambajan Chandiwala, or Long John Silver, the faithful guardian of Aurora's home, Elephanta – in the manner of his patron Hindu god, Ganesha – and a 'teller of fabulous elephant-tales,' which he in turn gives back to her as an expression of his gratitude at not being abandoned to the fate of a cripple in India. Here we see Rushdie's belief in the imagination's ability to heal and to open new possibilities of living. We also see his humour, itself a necessary capacity in the face of misfortune and human perversity.

Aurora's paintings illustrate related ideas; they are symbolic vehicles through which the artist struggles against a reduction of human vision, and in this respect they have a poetic and salutary function. Just as Aurora heals the poor sailor whom she has maimed, imaginatively opening up another life for him to explore, so too her paintings envision possibilities of the real; they enlarge the real by disclosing what is hidden or concealed within it – and by superlatively adding to it. Moraes uses various terms to describe her mythopoeic vision: 'Aurorised [rather than Authorised] version of history,' 'Mooristan' and 'Palimpstine,' to mention just a few of his Joycean-like neologisms (225–7). In the painting entitled 'Last Supper,' Aurora mixes Christian and Indian religious imagery, at once mourning the loss of her mother and creating an allegory of contemporary India. Other paintings, particularly the 'Moor series,' treat related themes of loss and recovery by way of a mythopoeic vision. Aurora reimagines the legend of the fifteenth-century fall of the Alhambra and of Boabdil's (Mohammed XI's) departure from Granada; this legend, told and embellished by the American fabulist Washington Irving in *The Alhambra*, is then overlaid with elements of contemporary India and her own mother–son relationship with Moraes. Her paintings 'were attempts to create a romantic myth of the plural, hybrid nation; she was using Arab Spain to re-imagine India,' Moraes remarks (227). The various terms and neologisms that he uses to define Aurora's art, such as 'interweaving,' 'hybridity,' 'Mooristan,' and 'palimpsest-art,' convey a basic concept: an aesthetic of composite elements and a radical typology where something new emerges out of something old. Moraes calls Aurora's paintings a 'Bombay remix of the last of the Nasrids' (the last Moorish dynasty in fifteenth-century Spain), in which the Alhambra is placed on Malabar Hill in southern India (225). (Myth and word play, of course, go hand and hand in Rushdie's fiction, for the word 'Malabar,' we should note, is an anagram of 'Alhambra.') Aurora's paintings are fabulist, mythopoeic. In them the dividing line between land and water becomes a place of transformation where worlds collide and metamorphose; the paintings' backgrounds show new social orders in evolution. She 'seek[s] to paint a golden age,' Moraes explains. 'Jews, Christians, Muslims, Parsis, Sikhs, Buddhists, Jains crowded into her paint[ings] ... and the Sultan himself was represented less and less naturalistically, appearing more and more often as a masked, particoloured harlequin, a patchwork quilt of a man; or, as his old skin dropped from him chrysalis-fashion, standing revealed as a glorious butterfly, whose wings were a miraculous composite of all the colours in the world' (227).

But what can it mean, in the narrator's words, to 'us[e] Arab Spain to re-imagine India'? Can one cross borders so easily? Can the past of one society inform another society distant from it geographically and chronologically? For Rushdie, it is partly a question of history – Moorish Spain and the coastal cities of the Indian Ocean do share a multiculturalism – but it is more a question of myth, the cultural imaginary, and utopian possibilities. Rushdie wants to penetrate what Ricoeur calls the 'mytho-poetic nucleus' of society ('Myth' 482–3). He seeks to valorize this nucleus of Indian society – and that of our contemporary global society – and to invoke its possibilities of human development and enrichment. Aurora's paintings and Rushdie's novel are symbolic acts that resemble the invocations of the visionary poet in Coleridge's 'Kubla Khan.' By way of his typological reading of history and his mythopoeic narratization of twentieth-century India and the contemporary world, Rushdie makes the case for a 'plural, hybrid nation' and a new human order. Édouard Glissant calls this new order of relation the 'chaos-monde' and the 'tout-monde,' terms with different emphasis but used more or less interchangeably. The former term defines 'cette rencontre conflictuelle et merveilleuse des langues' ('this conflictual and marvellous meeting of languages'); the latter term denotes the presence of an entire world *within* each individual's limited place and consciousness. The world is being creolized, he contends; all cultures are being creolized today in their contact with one another. The ingredients vary, but the principle is the same; because of these cultural mixings, there is no longer a single culture that can call itself pure ('L'Imaginaire des langues' 13, 21).

Utopia/Dystopia

To claim that the project of *The Moor's Last Sigh* is partly utopian does not mean that it takes us down a yellow-brick road. A tale told against a backdrop of genocide, civil wars, and the rise of religious fundamentalisms, violence is everywhere. In a fit of black humour, Aurora exclaims: 'Human perversity is greater than human heroism ... or cowardice ... or art' (124). A remark of George Steiner would seem apropos here: 'Malraux said: "The twenty-first century will be religious or it won't be at all." I dare to contradict him: I fear that, if the twenty-first century is religious, it will cease to exist. I hope that there will be human beings who contemplate our human condition, rather than a transcendence of it. Would that ideological fanaticism be branded the original sin!' (Interview 9). Right at the beginning, Moraes informs us that his family history will be a violent one, but he transforms the violence into stories, appropriating it and taming it as does his oriental counterpart, Shahrazad, in her own stories invented against violence and tyranny. *The Moor's Last Sigh* is a modern *Arabian Nights*, and as in the latter, the storytelling, mythmaking process as vehicle of hope and emancipation stands as a kind of ultimate message. Rushdie dips into the treasure chest of myth and legend and opens an imaginary space that contemporary events would seem to bar; in critiquing fundamentalist and totalitarian ideologies, he separates 'myth' that masks from 'myth' that awakens and seeks to emancipate. The one is ideological, the other is utopian –

whether we work with Benjamin's definition, Bloch's, or Ricoeur's, the basic idea of a dualistic entity and two-fold operation would seem the same.

'Nothing is purely,' the Presocratic philosopher Anaxagoras claims (*Presocratics Reader* 59). Rushdie's novel makes a similar claim, and raises a similar question. What is identity? Toward what kind of cultural and social organization must the world today evolve? The novel convincingly portrays the profusion of the many, that is, cultural plurality, but does it give us some sense of a standard of acceptable human behaviour? In a world of cultural relativity, there still need to be values that apply across cultures. So Rushdie draws on myths and legends from around the world to illustrate a certain commonalty in the human predicament and to construct an implied set of values, thus reconciling the notions of cultural relativity and universal human rights and values. As some reviewers have suggested, the novel has its contradictions, one of which, in my view, is that its underlying message can be interpreted as just the opposite of what it appears: not as a plea for the triumph of the many over the one, but as a plea for the one that believes in the many, that is, for universal human values that prohibit exclusion and violence. One of the surprises of this novel, then, is that its message is one of conservation, just as much as it is one of subversion and rebellion. But isn't this the very nature of myth, to conserve as well as to transform, to draw something new out of something old? Using myth and legend to carry its message forward, *The Moor's Last Sigh* takes a stand against static notions of identity and exclusion based on essentialism, and stands up for the openness of societies and open-endedness of human stories. Drawing on ancient as well as modern stories from East and West, it is a book that believes in the power of myth and the imagination to liberate and to envision a better world.

6. Identity and Citizenship in a World of Shame

'J'appartiens à ce parti d'opposition qui s'appelle la vie.'

Balzac

The end of the twentieth century also marked the two hundredth anniversary of the birth of Honoré de Balzac, author of, among other books, *La Comédie humaine* (1834–7), a monumental work itself encompassing more than ninety novellas and novels. It goes almost without saying that Balzac was not a minimalist; in *La Comédie humaine* alone, the total number of named characters is estimated at 2472, to which can be added a further 566 unnamed characters. I begin this chapter with a quotation from Balzac because, as old-fashioned as these words might have sounded just a few years ago, today again they speak to us in their simplicity and profundity: 'I belong to that opposition party called life.' I like the spirit of universality that this quote conveys and its emphasis on attachment to experience rather than allegiance to ideologies. I also like its resolution of oppositions: a sense of self, coupled with a sense of involvement and participation in something larger than self; a refusal of categories yet an embrace of all that is, both large and small. In a world where identity and citizenship are defined narrowly along ethnic or national lines, we would do well to adopt a more Balzacian attitude, even at the risk of the impractical and the gargantuan.

Citizenship in the twenty-first century must be reconceived as a composite entity, whose allegiances extend from the culturally specific to the humanly universal. And because concepts of citizenship cannot easily be separated from concepts of individual and cultural identity, identity likewise must be reconceived as composite, its roots stretching

Identity and Citizenship in a World of Shame   177

across localities to regional and global distances – and along with this extension, an expansion of the responsibilities of our citizenship in the world. Identity comprises the actual and the potential; embodied in the biological and in history and cultural tradition, it is equally a situation, a recursive event, and a work in progress that remains incomplete and unfinished. The identity of an individual (or a group) has its own particularities, yet it is also dependent on and interrelated to the identities of others. It is a system within a system, a network within an immense living network, whose linkages have a past, present, and future and whose material of exchange consists of all manner of information, from DNA to history and the stories of the literary, cultural imaginary. To elaborate contemporary ideas about identity and citizenship, this chapter will draw principally on works of Édouard Glissant (*Introduction à une poétique du divers; An Introduction to a Poetics of Diversity*) (1996), Amin Maalouf (*Les Identités meurtrières; Murderous Identities*) (1998), Tzvetan Todorov (*L'Homme dépaysé; The Disoriented Man*) (1996), and V.S. Naipaul (*Beyond Belief: Islamic Excursions among the Converted Peoples*, 1998), and secondarily on a disparate group of philosophers, sociologists, scientists, a composer-musician, a designer, literary scholars, and intellectuals, including Paul Ricoeur, George Steiner, Ernst Bloch, Emmanuel Lévinas, Gianni Vattimo, Matthieu Ricard, Trinh Xuan Thuan, Neil Bissoondath, Paco Ibañez, Karl Lagerfeld, Henry Louis Gates, Jr, and Paula Gunn Allen. Identity and citizenship will be considered from 'Eastern' as well as 'Western' perspectives – if one can still speak in such broad categorizations – with an emphasis perhaps on the contention that contemporary Western conceptions of identity find correlates in ancient Eastern religion and thought. Scholarly studies such as Matthieu Ricard's and Trinh Xuan Thuan's *L'Infini dans la paume de la main* (*Infinity in the Palm of the Hand*) and Reinhard May's *Heidegger's Hidden Sources: East Asian Influences on His Work* illustrate interesting intersections of the two traditions. I will compare and contrast these diverse perspectives and use them as a foundation for further conceptual development of frameworks of contemporary identity and citizenship. Intrinsically related to these issues is what I have referred to in the title of this chapter as 'shame.' The political, cultural, and social environment in which we live today is marked by enormous discrepancies and inequalities; concepts of identity and citizenship would be empty indeed if they were to ignore this situation and not respond to the shame of our twenty-first-century world or the shame of being citizens in societies that overconsume and waste resources, contaminate the planet through industrial and other pollution, and tolerate the enormous gap between 'rich' and 'poor' countries. The discrepancies between have's and have not's grow larger each year; those who 'have' must effectively address the plight of those who 'have not' – morally and imaginatively – or all claims of individual and communal identity and citizenship will be rendered hollow and irrelevant in the face of this human catastrophe.

Perspectives on Identity and Citizenship

Caribbean poet, novelist, and intellectual Édouard Glissant has published numerous works that conceptualize the notion of creolized identity, works including *Le Discours antillais* (*Caribbean Discourse*, 1981) and *Tout-monde* (1993). One might summarize the main ideas in Glissant's treatise on this subject, *An Introduction to a Poetics of Diversity*, as follows: today's world is undergoing a pervasive process of creolization, or interaction and mixing of cultural identities, whose consequences are unpredictable though potentially enormous. Glissant prefers the word 'creolization' to 'hybridity' because the latter term connotes a certain control and predictability, whereas what is happening today is limitless and often chaotic. This process of creolization renders obsolete notions of uniquely rooted identity, which have been the foundation of the nation-state since the European Renaissance and subsequent centuries of colony and empire. In general, Glissant demythifies notions of essentialist identity; he conceives of identity as something heterogeneous, that is, as a field without a centre, a rhizomic tissue of cultural qualities and values that interact.[1]

Given this pervasive creolization of the world, one important question for communities becomes how to delimit a sociocultural space without excluding cultural otherness and how to incorporate cultural otherness without fracturing the well-defined community. How can a community simultaneously be open to all thoughts and all people yet remain a particular place with its own cultural contours and predilections? Is there some point where Portugal, for example, creolized by influences from Europe, South America, and Africa, not to mention North America, would cease to be Portugal? These questions, although they do make sense, are misleading, at least to a degree. For the phenomenon of creolization, as Glissant comprehends and conceives of it, is a situation that we are already within; this creolization has become a part of our living experience just as tradition constitutes the given of our 'prejudice' (i.e., pre-judgments) and our contemporary situation. To designate the individual interiority of this creolizing world of globalization, these swift and multiple cultural interactions and superpositions that strike the individual consciousness, Glissant coins the rubric of the *tout-monde*. Here we see perhaps the influence of Heidegger and other thinkers who work with the concept of 'Dasein,' for this creolization is an event situated equally in consciousness and the world. The word 'diversity' in the title of Glissant's book *An Introduction to a Poetics of Diversity* is a key one; this diversity emerges from and as a result of the cultural interactions and clashes within the *tout-monde*, a kind of universal situation and event at the end of the twentieth and beginning of the twenty-first century. It would seem that Glissant seeks to integrate the notion of 'universality' with the notion of 'difference,' although he would reject or at least be suspicious of the term 'universal.' He does *not* believe that the twenty-first century will be one in which standardization, or global sameness, is inevitably the sad result. The contemporary sociocultural world is not deterministically of one sort or another, if only because the consequences of creolization within the individual consciousness and within communities are incalculable. The *tout-monde*, it should be made clear, is something concrete and historical, yet virtual as well. To describe it and envision its possibilities demands a new poetry and literature; nevertheless, everyone today is already living within this linguistic and cultural upheaval and reformation, whether they are conscious of it or not. The distinguishing mark of today's world is relation within a network of difference. Although languages and dialects are tragically and rapidly disappearing – of the estimated six thousand languages spoken in the world today, 90 per cent will no longer exist by the end of this century – particularities and idiosyncrasies do not necessarily diminish or vanish from the linguistic and cultural landscape (Wheeler, 'The Death of Languages' 9); they may become more complexly interrelated to other linguistic and cultural entities.

Writers today write in a multi-linguistic environment; whether a writer speaks several languages or only one, the presence of languages – and variations of languages – impacts on his/her consciousness:

> [W]hat characterizes our age is what I call the imaginary of languages, that is to say the presence of all languages of the world ... Today, even when a writer knows no other language, he takes into account, whether he is aware of it or not, the existence of those languages surrounding him in the process of composition. One can no longer write in a language in a monolingual manner. One is obliged to take account of the imaginary of languages. (Glissant, 'L'Imaginaire des langues' 12)

It would be wrong to equate the *tout-monde* as a concept with the linguistic world of *Finnegans Wake*, but it would not be entirely wrong. Joyce was a precursor of our contemporary world of languages and cultures that interact and mix, often in surprising and chaotic ways; in his own way, he inhabited that world in advance.

Although Glissant does not directly address the question of citizenship in such a creolizing world, the concept of the *tout-monde* would also seem to bring in its train a new notion of the citizen, who would likely have a double responsibility: first, to cultivate what is worth safeguarding in a communal identity and a locale, realizing at the same time that this local identity is already itself creolized; second, to envision that locale in all its relations to otherness, and to cultivate and celebrate the vitalizing diversity created in this interaction.[2] Citizens have a right to defend their specialness, their tradition, which in the case of many but not all cultures has itself come about through the process of diversifying creolization; and in defending this local specialness they also embrace the principle of the specialness of all cultures. This is their solidarity with the world of all languages and cultures. Although it is clearly diversity that Glissant celebrates, this diversity develops from a universal situation and event, that is, the *tout-monde*, this interiority of creolization of cultural identity that takes place everywhere and within everyone, although differently in each. By analogy, the particulars of citizenship in this creolizing world will be just as diverse, though all are grounded in the same universal phenomenon. To my knowledge, Glissant does not address the question of universal human rights, but it would seem that diversity itself depends on some common measurement, base, or foundation.

In *Les Identités meurtrières* Lebanese-French author Amin Maalouf, winner of the Prix Goncourt (*Le Rocher de Tanios*, 1993) and author of the historical study *Les Croisades vues par les Arabes* (*The Crusades Viewed by the Arabs*, 1983), makes four principal points concerning identity, and by extension, its implications for notions of citizenship. First, identity is composite. If each of us were to take an 'identity test,' Maalouf argues, we would soon realize that multiple elements make up our identity and that to select any one of them as the 'essential' element of this complex conglomeration would be both arbitrary and potentially dangerous. 'I search my memory in order to bring to light the largest number of elements of my identity,' he explains; 'I assemble them; I line them up; I do not disown any of them' (*Identités* 25). The various elements of individual identity have a double effect: on the one hand, they connect us with people with whom we share the same or a similar element and, on the other hand, they differentiate us from those others with whom we share one or some elements though certainly not all. 'Each one of my associations links me to a large number of persons; however, the more associations I take into account, the more my identity proves to be particular' (27). Each person is truly different precisely because of his or her composite identity: 'All of humanity is made up of individual cases; life is the creator of differences ... Each person, without exception, is endowed with a composite identity; one has only to ask oneself several questions in order to bring to light forgotten fractures, unsuspected ramifications, and to discover that one is complex, unique, irreplaceable' (30). Just as Glissant believes that creolization operating globally produces not uniformity but local diversity, so too Maalouf argues that at the level of the individual we always encounter diversity, even uniqueness. Life and life experience are the universals that generate a gamut of individual differences; essentialist categorizations, conversely, distort by elevating one element out of many into prominence and then mapping it across a gamut of differences, in the manner of a swipe of a paint brush in a single colour.

Maalouf's second point is that identity is dialogic; actually, he does not use this specific, Bakhtinian term, but his entire discussion in the section entitled 'Quand la modernité vient de chez l'Autre' ('When Modernity Comes from the Other') constitutes a reflection on the interrelation between a sense of self and the manner in which other people look at, think of, speak to, and treat us. 'What happens to us is always slightly others' fault, and what happens to others is always slightly our fault' (*Identités* 111). Neither individuals nor groups construct their identity in isolation, without a context of relations already in place; the individual and the group are constructed in their interactions with others. These remarks occur during Maalouf's discussion of the late-twentieth-century phenomenon of Islamic fundamentalism; they encapsulate his argument that the 'regard' (attitude) of the West, by way of modernity and globalization, is part of the dialogic process of identity construction for individuals and groups in countries where fundamentalism has flourished, where it has sometimes become a hostile response to Western others.

Maalouf's third point treats common fallacies in the conceptualization of identity, and here we find a resemblance with Glissant's concept of the *tout-monde*. Identity, Maalouf argues, has a double aspect, vertical and horizontal, the latter of which is often overlooked in essentialist definitions of identity. '[E]ach one of us is a storehouse of two heritages:

one 'vertical,' which comes from one's ancestors, the traditions of one's people, from one's religious community; the other, 'horizontal,' comes from one's era, from one's contemporaries. The latter ... is the most decisive, and it becomes a bit more so each day' (ibid. 137). All of us are 'infinitely closer to our contemporaries than to our ancestors,' Maalouf points out (136). 'I have more things in common with a randomly chosen passerby in the streets of Prague, Seoul or San Francisco, than with my own great grandfather,' he argues (136). This is the case not only for aspects such as dress and lifestyle, but also for habits of thought and moral conceptions (136). Given the innumerable connections that link an individual's destiny with that of his or her contemporaries, we ought to broaden and compound our sense of identity rather than privilege the vertical dimension and ignore or relegate the horizontal dimension to a minor status.

These reflections lead Maalouf to his fourth point, the predominance of the universal: that is, we all belong finally and most importantly to the human community. Globalization impels us to consider the notion of the universal from a new perspective, but globalization in itself is neither good nor bad. It depends. Economically speaking, globalization may lead to a more unjust, crueller world – that seems to be its direction at this time. But globalization might also mean a world less vulnerable to violent conflicts and genocide. As Jean-Baptiste de Foucauld points out in *Les 3 cultures du développement humain*, economic globalization means something distinct from globalization of human values. One can be against certain forms of globalization (e.g., multinational companies eliminating locally based agriculture) yet in favour of others (e.g., education for all children of primary school age): 'What is at stake is the formation of a global human community. It exists as an objective, biological fact. It is inscribed, in principle, in the charters of the world institutions at the United Nations. But it is not lived as such; it is not a reality. We are only very virtually world citizens. That, however, is the barrier to be crossed' (Foucauld, *Les 3 cultures* 373). Maalouf calls for a reconceived notion of individual and human identity, sketched along the lines of the above points, to carry us toward a better world. 'If the new methods of communication bring us closer together much too quickly ... , they also make us notice our common destiny. What makes me think that the current evolution, in the long run, could be favorable, is the emergence of a new approach to the notion of identity. An identity that would be perceived as a sum of its parts, and at the heart of which, an attachment to human community would become more and more important, until one day it would take on a principal role, without erasing our individual particularities ...' (133). This is the trend that Maalouf perceives, and he modestly concludes with the hope that humanity will overcome its growth pains and that his book, having been overtaken by the times, will be relegated to some dusty library shelf.

In Maalouf's commentary we hear echoes of Glissant, who insists that identity today must be reconceived as rhizomic rather than rooted, for all of our experiences are situated within the *tout-monde* of creolizing cultural elements. The implications in terms of notions of citizenship are not difficult to draw; here I will simply indicate that, for Maalouf, citizenship has both a singular and a multiple meaning. Our passports register us as citizens of one or another political state, but this registration does not encompass our allegiances and attachments, which may extend to several communities and more than one country. Literary critic and intellectual George Steiner would take Maalouf's ideas even further. Having lived in Germany, England, France, Italy, and the United States, not to mention more temporary sojourns in China, Japan, and other countries, Steiner rankles at the notion of an identity equated with nationality; he sees himself as 'international,' as someone with attachments and a sense of belonging much more personal and expansive. Steiner tells an anecdote of his first days at a university in Beijing and his feeling of estrangement and twinge of disappointment upon taking up his dilapidated office quarters; the arrival of a student, demanding information about the first reading assignment, suddenly knocks him out of this mood, however, and makes him realize that, yes, in this role as professor, in this relationship with his students he feels a sense of belonging and takes his identity from this activity and relationship. Whether the exchange occurs in Beijing, Oxford, Paris, or Cambridge, it does not matter in the end ('Les Aventures d'une pensée'). Composer-musician Paco Ibañez, who, in his own words, 'speaks Basque from childhood, Castilian [Spanish] from school, French by way of exile, Italian by choice, Hebrew because of friendship, and Catalan by the luck of a [musical] tour,' would take these ideas even a step further (quoted in Lachaud, 'Ibañez pour l'espoir'). To the question, What is identity? Ibañez responds: 'Identity is what one loves.' It is not something geographic or biological; it is our reaching out to and claiming those elements in the world that we recognize within ourselves and admire in others. Identity is something in the heart. We become what we love. This is certainly an instance of what it means to conceive of identity horizontally – a reaching out toward what we admire and most care for.

Paco Ibañez's commentary on identity as desire and aspiration – that which one loves and hopes to become – places it within another realm that demands consideration. First, we can consider identity as a work, or as a project, which is an idea that one finds in the writings of Paul Ricoeur and Jean-Baptiste de Foucauld. For Ricoeur, identity is formed and evolves in a dialogic process through interactions with otherness. '[L]a conscience est une tâche,' he writes, and this task, or work in progress, passes through the detour of the other and otherness [*Le Conflit des interprétations* 20, 321]. Identity formation takes the 'long' rather then the 'short' road to its realization. This otherness with which consciousness engages may be, for instance, the relationship with another person or the tasks or professional activities that one regularly performs, reading a book, talking with a colleague, writing a letter, and so forth. Describing the plight of the individual in the modern world, Foucauld remarks that modernity has profoundly reopened the questions of identity that once seemed closed and answered for all time. Identities that were once given or imposed at birth or by the family, community, society, and work no longer define or contain the individual; in the words of Patrick Boulte, an individual's identity lies largely fallow ('en friche') and in need of development. The old social and religious anchors have been hoisted or discarded, nor do professional identities contain the whole individual. In short, the individual must *labour* or *work on* his/her identity in order to develop it:

> In fact, each person today is responsible for the formation of his/her identity, which is less a given than it once was and more something to be built. Identity results from a double intersecting view of self vis-à-vis self and others vis-à-vis self. This interaction simultaneously brings into play, on the one hand, the contemporary world and the consciousness that one has of it and that others have of one's self, and (on the other hand) an ensemble of desires, projects, and intentions for the future ... So that, identity passes much more by the route of choices made, by the direction/meaning that one wants to give to one's life (or such as other people feel it), and by interiority put into relation with these other people. That is to say, identity depends less on the exercise of a role than what P. Boulte calls the requests of others or the exigencies of the construction of the self ... In other terms, the construction of the person, identity, meaning, and social links form together by a voluntary, conscious, and sustained effort. (Foucauld, *Les 3 cultures* 20–1)

Only through this double engagement of self with self, and self with otherness can an individual construct his/her identity; and so identity should be viewed as a dialogic process rather than solely as some given essentialist features or characteristics. Taking into account the undeniable importance of our genetic imprint/heritage and our inability to choose the cultural, social environment into which we are born, there still remains a laboured and sustained formation of identity that continues throughout our lives; this is true today more so than ever before. Thus, we can speak of an individual's identity-in-progress as having a past, a present, and a future; we can also speak of this identity as forming concurrently with a sense of becoming a citizen or a member of a community and society. Philosopher Emmanuel Lévinas also considers identity as a work-in-progress, and he gives this work a utopian direction: to go beyond the self, toward otherness: 'Our responsibility for others is the place where the non-place of subjectivity is located and where the privilege of the question of "where" disappears'[3] (*Autrement qu'Être* 24). Others (*all* other people) define one's identity in its subjectivity and ethical responsibilities; the notions of neighbour and stranger lose their meaning in this movement outward toward otherness. Each individual – humanity as a whole – is incomplete in the sense that there will always be this challenge and possibility of otherness that dialogically shapes identity, itself extending into the strangeness of strangers. Utopia becomes not a place, but a human ex-centricity, a going beyond to encounter the otherness of others – the need and the ethical responsibility to do so.

As a process and situation, identity has a prospective quality. Although it is anchored in genetic and social realities, at the same time it is linked by its hopes and desires with a projection into otherness and a cultural imaginary that encompasses the themes and models of humankind. Without this prospective quality of identity, its evolution and development would grind to a halt. Each situation and each otherness with which we interact engages something actual and something potential but not yet realized in our identity. In this sense, we are made of both presences and absences, of concretized moments, recollections, and virtualities. Our lives are both actualized configurations and virtual possibilities, with each imparting and shaping the other.

In *L'Homme dépaysé* Tzvetan Todorov, another well-known European literary critic and intellectual, reflects on the experiences and attachments that have grown out of his peripatetic life in three countries: Bulgaria, where he was born and grew up; France, his adopted home; and the United States, where he has taught and conducted research at various American universities. Although Todorov does not use the same terminology as Maalouf or Steiner, he too conceives of identity more on a horizontal than a vertical plane: 'The only thing that [Bulgaria, France, and the United States] ... have in common for me ... is that I have found friends there with whom I continue to live today, whether present or absent' (26). Out of necessity these kinds of horizontal relationships constitute the principal base of identity formation for persons who have emigrated from one country or society to another. Todorov is sceptical of notions such as cultural hybridity and pluralistic identity, for his own personal journey has been marked with difficulty and pain. For a long period after his immigration, he felt ill at ease both in France and (upon return) in Bulgaria: 'I found myself split into two halves, both equally unreal' (17). Quoting T.E. Lawrence by way of André Malraux, he ponders whether any person with an allegiance to two cultures inevitably loses his or her soul (21). Todorov thinks of himself, and others like him, as persons who undergo a process of transculturation, itself neither loss nor assimilation, but rather the acquisition of a new cultural code without the former code being completely dropped (23). Language acquisition – its possession and mastery – is the crucial component for him in this transcultural process. Todorov is certainly right about this. It is interesting, though, to contrast his experiences with those of other European émigrés. George Steiner, for example, who grew up perfectly at home in three languages – German, French, and English – and has acquired others, overcame the obstacle that language acquisition poses to cultural belonging at an early age; that Steiner feels less bound by cultural difference than does Todorov is not therefore surprising. Renowned designer Karl Lagerfeld presents another example along the lines of Steiner, but with a twist. Lagerfeld feels perfectly at home (and strange) in the three or four languages that he speaks and writes fluently. His mother tongue is German, but he confesses that he writes best in English; he has not tried to erase his German accent when he speaks English, French, or Italian, but instead has made a point of retaining it for a certain individuality of style. Different rooms in his house are reserved for different languages and different language activities. Although he has lived primarily in France for a number of years, he has no desire to become a French citizen and retains a German passport. He thinks of himself not in terms of nationalities but as someone 'cosmopolite' ('Interview').

In *L'Homme dépaysé,* as well as in *Nous et les autres: La réflexion française sur la diversité humaine* (1989), Todorov moves from literary theory and criticism to cultural studies. Still, the traces of old interests and influences, especially the influence of Bakhtin and dialogism, itself the subject of an earlier study, remain.[4] As I have already suggested, Todorov conceives of a sense of belonging and personhood as something largely dialogically formed: 'Humanity, even that of the individual, is a product of the plurality of men. "Man becomes a man only among men," Fichte ... argues' (quoted in Todorov, *L'Homme dépaysé* 174). The dialogism of identity formation is quite complex; to be 'among others' does not simply mean having a role within society and having acquaintances and friendships. Other kinds of relationships also contribute to this formation. In our discovery of the world, books, especially literary works, may be more effective than actual social exchange, Todorov insists: 'in order to be understood, the real world must be doubled by an imaginary world' (ibid. 169).[5] The principle of dialogism can also be extended to the realm of education, that is, the education of better citizens. It is worth studying cultures and epochs other than our own precisely because such study engages us in a potentially illuminating historical and cultural dialogue. We are interested in other times and other places, 'not to judge them by today's criteria, but, on the contrary, to enlighten the present by the past, the here and now by the elsewhere. The study of cultures that are distant from us and, for this reason, more difficult to accept are perhaps, particularly useful here' (212). Making a plea for a broader humanist education, Todorov argues that we should maintain the study of Western civilization, while complementing it with the study of non-Western civilizations and 'marginalized traditions' (212).[6] This effort of expanded study is the price that must be paid, not only to produce experts in varied disciplines, but also to foster 'better citizens' (212). To sum up, the concept of locale remains important to Todorov, yet it must be compounded by a dialogue beyond itself (237).[7] The notion of citizenship should not be so exclusive to a particular country, or a particular locale, that the dialogue with otherness – other places, other cultures – remains unengaged. The notion of universal human values to which all citizens would hold allegiance is more democratic than ideologies of difference that conceive of the world divided into camps of races, nations, classes, or sexes (209). This universalist argument incarnates the spirit of dialogic cricitism, whose rationale and ideal Don Bialostosky explains in these words:

As a self-conscious practice, dialogic criticism turns its inescapable involvement with some other voices into a program of articulating itself with all the other voices of the discipline, the culture, or the world of cultures to which it makes itself responsible ... Neither a live-and-let-live relativism nor a settle-it-once-and-for-all authoritarianism but a strenuous and open-ended dialogism would keep them talking to themselves and to one another, discovering their affinities without resting in them and clarifying their differences without resolving them. (Quoted in Abrams, *Glossary* 64)

Identity as well as citizenship formation depend on such engagement, such interplay of diverse elements.

Having briefly considered ideas of Glissant, Maalouf, and Todorov, to add V.S. Naipaul, winner of the Nobel Prize in Literature 2001, to this list would seem to make for strange literary bedfellows. These four writers do have something in common though: all were born in places outside the intellectual centres of Europe and North America – in Martinique, Lebanon, Bulgaria, and Trinidad respectively; all reject essentialist and divisive notions of identity and citizenship. Naipaul's book *Beyond Belief: Islamic Excursions among the Converted Peoples* and a short article entitled 'The Universal Civilization' (1992) throw light on the consequences of ideology on individual identity and social structures in Middle Eastern and Asian countries. Before turning to this book and essay, I want to highlight remarks drawn from 'Two Worlds,' Naipaul's Nobel lecture (2001), which suggest a certain concept of identity, in particular an identity of the writer. For Naipaul, identity is not primarily something given, but something that takes shape and evolves. Proust talks of talent, Naipaul talks of labour and luck. Proust contends that '[t]alent is like a sort of memory which will enable [artists] finally to bring this indistinct music closer [i.e., the beautiful things they have to write], ... to note them down,' whereas Naipaul counters: 'Talent, Proust says. I would say luck, and much labour' (ibid. 486). Naipaul emphasizes that 'intuition' has always been his guide: 'I have no system, literary or political' (486). Writing, which involves researching a subject matter, leads to a quest for otherness, for understanding the 'darkness' in one's world. Each of his books, Naipaul says, has been an attempt to shine the light on a bit more of that area of ignorance and mystery: 'When I became a writer those areas of darkness around me as a child became my subjects. The land; the aborigines; the New World; the colony; the history; India; the Muslim world, to which I also felt related; Africa; and then England' (484). A recursive process of the writer's identity emerges: 'Each book, intuitively sensed and, in the case of fiction, intuitively worked out, stands on what has gone before, and grows out of it. I feel that at any stage of my literary career it could have been said that the last book contained all the others' (480). Naipaul follows the winding tracks of his writer's identity formation, yet concludes by emphasizing that there remains something that cannot be traced, a beyond still in darkness: 'the greatest miracle for me was getting started. I feel – and the anxiety is still vivid to me – that I might easily have failed before I began' (486). Although Naipaul has written all of these things before in one place or another, this Nobel lecture is still a moving (and certainly modest) account of his becoming a writer and of the inexplicable nature of an individual's relation with the world and his destiny in it.

Beyond Belief: Islamic Excursions among the Converted Peoples (1998) records Naipaul's journey through four Asian countries – Iran, Indonesia, Pakistan, Malaysia – and recounts the stories of the people whom he meets. Both travel book and sociocultural study, it treats the impact of fundamentalism and globalization on cultural identity and citizenship. Like Glissant and Maalouf, Naipaul views individual identity as richly composite; cultures and societies that attempt to force this complex interrelatedness into a uniformity end by spawning monsters. Identity viewed as essence leads backward into rivalries, fatalism, and old social injustices. A sequel to *Among the Believers* (1981), this is likewise a controversial book, praised by many reviewers while pilloried by a few others. Writing for the *New Republic*, Fouad Ajami mounts what is perhaps the most thoughtful attack; subtitling his review 'V.S. Naipaul's Misunderstanding of Islam,' he finds the book seriously flawed: it is 'opinion through and through. And it is ill-considered opinion, too.' The central flaw of the book, in Ajami's view, is its falling in with the 'contemporary tendency to reduce the politics of Muslim societies to Islam, to religious categories' (30). The role of religion is not as totalizing as contemporary analyses, including Naipaul's, make it seem (31). Naipaul falls short, on the one hand, of good ethnography, as in Clifford Geertz's durable study *Islam Observed*; and, on the other hand, of good art. Ajami concludes the review by contrasting Naipaul with Conrad, much to the latter's advantage. Unlike Conrad, who in his Southeast Asian stories gives us the 'whole wonder of the world,' Naipaul gives us instead a 'simplified political and religious creed.' He fails to capture 'the pain of modernity to which men and women submit, against which men and women rebel' (33).

Ajami may be right about all this, but at the same time *Beyond Belief* also offers its readers a penetrating treatment of the dangers of defining identity and citizenship according to essentialist ideologies. In the section entitled 'Dropping Off the Map,' Naipaul looks at the results of one country's attempt to establish a pure Islamic state, along the lines of its founder-poet Mohammed Iqbal:

> What Iqbal [says] in an involved way is that Muslims can live only with other Muslims. If this was meant seriously, it would have implied that the good world, the one to be striven after, was a purely tribal world, neatly parcelled out, every tribe in his corner. This would have been seen to be fanciful.
> What is really in the background of this demand for Pakistan and a Muslim polity, what isn't mentioned, is Iqbal's rejection of Hindu India ...
> The speech is full of ironies today. Pakistan, when it came, disenfranchised the Muslims who stayed behind in India. Bangladesh is on its own. In Pakistan itself the talk is of dissolution. The new Muslim polity there has turned out to be like the old, the one Iqbal knew: you don't have to go down far before you find people who are voiceless and without representation as when Iqbal made his speech in 1930. (269–70)

Women in particular are without voices – and faces. In a shelter for the battered, Naipaul meets a thirty-five-year-old woman whose husband has 'butchered' her nose; a human-rights lawyer calls her a 'victim of feudal society' (272). In the twenty-first century, in more than one region of the world, women can still be reduced to slaves of one sort or another; the Nawab of Bahawalpur had three hundred and ninety concubines, a Pakistani journalist recounts to Naipaul: 'Most of them had slept only once with him; but then they could sleep with no other man ... Always in the harem he had sixteen or eighteen women on whom he would call' (355). Sensationalist as this sounds, we know now, after outcries concerning the plight of women in neighbouring Afghanistan, that it is not. The paradox of the state dedicated to a fundamentalist identity Naipaul sums up in this way: 'Where there was no law, no institutions that men could trust, the code and idea of honour protected men. But it also worked the other way. Where the code was strong there could be no law ... In the frontier ... the modern state was withering away; it was superfluous. People were beginning to live again with the idea of clan and fiefdom' (351).

Whereas *Beyond Belief* looks at the breakdown of societies who conceive of identity and citizenship along the lines of fundamentalist ideologies, Naipaul's essay 'Our Universal Civilization' (1991) – originally an address given at the Manhattan Institute in New York – makes a plea for transcultural values. Just exactly what Naipaul means by 'universal civilization' is not totally clear, since he speaks of it chiefly in reference to his own life and development as an intellectual and writer. The universal civilization 'has been a long time in the making,' he remarks (25). It wasn't always universal, it wasn't always attractive; '[t]he expansion of Europe gave it for at least three centuries a racial tint,' he notes, but adds that, since the end of the Second World War, this civilization has made an 'extraordinary attempt ... to accommodate the rest of the world, and all the currents of that world's thought' (25). Terminology becomes problematic here, for it would seem that the 'universal civilization' is not universal in the sense that everyone shares its benefits; rather, it is universal in a much more restrictive sense: it is not the property of any one culture or society but, like the individual, a composite of many cultures and societies, and continues to evolve as a transcultural identity. A reliance on democratic institutions to regulate the communal life of the society and to protect the individual, the fostering of a spirit of inquiry and criticism, the ideal of equality, and hope for a better life: these are values that Naipaul locates in this civilization.

In spite of problems related to the term, the idea of universal human values is re-emerging today with a new force and conviction. Amin Maalouf, for example, develops similar ideas in *Les Identités meurtrières*; both Naipaul and Maalouf contend that the basic rights of human beings are transcultural. These include, among other principles, the right to knowledge; the right to choose freely one's life path, loves, and beliefs, while respecting the liberty of others; the right to health; the right to live a decent and honourable life (142–3). André Comte-Sponville's and Luc Ferry's *La Sagesse des modernes* (*Wisdom of the Moderns*) and Tzvetan Todorov's *L'Homme dépaysé* also put forward the concept of universal values. Although Naipaul is certainly right about transculturalism, what is perhaps most striking about civilization today is its inequalities – the discrepancies within societies and between nations and regions of the world. Jean-François Fourny remarks: 'Perhaps Dostoevsky observing nineteenth-century London, Dickens, and the Marx of Chapter 25 of Book 1 of *Capital* were unknowingly right for what they described was to repeat itself twice: the end of the nineteenth century and that of the twentieth century coincide in terms of poverty, hardship, and human suffering' (Fourny, Review 150). Regis Debray, author of *Le Fe sacré*, observes that 'the more the world economy turns global, the more politics reverts to the archaic tribal and religious past as if we were caught between two competing histories, one going forward, the other walking backward' (quoted ibid. 152).

Debray's observation hits the mark, suggesting not only a large-scale disjuntion of human developments but also the misplaced priorities that such a disjunction engenders. Here is one small example of many that could be cited: although insulin was discovered eighty years ago and today is a relatively inexpensive medication, thousands of men, women, and children have no or limited access to it. In contrast, during the war in Iraq (2003), billions of dollars were spent on bombs and armaments of one sort of another, and thousands of people died in these bombardments and offensives. That we as citizens of various countries live in a world where these acts and policies are common, and are tolerated, accepted, and/or ignored, is part of what 'shame' means in the title of this chapter.

In terms of opportunities and quality of life, the gap between regions of the world is widening. Two events of the year 2002 that might serve as barometers of this gap were the World Summit on Sustainable Development in Johannesburg, South Africa and the World Soccer Cup in Japan and Korea. Statistics do not convey the full misery and peril, but they perhaps give a sense of scope and dimension. Here are a few estimates that fall within the categories of 'sick planet' and 'suffering humanity':

- About 50 per cent of all fish stocks are fully exploited; 20 per cent are overexploited; 15 per cent of all forest species will be extinct by 2025.
- Three million people die each year due to air pollution.
- According to the World Bank, twelve million people die each year from polluted water or lack of water.
- UNICEF reports that four million children die each year from drinking dirty and unsafe water.
- According to the United Nations, 20 per cent of the world population, or 1.1 billion people, have no access to fresh water, while 40 per cent, or 2.4 billion people, lack adequate sanitation. Tricia Barnett, director of Tourist Concern in the United Kingdom, a charity that campaigns for responsible approaches to travel, observes: 'Tourists in Africa will be having a shower and then will see a local woman with a pot of water on her head, and they are not making the connection. Sometimes you'll see a village with a single tap, when each hotel has taps and showers in every room.' Along the same lines, it would seem that golf courses take priority over thirsty men, women, and children:

an eighteen-hole golf course in a dry country consumes as much water as a town of 10,000 people.
- Rich countries gave about US$54 billion in development aid in 2001, but paid more than US$350 billion to their own farmers; a World Bank official commented: 'The average cow is supported [at] three times the level of income of a poor person in Africa.'
- Eighty per cent of global finance flows went to rich countries in the year 2000, with the entire African continent receiving less than 1 per cent of direct foreign investment.
- Twenty per cent of the countries of the world control 80 per cent of the planet's riches.
- According to the United Nations report 'La Pauvreté dans le monde' (2000), 2.8 billion people, or half of the world population, live on less than two dollars a day; 110 million children (two-thirds of whom are girls) do not go to school and 250 million children work; all the ecosystems of the planet are in decline and a third of the natural resources have disappeared in the brief period of thirty years.
- It is estimated that 200 million children work in factories controlled directly or indirectly by Western companies, that almost 50 per cent of young Black Americans will spend time in prison, and that there are a half-billion firearms in circulation.[8]

Médecins Sans Frontières use a simple analogy to convey the scope of the human predicament:

If the world were a village of 100 people ...
1 is dying of famine;
15 are dying of epidemic diseases;
20 are malnourished, living in fear of bombardments, armed attacks and landmines;
25 do not have a shelter, access to health care or access to clean water.
(*Médecins Sans Frontières Newsletter*, September 2002)

It goes almost without saying, to quote James Wolfensohn, president of the World Bank, that 'an unjust world is a dangerous world' ('Un Monde injuste' 28).

In his chronicle for *L'Express*, 'La "Coupe du monde,"' Jacques Attali takes the occasion of the World Soccer Cup 2002 to reflect on the state of the world; the title of the essay plays on the word 'coupe,' which means both 'cup' and 'cut' in French. This event not only separates the winning soccer teams from the losers, but also clearly demarcates humanity into two distinct groups, the have's and the have not's. Around the world, rich and poor alike passionately watched these soccer matches; however, those in the latter category had much less opportunity to do so, given that a third of humanity has neither electricity, telephones, nor, much less, television sets. World soccer means big money, with the top players making millions of dollars each year; given that a billion human beings in the world must survive on less than one dollar per day, the gap between the two realities is vertiginous. Can anything be done? Attali has a suggestion: if the sponsors of the World Cup would contribute 1 euro/dollar for every television spectator – more than a billion euros/dollars – each year until the next Coupe du monde, sufficient funds would be created to make loans to 8000 well-proven institutions of microfinance around the world; these institutions could then provide the means for ten million men and women each year to create their own employment rather than depend on their families or charitable organizations. Attali estimates that, in four years' time, this method would help 200 million human beings climb out of misery and poverty. He concludes: 'The Coupe du monde could thus help to reduce the "coupe du monde," and humanity could win its most stunning victory. Against itself' (17).

Any notion of citizenship today must take into account the 'coupe du monde' – these 'two competing histories' of humanity – as well as changes in individual and cultural identity that the twentieth century has fostered. Emancipatory groundlessness, on the one hand, and a revised notion of human universals, on the other, constitute two opportunities for constructing new ideas of citizenship. These are not two hopelessly incompatible positions, but rather potentially complementary ones. I use the term 'emancipatory groundlessness' rather then 'nihilism,' because in common parlance the latter has negative connotations that are almost impossible to overcome. In Italian philosopher Gianni Vattimo's view, nihilism is an often misunderstood term; it does not designate the disappearance of all values, but rather the highest value, that is, Truth with a capital 'T.'[9] A world with no values whatsoever – with no prejudices, no traditions – would be unimaginable; as Vattimo argues in *The End of Modernity*, the disappearance of the highest value 'liberates the notion [of value] in all its vertiginous potentiality,' with all values now possessing 'the capacity for convertibility and an indefinite transformability' (21). In *Beyond Interpretation* Vattimo contends that a properly understood nihilism can be a useful vantage point from which to argue against 'the fundamentalisms and communitarianisms reappearing all across the late-modern world' (39). It is also a useful vantage point from which the notions of nation and citizenship can be demythified, which is, in one sense, what Glissant attempts in his *Introduction à une poétique du divers*, where he argues that European nation-states are built, in part, on founder myths that became distorted into ideologies of exclusion. Nihilism levels hierarchies, and in this capacity it contains the potential of democratization and egalitarianism; it can, perhaps, free us from notions of allegiance and citizenship that are no longer compatible with the contemporary world, with its delocalizing and globalizing forces. 'Instead of reacting to the dissolution of the principle of reality by attempting to recuperate a sense of identity and belonging that are at once reassuring and punitive, it is a matter of grasping nihilism as a *chance* ... of emancipation,' Vattimo concludes (*Beyond Interpretation* 40).

Emancipatory groundlessness and universalism are incompatible with a citizenship founded on notions of cultural relativism, which has been proposed (though never convincingly) as a viable response to the cultural, social transformation of the postmodern world. As early as the 1980s, Vattimo began attacking separatism and relativism as a contemporary myth, more of a belief than a well-founded concept. Cultural relativism, he argues, 'ignores both (a) the effective context in which the thesis of the irreducible plurality of cultural worlds is put into place, and (b) the effective impossibility of isolating one cultural world from another.' In Vattimo's view, cultures interact 'like speakers in a dialogue'; once this is recognized, 'the question must then be raised of the common horizon on which the dialogue itself takes place.' And this kind of question 'invalidates from the first any project – like that of cultural relativism – to represent "other" cultures as isolated objects' ('Myth' 33). Relativism, especially as it is translated into the popular concept of multiculturalism, came under increasing attack in the 1990s, and not just from the far right of the political spectrum. Neil Bissoondath's *Selling Illusions: The Cult of Multiculturalism in Canada* (1994) is one such attack.[10] Bissoondath[11] argues that multiculturalism is a flawed concept, first, because it is essentialist and ahistorical, fixing people forever in frozen identities, and second, because its application is superficial, 'reduc[ing] cultures hundreds, sometimes thousands of years old to easily digestible stereotypes' (84). Scholars of ethnic studies such as Henry Louis Gates, Jr and Paula Gunn Allen also question the continuing usefulness of multiculturalist concepts and binarisms like center-margin that have informed post-colonial and minority literary studies during the past decades. 'All definitions of ethnic tradition,' Gates points out, 'ultimately are both tautological and essentialist' ('"Ethnic and Minority" Studies' 293). '[R]itualized invocation of otherness,' he continues, 'is losing its capacity to engender new forms of knowledge and ... the "margin" may have exhausted its strategic value as a position from which to theorize the very antinomies that produced it as object of study' (ibid.). I believe that multiculturalism can serve as a viable social concept only if it is understood as cultural interrelatedness, not as a gamut of essentialist identities. Defining her own position as woman, Native American writer, and intellectual vis-à-vis the exclusions of Eurocentric traditions, Allen opts for the (Buddhist?) term 'the Void,' a place from which 'all arises' and 'all returns' ('"Border" Studies' 304). She coins the term 'self-in-relation' to designate the primary characteristic of individuals in society, and calls for a reading of texts and cultures 'that places the twin concepts of I and thou securely within the interconnected matrix of all and everything, one that uses the presence of absence to define the manifest and that uses the manifest to locate and describe the invisible' (314).

Before turning to a revision of notions of identity, citizenship, and human universals, I want to discuss Asian, and specifically Buddhist, perspectives on identity. British historian Arnold Toynbee once remarked that the arrival of Buddhism in the West could turn out to be the most important event of the twentieth century (quoted in Jean-Sebastien Stehli, 'Rester Zen' 35). Although he may have miscalculated the precise moment, in Europe as well as North America the presence and impact of Asian cultures has become increasingly evident.[12] In *L'Infini dans la paume de la main*, biologist-turned-Buddhist monk Matthieu Ricard,[13] through a dialogue with Trinh Xuan Thuan, an astrophysicist at the University of Virginia, elaborates the Buddhist concept of nonintrinsic identity and explains other key ideas such as interdependence, impermanence, the void, compassion, and awakening (or mindfulness). In Buddhist thought, neither things nor individuals have an intrinsically independent existence; everyone and everything in the world is interrelated in the network of life. Agreeing with Ricard, astrophysicist Trinh Xuan Thuan remarks: 'We are all made of star dust. The brothers of wild beasts and cousins of the flowers of the fields, we all carry within us cosmic history. The simple act of breathing connects us with all the beings who have lived on this planet. Even today we continue to inhale millions of atoms that went up in smoke during the burning-at-the-stake of Joan of Arc in 1431, and some come from the last breath of Julius Caesar' (107). Interdependence in a Buddhist sense means still more than this, though; because all phenomena are impermanent and because what we call our ego, our 'I,' is part of that impermanence, not itself intrinsically independent, human beings cannot step out of, or transcend, this network of interdependent relationships. Because the world – and everyone and everything part of it – is in a process of flux, to assign an identity to any impermanence would be to elevate one of these moments from that stream of continual change. Interdependence helps clarify a related concept, that of the 'void' or 'non-reality.' Buddhists believe that all is an emptiness; life neither is nor is not – it is beyond conception. Ricard explains: the void is 'the non-reality of animate and inanimate phenomena, their true nature[;] in no case [does it mean] nothingness. The clear recognition of the void and the emergence of compassion in regard to all human beings without distinction is simultaneous' (455). The world is the continuous transformation of this void, and to become mindful of this is a step toward liberating oneself from the sufferings of this world, which are tied to illusions about it. Interdependence of phenomena equates with universal responsibility, so identity in Buddhism implicitly ties in with ideas about community and citizenship (though Buddhists do not use the latter term, as far as I know). These 'Eastern' concepts may seem radical or mystical, but they find correlations in quantum mechanics and physics, which is the whole point of the extended dialogue between the scientist-turned-Buddhist monk and the astrophysicist with Buddhist leanings. Trinh Xuan Thuan quotes Einstein more than a few times, as in these sentences about interdependence and universality:

> A human being is a part of all that we call the universe, a part limited by time and space. He experiences himself, his thoughts and his emotions, as if they were events separated from the rest of the world, this is a kind of optical illusion of his consciousness. This illusion is one form of prison for us, because it restrains our personal desires and constrains us to reserve our affection for a few persons who are the closest to us. Our task should consist of liberating ourselves from this prison by enlarging the circle of compassion such that it would include all living creatures and all nature in its beauty. (105)

This idea approaches the idea of 'otherness' that we find in the philosophy of Lithuanian-French philosopher Emmanuel Lévinas, who locates subjectivity in others, in the stranger, whom we have the responsibility to go toward and address as 'tu' (as a friend).

Reorientations of Identity and Citizenship

Having examined the concept of identity from various perspectives, I want to bring these perspectives together to sketch 'new' concepts of identity and citizenship. Identity, citizenship, and universal rights might all be formulated as entities, processes, and/or recursive systemic networks. Two components emerge as crucial to a reconception of identity along non-essentialist lines: first, identity has a time component, with a past, present, and future; second, identity has a spatial component, with links to otherness of all sorts. These two components 'expand' or 'spread out' identity into a much larger area than we are accustomed to imagine; conceived in this manner, identity should be thought of not as a centre, but as intersecting networks of moments and linkages. An objection might be raised that identity, no matter what we say about it, still has a core of genetic, historical, cultural, and social material that determine an individual's make up and behaviour. Certainly, identity has a heritage – it is embodied – yet it is difficult to ascertain where this heritage begins and where it will lead. Genetic, historical, and social imprints provide a context for identity, yet this context interacts dialogically with each situation and event in an individual's life, and these situations and events construct identity in conjunction with its previous contexts. We might think of identity, then, as composed of a context (genetic and social imprints) and of situations and events; identity evolves in a performance that dialogically connects them. This is a recursive process with feedback loops that repatttern the individual. When we look for an anchor for identity, we find that only through isolating a particular moment or through selecting some characteristic out of many can we impose a definition or a stability on the flow and expansion that constitutes an individual's evolution. Identity emerges from the processes of a systemic network. Along a time coordinate, identity has a past, present, and future. The past, including its genetic and social heritage, is always something considered through the lens of the present; in the process of the translation – crossing over into a contemporary moment – the past becomes different. The present itself is a work in progress; with each moment, an individual's identity undergoes subtle or perhaps significant changes. Identity also has a future aspect, but this futurity has an anticipatory, not-yet, prospective quality. So one could say that, given these three temporal components, that identity stretches out across time, and that it has a virtual as well as an actual quality. Spatially, identity also spreads out into all the relationships that connect us with other persons and other things; it spreads into the work we do and tasks we perform, into the books we read and all the histories and stories of which we have become vicariously part. This double network in time-space, which comprises processes as well as linkages, maps an individual's identity; furthermore, the network interacts with the network of other individuals, so any attempt to define an individual's identity extends into other individuals' identities. Because these interrelated networks constitute recursively operating systems, altering according to 'new information,' the reality of an individual is less a *given* than an *emergence*. An individual's identity has no intrinsic autonomy; it is more of a 'becoming' than a 'being,' and in this sense it neither is, nor is not – it is always changing and in evolution. In this profound sense, identity, like the Buddhist conception of the world, is an emergence and an impermanence. We need, then, to reorient our conception of identity away from the notions of core and certainty and toward the notions of changing fields or networks, which themselves are full of potential, virtual elements. East Asian philosophy emphasizes process and relation; the Western concept of identity needs to reincorporate these ideas, which perhaps were part of a Presocratic way of looking at the world but were displaced by stabilities and certitudes. With a reoriented notion of identity, one can see more clearly the demands of individual responsibility and citizenship in the contemporary world.

Because cultural diversity is dialogic, not essentialist, and because cultural difference has been depleted by processes of Westernization and homologation,[14] the concepts of commonality and universal rights lay a stronger basis for constructing an idea of citizenship. A logic of difference leads away from, not toward community: 'If I were to argue always and necessarily as a French man, born in a particular family, belonging to a particular social class, and a particular sex,' philosopher Luc Ferry explains, 'I would be, by definition, relegated to these natural, ethnic communities. And I would be incapable of raising myself above my condition in order to reach whatever form of universality. In brief, I could not be an authentic citizen of either a real or an ideal republic' (Comte-Sponville and Ferry, 'La Sagesse des modernes' 82). Elevating difference to a supreme value, Amin Maalouf points out, can lead to the logic of murderous identities. Without a sense of interrelatedness, the group as well as the individual is relegated to its own ghetto of thought and values; identity becomes frozen, ideological. A sense of interrelatedness, then, is crucial. Like identity, universal rights ought to be viewed as constructions and works in progress, open to interpretation in their meaning and application; they do represent, however, a platform within which differences can be organized. According to Foucauld, nations of the world need to 'move from affirmed differences in the face of universalism to differences organized within a truly commonly held system.' This can be accomplished by putting the emphasis on the 'theme of human development,' which includes cultural diversity but which can also serve as 'a support for [a] supple and progressive convergence' of ideas (*Les 3 cultures* 373–4). World citizenship emerges then from practical interactions and interpretations of a recursive sort across the network of cultures and societies, all of which have a stake in human development.

Universal rights need not be a political tool to enforce the order of the industrialized nations; the universal can equally demand a world order that will not tolerate the misery and indignity that claims the majority of the world's inhabitants today. A sense of interrelatedness enlarges understanding, the kind of understanding that Hans-Georg Gadamer delineates in *Truth and Method*:

> If we put ourselves in someone else's shoes, for example, then we will understand him – i.e., become aware of the otherness, the indissoluble individuality of the other person – by putting *ourselves* in his position.
>
> Transposing ourselves consists neither in the empathy of one individual for another nor in subordinating another person to our own standards; rather, it always involves rising to a higher universality that overcomes not only our own particularity but also that of the other. (304)

I think of citizenship in this light: it consists of acts of interpretation, acts of understanding in which we view ourselves and others within the horizon of universal values and responsibilities. It consists of a translation. Gadamer puts the accent on transcendence, but I think of this more as a sideways movement, a going outward that will certainly confront obstacle after obstacle and will therefore need to reorient and improvise along the way. It will not be anything automatic, and it will never be something that comes to an end. It is a living project.

Today, the whole world enters our consciousness daily; we cannot easily keep it out. When we watch the televised news, for example, we see images that will not allow us to remain safely where we are; whether we recognize their effects or not, they haunt us – sometimes with wonder, more often with a dissatisfaction and diminishment. The psychological effects of this *tout-monde* resemble those that writers of earlier generations recorded during their travels and sojourns in former European colonies. In *An Experience of India* Ruth Prawer Jhabvala observes: 'Having once seen the sights in India, and the way it has been ordained that people must live out their lives, nowhere in the world can ever be all that good to be in again' (10). All things are related, Jhabvala's observation implies; one place is linked to other places, and the life of each person is related to the lives of all others.

In this age of global images, the reading of literary texts still has something to offer as a mediation between the particular and the universal. Literature helps us touch the universal – within ourselves and others. My rereading of Camus's *La Peste* (*The Plague*) comes to mind – especially now, in April 2003, when Hong Kong is confronting the atypical pneumonia (SARS) virus and has been declared a place at risk by the World Health Organization. Perhaps from his childhood in an Algiers ghetto, or from his travels in the impoverished Kabylie region of Algeria, Camus came to understood the kind of diminishment of which Ruth Prawer Jhabvala writes in *An Experience of India*. In *The Plague*, an inquiry into the meaning of citizenship in a world of nihilism, the narrator speculates: '[N]o one will ever be free so long as there are pestilences' (37). We have the plague within us, observes Tarrou, a principal character in the novel, an observation that would also seem true of the hidden impact of what Glissant has called the *tout-monde*. To be a citizen today is to become 'mindful of' (a Buddhist phrase), and act according to, the interrelated networks that embody each of us in the world. Furthermore, a mindful and practical citizenship will address the dangers and shame of inequalities of human development between societies and geographic regions. In 1950 the world population totaled about 2.5 billion; in 1991 it had reached 5.3 billion; by 2025 it is projected to be 8.6 billion inhabitants, of which 7.2 billion will live in less-developed countries.[15] That is to say, 84 per cent of the world's inhabitants will reside in countries with low per-capita incomes. These countries remain a third or fourth world, that is, a periphery of underdevelopment – but in another sense there is no longer a periphery.

The greatest task that an individual faces is to live his or her values, and this is an idea that links East and West – Buddha to Confucius to Socrates – but which the West has largely put aside as too simplistic for modernity. A wise person is not only an intelligent person, but one who puts into practice his or her beliefs. Western notions of knowledge and wisdom need to be reoriented in this direction. In doing so we will reorient the notion of citizenship in directions that include resistance (e.g., critiques of power and impositon) as well as formation of prospective models of citizenship in a world of inequalities and injustices, where shame allows us not to forget that self is other. 'One wonders whether clothing the naked and feeding the hungry is not the true access to otherness (altérité),' Emmanuel Lévinas ponders (quoted in Calvora, 'Levinas' 131); it is a question that now confronts us almost daily no matter where we live or how we live our lives. Still, I want to conclude on a different note, one that Lévinas, the philosopher of the *au-delà*, would perhaps appreciate. At the end of Amin Maalouf's *Léon l'Africain*, a novel that imaginatively treats the expulsion of Arabs and Jews from fifteenth- and sixteenth-century Spain, a father speaks to his son these words that ring as true today as they might have at that time:

> No matter where you are, there will be some who will want to judge you by the color of your skin and pry into your prayers. Take care not to flatter their instincts, take care not to bend before the crowd! Moslem, Jew or Christian, they should accept you as you are ... When the spirit of men seems narrow, tell yourself that the lands of God are vast, and large are His hands and immense is His heart. Don't hesitate to wander far and wide, beyond all seas, beyond all borders, of all countries, of all beliefs ... Toward that final place where no one is a stranger before the face of the Creator. (473)

The destination is Heaven, but that place is also a 'nowhere,' a utopia of the human spirit.

Neither Subjects nor Objects:
In the Middle Way

Nothing is found that is not dependently arisen.
For that reason, nothing is found that is not empty.
>D. Kalupahana, *Nāgārjuna: The Philosophy of the Middle Way*

Reality is endless, it is transformed and becomes an eternal story, where everything always starts again.
>Ricardo Piglia, 'Afterword' to *The Absent City*

Critical thinking today faces two conceptual challenges: on the one hand, the challenge of fundamentalisms, whether political or religious, with their frozen pictures of identity and society; on the other hand, the challenge of groundlessness, or the growing awareness of the lack of foundations for cherished notions such as self, culture, and world. We see the damage of fundamentalisms – 'murderous identities,' to recall Amin Maalouf's phrase – in the various confrontations, declared or otherwise, between East and West, North and South, and rival ethnic groups in one geographic region or another. Although the second development concerns something much less tangible and dramatized, the first development would seem in part a reaction to it. 'Whether we want to be there or not,' argues Hilary Putnam, author of *Reason, Truth and History*, 'science has put us in the position of having to live without foundations. It was shocking when Nietzsche said this, but today it is commonplace; *our* historical position – and no end to it is in sight – is that of having to philosophize without "foundations"' (quoted in Varela, *The Embodied Mind*). So we might say that the first challenge is the challenge of (mistaken or falsely perceived) foundations, while the second is the challenge of the lack of foundations. The epigraphs with which I begin this chapter and résumé of the book's project suggest attitudes and methods to respond to those challenges. The first epigraph proposes the response of Buddhism, or a certain interpretation of Buddhism, which insists that phenomena are interdependent and therefore empty of an intrinsic reality. Such a stance and strategy of thought constitutes a powerful tool in breaking up fundamentalist assertions; all fundamentalisms, whether political, religious, or ethnic, fall into the grips of stasis and essence in a world of metamorphosis and transformation. The second epigraph, which also has a Buddhist slant, proposes a complementary idea: reality emerges from translations, and it continues to do so without limit or finality. These are not two antithetical ideas; according to Buddhism, 'emptiness is not only the ultimate nature of phenomena, but also the potential that permits these phenomena to manifest infinitely' (Ricard and Trinh, *L'Infini* 52). The response to the second challenge, then, need not be nihilism understood in its negative sense of nothingness; there can be a positive response that opens into the possible, the not-yet conceived, and the hopeful. I have sought to incorporate within my translational approach to texts these Buddhist reorientations of foundations of critical thinking, and I believe this is a crucial task.

The translational approach, which takes a subject matter and changes it from one place, state, form, or appearance to another, recomposing it in other registers, involves three linked processes: (1) resistance, (2) identity shedding and identity making, and (3) possibility seeking. First, translation resists the imposition of ideologies, packaged meanings and messages, for we live increasingly in a society of the spectacle, where we are surrounded in every aspect of life by manipulative performances and the mediatized presentation of reality; ours is a world where there is little visible truth. The Iraq crisis and war is a sterling example, and there are numerous others.

Translation resists the imposition of meaning by shifting the subject matter into other registers, by giving it other interpretations that need, in principle, never come to an end. It resists fundamentalisms and ideology when understood pejoratively as a fixed, frozen picture or position; since any representation tends to become reified, translation as a recursive operation works to destabilize what becomes intransigent and enclosed. It insists on movement and openness as a protection against imposition and as a preparation for other processes or operations.

Translation resists false truths; in this aspect, translation has the quality of a critique. Second, translation involves the shedding and making of identity, and this is an ideational operation. In its basic meaning 'ideology,' Paul Ricoeur points out, denotes a 'conception, idea, or representation' (*Ideology and Utopia* 75); we can hardly live without ideas and identities, but we must recognize their intrinsic instability and maintain the flexibility to shed and alter them. Translation attempts to make sense of something and in making sense it sheds old identity and makes new identity; it engages in a dialogue with the world that also repatterns the interpreter/translator. The dialogic nature of translation demands that the individual constantly readjust and readapt in order to manage the shiftings of the self-otherness implication; comprehension involves patterning, then repatternings. Third, translation seeks possibilities. It strikes outward into a liminal space, where it seeks to become more 'mindful,' to use a Buddhist term, and to discover reality. In cognitive terms,

> knowledge is the result of an ongoing interpretation that emerges from our capacities of understanding. These capacities are rooted in the structures of our biological embodiment but are lived and experienced within a domain of consensual action and cultural history. They enable us to make sense of our world; or in more phenomenological language, they are the structures by which we exist in the manner of 'having a world.' (Varela, *The Embodied Mind* 150)

To respond to the dual challenges of fundamentalisms and groundlessness, interpretation has need of all three aspects of this heuristic operation. Without an aspect of resistance (i.e., critique) and the shedding and making of identity, the exploration of possibility would turn into an idle fantasy or a utopian quest in the pejorative, pathological sense of the word. As we have noted, ideology and utopia constitute different sides of the same coin: without a reaching toward something beyond itself, the ideational turns into a frozen picture, a fixation; without an embodiment in culture and the world, possibility seeking is fruitless fantasy.

In Wolfgang Iser's words, interpretation translates 'something either verbal or nonverbal into a register that is linguistic in nature.' This transposition may be from one text to another, but it is not limited to something textual; it may be from 'a past into a present' or 'a hidden life into a transparency.' It can equally apply to 'the control of entropy, the processing of a heritage, all encounters between cultures, and the telescoping of different cultural levels' (*Range of Interpretation* 135). Emergence distinguishes acts of translation in the double sense that their transpositions bring about (1) readjustments of their own procedures and (2) 'mapping[s]' of new phenomena (183). These mappings reverse the usual map/territory relationship: 'Instead of denoting a territory, the map enables the contours of a territory to emerge ... Therefore the map adumbrates the conditions under which the not-yet-existing may be conceived' (186).[1] In short, interpretation as translation seeks to discover, and that, Iser contends, is its anthropological rationale: humans' need to understand themselves and the world, and to try to reach the unreachable. In each chapter of this study something has been translated, and with each act of translation new obstacles and possibilities have arisen, blocking the way in some directions and opening it in others. A schema of interpretive paths that were followed might look like the following, where 'SM' stands for subject matter, 'R' for register, and 'ER' for emergent reality. As I have suggested in the introduction, we might distinguish between the singular and plural of the word 'Orient' in this framework by designating the singular form as the subject matter and the plural as the liminal space or emergent reality.

Chap. 1 SM: Borges's *Historia universal de la infamia*
R: Mystery, Islam, Gnosticism, Buddhism
ER: Orients as intertextuality, or the world as library

Chap. 2 SM: Bowles's short fiction and travel writing
R: Travel as performance; mimesis versus translation
ER: Orients as counter-Western discourses and existential transformations

Chap. 3 SM: Hong Kong as place; Wong's *Hong Kong Stories*
R: Recursive systems and narrative networks
ER: Hong Kong identity as living labyrinth

Chap. 4 SM: Ishiguro's *When We Were Orphans* and Piglia's *La ciudad ausente*
R: Existentialism; narrative networks; landscape
ER: Consubstantiality of place and identity

Chap. 5 SM: Rushdie's *The Moor's Last Sigh*
R: Rewritings of history, myth, and legend
ER: Utopia/dystopia and a new, multicultural world of possibility

Chap. 6 SM: Identity and citizenship
R: Composite entities, Buddhism, creolization, virtuality
ER: Identity as a multi-dimensional field of relationships

The first part of the study, chapters 1 and 2, addressed the Orient first as texts and then as experiences; these are two basically different orientations that might be used to categorize the tendencies in individual apprehension of things Oriental and exotic. Chapter 1 took the subject matter of Borges's *Historia universal de la infamia* and considered it from the perspectives of mystery, Islam, Gnosticism, and Buddhism; Borges's tendency is to transpose all experience into texts, and one might say that his Orients are a vast intertextuality. Chapter 2 considered voyages in Paul Bowles's short fiction and travel writing, focusing on the performative process of travel/voyages in terms of mimesis versus translation. The Orients that emerge in Bowles's works are of two sorts: counter-Western discourses and existential transformations of the traveller/voyager. For Bowles, the Orient is a threshold experience, a transformer. The second part of the study, chapters 3 to 6, reorients the discussion in the direction of post-colonial, postmodern writers and contemporary issues, with Buddhist concepts constituting an important current informing that discussion. These chapters treat reorientations of ideas and concepts such as the city, place and identity, citizenship, East and West, and approaches to literary studies. Chapter 3 considered Hong Kong as place and David T.K. Wong's *Hong Kong Stories*, which it read as an anthologic translation of city into situations, events, and stories; the registers of interpretation were recursive systems and narrative networks. In the physical and virtual space of the urban world, individuals move in a living labyrinth of predicaments and transformations; the city becomes a phenomenological experience from which individual identity emerges and reality is mapped. Chapter 4 continued the examination of place and identity in two books, Ricardo Piglia's *La ciudad ausente / The Absent City* and Kazua Ishiguro's *When We Were Orphans*. Using phenomenological, existentialist perspectives based on the implication of consciousness and world, this chapter translated place and identity into consubstantiality and networks of virtual relations. Using the registers of history, myth, and legend in Salman Rushdie's *The Moor's Last Sigh*, chapter 5 sketched a reorientation of literary, cultural imaginaries by way of an ideological critique of fundamentalisms, and a recomposition of East/West histories and stories as an awakening to the utopian possibilities for a contemporary world of multicultural societies. Drawing on writers, artists, philosophers, scholars, a monk, and scientists, chapter 6 translated the concepts of identity and citizenship. Through the registers of composite (rather than essentialist) entities, Buddhism, creolization, and virtuality, identity was seen to be a network of interrelationships, many of which are virtual and prospective. Identity is spread out in time and space, and it is something that evolves, though it remains incomplete, a certain untranslatability and a reaching-toward-the-unreachable becoming a motor of the development itself. Identity was translated into a dialectic of context and situation; contemporary concepts of identity and citizenship were reoriented toward Buddhist notions of interdependence and universal responsibility.

Neither Subjects nor Objects

What can the translational approach contribute to post-colonial and contemporary literary studies? We have already said that interpretation as acts of translation has the capacity to respond to the dual challenges of fundamentalisms and groundlessness. In terms of approaches to literary and cultural studies, there are four points that I wish to underscore. First, the translational approach brings the reader into a primary position in the interpretive equation. In the sciences as well as the humanities, it has become apparent that the observer, or the observer community, affects all attempts to know and understand; approaches to literature and culture must incorporate this fundamental factor. Second, the translational approach addresses utopia as well as ideology. It can focus on what is *in front of* the text as well as what is behind it. Much of late-twentieth-century literary theory has a deterministic and reproductive slant, which is fatal to any approach that seeks to be heuristic. The translational approach can integrate the concept of cultural and historical embodiment without entangling itself in a deterministic net; this approach highlights 'net' as network of connections rather than skein of entrapment. Third, the translational approach is neither subject- nor object-oriented; it takes the middle way. The concept of liminal space, which I have called emergent reality, implicates subject and object in a bond. This bond may be viewed from different perspectives, which is why the translational approach can respond to fundamentalisms on the one hand (i.e., critiquing the illusion of intrinsic entities) and groundlessness on the other (i.e., shifting the focus from pejorative nihilism to transformative potentiality). Fourth, within acts of translation neither the approach nor the world is treated as complete or final; each translational act generates ramifications on the method as well as its mapping of reality. Nothing is final or at rest; everything evolves, whether we focus on the method or on what the method tries to comprehend.

We have said that the translational approach involves three linked processes: resistance, the shedding and making of identity, and possibility seeking. These linked processes might also be described as three movements and heuristic formulations: circularity, sideways movement (e.g., metonymy), and projection toward an absence (i.e., toward 'something missing'). In the following paragraphs I will consider these movements as they might relate to Orients as emergent reality, thinking about them broadly rather than specifically (as I have tried to do in previous chapters). For the Buddhist, as well as the hermeneuticist-phenomenologist, subjects and objects are implicated one in the other. To separate them is to begin to go astray, so any Orient defined as or equated with a geographic entity or *topos* inevitably leads back to the subject (i.e., the reader/participant/observer), where it takes on an aspect of consciousness. The Orient is circular in the sense that Orient as liminal space and reader share a bond as emergent entities. In Iser's words, 'interpretation highlights the fact that human beings live by what they produce, which points to an important facet of the human condition: humans appear to be an unending performance of themselves' (*Range of Interpretation* 187). There is circularity in the process of interpreting an Orient, and this process has a double aspect: a *transformation of the foreign* and a *foreign transformation*, which translates the text or experience into the interpreter's familiarity with the world and translates him or her toward the alien-ness of the text or experience. This recursive movement resists totalized representation, which would stop the cycle in one of its loops and define that loop as the terminus; it generates a 'middle way' of neither subject alone nor object alone, dependent on the bond between observer and observed, interpreter and interpreted.

Each Orient emerges from a sideways, metonymic movement of translation; there is no limit to the identities that emerge, given different highlightings, and this is one sense of Ricardo Piglia's remark that '[r]eality is endless,' in constant transformation. Here we also see another aspect of translational approaches' resistance to reification, their capacity to deny political, ethnocentrist, and fundamentalist representations. This sideways movement of translation, coupled with its circularity, functions as both a reality check and reality maker; the movement is recursive and depends on a feedback loop, which provides corrective adjustments. Metonymy, which exchanges the name of one thing for that of another of which it is an attribute or with which it is associated, initiates an imbalance that pushes the exchange forward into new shapes and terms. The subject matter eludes the grasp of the register, which attempts to represent it; the attempt at representation exposes new aspects of the subject matter and the limitations of the register. The sideways movement continues to be fuelled by this resistance and, along with it, transformations in the manner that the subject matter is perceived and can be represented. Any attempt to represent *the* Orient leads to *Orients*. All translations are metonymic, for within the rhizomic network of language and reality, centres become provisional points of momentary focusing; because of the imbalance between subject matter and register, the sideways motion of translation never stops, the network shifts, and a new configuration emerges. In reading and writing, and in other activities that call for interpretation, we spend all our lives moving sideways.

We have said that Orients are emergent phenomena, so one question that we must ask is *why* these phenomena emerge. Edward Said provided one answer, linking Western ethnocentrism with power and imperialism; through discourse analysis he exposed the ideological nature of Orientalism. However, as John MacKenzie later pointed out, Western interest in the 'Orient' must be linked with a reaction against industrialization in nineteenth-century Europe and with counter-culture discourses; in other words, the motivation of the Orientalist may be more utopian than imperialist or ideological. I would like to extend this insight with reference to a conversation between philosophers Ernst Bloch and Theodor Adorno concerning utopian longing, because Orients as emergent realities can be viewed as manifestations and expressions of utopian urges. In this conversation Bloch makes the point that for human beings everything depends on a 'totality'; if this sense of totality is shattered, then the urge for meaningfulness will seek other outlets and grasp what can be grasped. He cites Wilhelm Raabe, who in the middle of the nineteenth century wrote: 'When I get up in the morning, my daily prayer is, grant me today my illusion, my daily illusion' (*Utopian Function of Art and Literature* 14). Raabe's prayer testifies that illusions become necessary in a world 'completely devoid of a utopian conscience and utopian presentiment' (14). Orients manifest a utopian urge, a motivation succinctly summed up in Bertolt Brecht's phrase 'Something's missing' (15). Orients often contain but also exceed the ideological; they shift the ideational toward an absence. As otherness, as the beyond, Orients convey imaginative and existential possibilities. Philosopher Emmanuel Lévinas would say that they convey the incompleteness within human beings that strives for something beyond – for the encounter with the stranger or, in other terms, for the what-is-missing. The Orient as utopian possibility stands as metaphor for an *au-delà*; it is not a location, but an ex-centricity, a search and a hope. In sum, these three dimensions of the translational approach – circularity, sideways movement (e.g., metonymy), and projection toward an absence (i.e., toward 'something missing') – complement one another and serve as checks and balances. The interpretive processes of resistance, identity shedding and identity making, and possibility seeking stand in relation and are mutually dependent.

In words that echo the Presocratic philosopher Heraclitus as well as Buddhist thought, Norman Wiener, father of cybernetics, likens human identity to whirlpools in a river that flows without end (quoted in Ricard and Trinh, *L'Infini* 177). A basic reorientation of this study has been to define place and identity as transformative, mutually implicated relations. Identity comprises a given (a heritage, genetic and social imprints, a past) and a virtual component (prospective, future possibilities). Place and identity are consubstantial, linked in transformative relationships. Buddhists have known this for thousands of years; in the twentieth century the West also began to learn that place and identity resemble fields of interrelationships that are just as much virtual as actual. Bringing Buddhist viewpoints and concepts to registers of interpretation may help formulate appropriate responses to the double challenge of fundamentalisms and groundlessness in the contemporary context. Some of the pre-eminent Western scientists of the twentieth century have underscored the congruencies between modern scientific theories and Buddhism and other Eastern thought, and have signalled the need to rethink notions of place and identity along those lines. For example, in University of Virginia astrophysicist Trinh Xuan Thuan's words, quantum mechanics modifies our notions of locale, conferring on space a holistic influence; in the big picture, 'here' and 'there' make no sense because here is implicated in there, a concept that physicists refer to as 'non-separability.' For Foucault's pendulum, all directions are equal, since it adjusts its oscillation not according to a local environment but in conjunction with the farthest galaxies known to human beings (ibid. 103). Physicist Niels Bohr offered this reorientation of the

Western separation of subject and object: '[W]e must turn toward the epistemological problems that thinkers like the Buddha and Lao-tseu have already confronted, and in so doing attempt to reconcile our situation of spectators and actors in the great drama of existence' (quoted ibid. 177). Albert Einstein has remarked: 'If there exists a religion that might be in accord with the imperatives of modern science, it is Buddhism' (quoted ibid. 414). The Buddhist concept of the vacuum, for example, finds a correlate in modern atomic theory: 99.9 percent of the mass of the atom – or of all matter, if you prefer – consists of a cloud of rapidly revolving electrons; that is to say, all mass consists primarily of a quasi-emptiness. The Buddhist concepts of flux and interdependence parallel scientific theories of evolution: from the smallest atom to the entire universe, passing by way of galaxies, stars, and human beings, all is in movement and transformation (ibid. 90–1). Astrophysicist Hubert Reeves takes as the title of one of his best-known books *Patience dans l'azur: L'évolution cosmique*, a phrase from these Buddhist-sounding lines of Paul Valéry (quoted ibid. 19):

Patience, patience,
Patience dans l'azur!
Chaque atome de silence
Est la chance d'un fruit mûr!

These lines beautifully suggest the history of the cosmos, its transformation – one might say – from emptiness into infinity. Reeves is well aware of Hindu and Buddhist traditions, and he sometimes alludes to them in his narratives and explanations. For example, the 'real question' about the universe is, he states: 'Why is there something rather than nothing?' (76) The long history of cosmic evolution – nuclear evolution to chemical evolution, biologic evolution, and finally anthropologic evolution – might be thought of, in Buddhist terms, as a continual transformation from 'emptiness' into infinity. How old is the universe? One of Reeves's responses takes the form of an anecdote from Hindu tradition, with its notion of cycles of destruction that occur after a period of time known as a *kalpa*; the Buddha recounts: 'Every one hundred years an old man brushes a mountain higher and more solid than the Himalaya with a handkerchief made of the finest silk of Bénarès. After a *kalpa*, the mountain will be razed to sea level' (quoted ibid. 77). For his own mathematical amusement, Reeves has calculated – he gives the figures in an appendix – the time it would take the old man to wear down the mountain: approximately 10^{32} years, which roughly corresponds to the scientifically estimated age of the universe. This example is, of course, more light-hearted than dogmatic.

In short, there is interest in Buddhist and Eastern thought across a range of disciplines from cognitive science to biology, quantum physics, and astrophysics. Yet critical thinking and literary theory, too, can draw insights from Buddhism in the task of sorting out rival claims of subjective versus objective theories. The Buddhist concept of the middle way effectively refuses subjects and objects by insisting on interrelationship; it refuses foundations by insisting on the emptiness of all phenomena and the world, but this refusal does not lead to a pejorative nihilism. Rather, it is the initial step in an evolution toward compassion and responsibility – so the refusal has a positive quality. Buddhists question all notions of inherently stable entities; they respond to ethnocentrism by acknowledging that we are creatures of habit and prejudice but that we can learn to break the cycle of the habitual and the automatic. Buddhism might be considered 100 per cent post-colonial in that its origin is non-Western, nor does it depend, even in this era of globalization, on a solitary Western concept. In fact, Buddhism can perhaps give a corrective and creative nudge to post-colonial theory, which has become narrow and rigid in its inquiries and possibilities. I am not suggesting that rose-coloured glasses replace the hard, shameful facts on which post-colonial literature and criticism focus. Bloch is right: 'People must first fill their stomachs, and then they can dance ... Only when all the guests have sat down at the table can the Messiah ... come' ('Something's Missing' 15). Beyond post-colonial and Marxist concerns, and in terms of literary studies as interpretative studies, there is an intersection, or meshing of concepts, between Buddhism and the translational approach. In particular, the concepts of codependency and codependent arising – of subjects and objects, things and their attributes, causes and effects – parallel concepts of the translational approach, where a subject matter and a register interact, generating an emergent reality that is neither wholly subjective nor wholly objective, but rather a dependent relationship linking the interpreter and what is being interpreted. Buddhism is above all experience-oriented, logical, and practical in its own terms. 'I feel the basic Buddhist attitude is quite similar to the scientists' attitude,' the Dalai Lama explains. 'Be open and investigate, find something, confirm it, then accept it. Whichever way you go [within the varieties of Buddhist thought], ... either way there is a strong emphasis on your own analysis and investigation and not simply a dogmatic adherence out of faith in the Buddha' (quoted in Hayward and Varela, *Gentle Bridges* 33). Points of commonality link the cognitive processes of translation, especially when it takes the form of a recursive loop, and the cognition of Buddhism, which also depends on feedback loops and therefore involves a process of adjustment and an analysis of emergent phenomena. The translational approach and Buddhist concepts mesh well: that has been one of the discoveries of this study.

In closing – and as a way of emphasizing that intersection of East-West – I want to consider two contemporary texts/performances, interpreting them in part from Buddhist registers of place and identity: John Neumeier's *Nijinsky*, performed by the Hamburg Ballet in Hong Kong in March 2003, and Hong Kong poet Agnes Lam's 'Writing in the Middle of the Road' (2001). The ballet treats the life, dance, and choreography of the Polish-Russian dancer Vaslav Nijinsky. 'All three aspects – the dancer, the choreographer and the person Nijinksy – form the starting point,' Neurmeier explains. He states a central problem that the ballet addresses in this manner: 'In creating a work about a historical person, what aspects should we concentrate on? ... The man? The artist? Which witness, what information can we trust, which theories should one follow? What points of view can we take towards the complex puzzle Nijinsky?' (Program notes). Neumeier faces a problem of interpretation/translation: what subject matter to select and which registers to highlight. We as viewers can better understand the ballet if we see it as an attempt to translate place and identity into idioms of music, body movement, costumes, and *mise-en-scène*. To convey the mystery and creativity of Nijinsky, Neumeier chooses the impressionistic and Oriental music of parts I, III, and IV of Rimsky-Korsakov's *Sheherazade* (1888), and to keep the ballet from falling into representation of a static, essentialist identity he employs several Nijinskys, all on the stage at the same time during the climactic end of Act I. There is Nijinsky as Harlequin in *Carnival*, as the Spirit of the Rose in *Le Spectre de la rose*, as the Golden Slave in *Sheherazade*, as the Young Man in *Jeux*, as the Faun in *L'Après-midi d'un faun*, as *Petrushka*, and as various ghostly shadows. These several dancers represent 'fragments of Nijinsky's persona,' Neumeier writes. The ballet commences in the Festsaal of the Suvretta-Haus, a hotel in St Moritz, which Neumeier treats as a place-identity branching into a complex network of past, present, and future: 'it is a moment of transition, a place of memory and premonition.' The 'Eastern' reality that emerges in this ballet is the world as inexhaustible spectacle of transformations; the viewer revels in the richness of the music, scenes, and dance, yet at the end a sense of transience and emptiness cannot be dispelled.

The speaker in Agnes Lam's poem 'Writing in the Middle of the Road' is a passer-by who sees a woman writing on a table in the middle of Pokfulam Road, a busy thoroughfare in Central, Hong Kong; the traffic rushes by, but the woman continues unperturbed in her activity from sun-up to sundown. The leaves of paper on which she writes are picked up by the wind and waft away to a nearby cemetery, which lies in the valley below; no car stops and no police arrive to question or remove the elderly lady from her open-air escritoire. The passer-by eventually decides to ask the women why she does not write at home instead of the middle of the road; her reply points out that customary ideas of place and identity cannot capture life's transformations – especially life in Hong Kong. 'What is home?' the woman inquires. In rapidly metamorphosing Hong Kong, today's buildings stand on yesterday's seabed. The middle of the road used to be a mountain, and the spot where the woman is writing, a hut. In the future, the middle of the road may revert to being someone's hut, or it may turn into something else. 'I am not at the wrong place,' the woman declares, challenging the perspective of the passer-by. 'Perhaps you are asking me from the wrong time? / Why should the present matter / more than the past or the future?' (stanza 4, ll. 12–15). When Hong Kong fiction writer and editor of *City Voices* Xu Xi read this poem in a talk at the Chinese University of Hong Kong, she spoke of its humour. Of course, it can be read as a humorous poem, but it can also be interpreted as an allegory or fable, or as a satirical commentary on Hong Kong, a place that its inhabitants call home but that doesn't stay the same long enough to allow anyone to rest. And with this thought we return to Heraclitus and the stream in which no one can step twice – or even once, in Cratylus's sophistic view. Interpreting the poem from the register of place and identity conceived of in Buddhist terms draws out other accents in the woman's response and leads to commentary on the impermanence of all things and on the arbitrariness of selecting one of them and calling it reality.

Lam's poem tells a story – whether real or invented it hardly matters, for the poem has convincingly translated an aspect of Hong Kong. '[L]ife – all life,' Jean-Didier Vincent writes, 'is a fable' (*La Vie* 15). It is because life is a fable (that is to say, a translation or transposition) that we need interpretation, for not all stories are true; some distort and propagandize. So it is the charge of interpretation to sort things out: to resist, to shed and make identity, and to seek the possible (the something-missing). When life becomes false, we intuitively turn to stories to look for truth and to reach toward an emergent identity for ourselves and the world. It is because life is a fable (a translation that is neither subject nor object) that there can always be hope.

Notes

Unless otherwise noted in the Bibliography, all translations are mine.

Introduction

1 A January 2003 database search of journal articles published on the topic of Orientalism and Edward Said resulted in 179 entries; other related topic searches would certainly result in numerous other entries. In the Bibliography I have incorporated a short list of articles and books that have responded to or developed further conceptualizations of Orientalism.
2 See *Orientalism*, 3, and 'Criticism between Culture and System' in Edward W. Said, *The World, the Text and the Critic* 178–225.
3 For a discussion of Buddhism and cognitive science, see Francisco J. Varela, Evan Thompson, and Eleanor Rosch, *The Embodied Mind: Cognitive Science and Human Experience*, and Jeremy W. Hayward and Francisco J. Varela, *Gentle Bridges: Conversations with the Dalai Lama on the Sciences of Mind*.
4 See Roman Ingarden, *The Cognition of the Literary Work* and *The Literary Work of Art*.
5 See Paul Ricoeur, 'What Is a Text? Explanation and Understanding.'
6 It may be helpful to contrast this position with that of Said in *Orientalism*. Although Said does grant that the Orient of Orientalism undergoes reinterpretation and restructuring, he emphasizes the building-up of the discourse formation and then its force or authority in extending and perpetuating itself in the institutions of a society. A phenomenological, hermeneutic reading of texts places more emphasis on the interplay between accumulation (tradition) and innovation (reconfiguration) in which writers and readers engage.
7 More than half a century ago Northrop Frye argued that the assumption of

an encompassing intertextuality was fundamental to any serious study of literature. See 'The Function of Criticism at the Present Time.'
8 Sze Kwan-neung, Program notes, for Giuseppe Verdi, *Nabucco*, Latvian National Opera, Hong Kong, 11 December 2002. Also see Provincia di Parma, 'Giuseppe Verdi – His life and works,' http://www.giuseppeverdi.it/ing/verdi/opere-23.htm.
9 In Buddhist thought, mindfulness involves a calming of the mind and, thereby, a making ready of it for understanding or insight. 'Traditionally, [Buddhist] texts talk about two stages of practice: calming or taming the mind (Sanscrit: *shamantha*) and the development of insight (Sanscrit: *vipashyana*) ... The purpose of calming the mind in Buddhism is not to become absorbed but to render the mind able to be present with itself long enough to gain insight into its own nature and functioning' (Varela et al., *The Embodied Mind* 24).
10 For a discussion of Katherine Mansfield and the Orient, see Timothy Weiss, 'Oriental Elements in Katherine Mansfield's *The Garden Party and Other Stories*.'

Chapter 1 Borges's Search, or the Bibliophilic Orient

1 This is the motto of Nielsen's Symphony No. 4.
2 Borges and Bowles are connected by an interesting link. Bowles was the first to translate 'Las ruinas circulares' into English; it later appeared in the collection of translations *She Woke Me Up So I Killed Her*.
3 If a translation in English of Borges's work is readily available, I have cited and quoted from it unless other editions of the work in Spanish or French contain information not found in the English translation that I must draw on for one reason or another.
4 In Borges et al., *Antología de la literatura fantástica* 158–9.
5 Buddhism is diverse; there are different interpretations of texts and beliefs just as there is diversity within Christianity and Islam.
6 See 'Mystery Religion,' *Encyclopaedia Britannica Online*, at http://www.britannica.com. One stereotype of mystery religions, Walter Burkert argues, is that they were 'Oriental in origin, style, and spirit.' 'The term "Oriental,"' he cautions, 'betrays the perspective of Westerners; ancient Anatolia, Egypt, and Iran were separate worlds, each in its own right, even if all of them are situated more or less east of Western Europe' (*Ancient Mystery Cults* 2–3). See also Marvin W. Meyer, ed., *The Ancient Mysteries: A Sourcebook*.
7 'Mystery Religion.'
8 For analyses of the logic of narrative, see Paul Ricoeur, *Temps et récit*, Vladimir Propp, *Morphology of the Folk Tale*, and Claude Bremond, *Logique du récit*.

Notes to pages 31–8 219

9 The original reads: 'las ciudades, climas y reinos en que se divide la tierra, los tesoros ocultos en el centro, las naves que atraviesan el mar, los instrumentos de la guerra, de la música y de la cirugía, las graciosas mujeres, las estrellas fijas y los planetas, los colores que emplean los infieles para pintar sus cuadros aborrecibles, los minerales y las plantas con los secretos y virtudes que encierran, los ángeles de plata cuyo alimento es el elogio y la justificación del Señor, las distribución de los premios en las escuelas, las estatuas de pájaros y de reyes que hay en el corazón de las pirámides, la sombra proyectada por el toro que sostiene la tierra y por el pez que está debajo del toro, los desiertos de Dios el Misericordioso. Vio cosas imposibles de describir, como las calles alumbradas a gas y como la ballena que muere cuando escucha el grito del hombre' (*Historia universal* 128–9).

10 The original reads: 'A esa curiosa variación de un filántropo debemos infinitos hechos: los *blues* de Handy, el éxito logrado en París por el pintor doctor oriental D. Pedro Figari, la buena prosa cimarrona del también oriental D. Vicente Rossi, el tamaño mitólogo de Abraham Lincoln, los quinientos mil muertos de la Guerra de Secesión, los tres mil trescientos millones gastados en pensiones militares, la estatua del imaginario Falucho, la admisión del verbo *linchar* en la décimotercera edición del Diccionario de la Academia ...' (*Historia universal* 17–18).

11 Fascinating but difficult to define, Gnostic beliefs can be summarized as follows:

In the Gnostic view, the unconscious self of man is consubstantial with the Godhead, but because of a tragic fall it is thrown into a world that is completely alien to its real being. Through revelation from above, man becomes conscious of his origin, essence, and transcendent destiny. Gnostic revelation is to be distinguished both from philosophical enlightenment, because it cannot be acquired by the forces of reason, and from Christian revelation, because it is not rooted in history and transmitted by Scripture. It is rather the intuition of the mystery of the self.

The world, produced from evil matter and possessed by evil demons, cannot be a creation of a good God; it is mostly conceived of as an illusion, or an abortion, dominated by Yahweh, the Jewish demiurge, whose creation and history are depreciated. This world is therefore alien to God, who is for the Gnostics depth and silence, beyond any name or predicate, the absolute, the source of good spirits who together form the *plērōma*, or realm of light.

See also 'Gnosticism' *Encyclopaedia Britannica Online*, at www.britannica.com.

12 The original reads: 'La música, los estados de felicidad, la mitología, las caras trabajadas por el tiempo, ciertos crepúsculos y ciertos lugares, quieren decir-

nos algo, o algo dijeron que no hubiéramos debido perder, o están por decir algo; esta inminencia de una revelación, que no se produce, es quizá, el hecho estético' (*Nueva antología personal* 260–1).

13 A short list of works would include the following. *Antología de la literatura fantástica* (1940), co-authored with Adolfo Bioy Casares and Silvina Ocampo, contains passages from the *Arabian Nights*, the Japanese author Ryunosuke Agutagawa, the Chinese philosophers Chuang Tzu and Liehtsé, the sixteenth-century Chinese author Wu Ch'eng En (Wu Chengen), the eighteenth-century Chinese novelist Tsao Hsueh Chin (Cao Xueqin), and translations and/or adaptations of Oriental material by G.K. Chesterton and G. Willoughby-Meade. *Ficciones* (1944) and *El Aleph* (1949) feature 'Two Kings and Two Labyrinths' and 'Abenjacán el Bojarí, Dead in His Labyrinth' as well as 'Averroes' Search,' 'The Garden of Forking Paths,' 'The Immortal,' and 'The South.' In *Historia de la eternidad* (1953), 'The Translators of the 1001 Nights' stands out as exemplary; in *El hacedor* (1960) and *Nueva antología personal* (1961), there are short pieces and poems such as 'Parable of the Palace,' 'Chess,' 'Limits,' 'The Other Tiger,' 'Aristo and the Arabs,' and 'Arte poetica.' *Historia de la noche* (1977) contains the poems 'Alhambra,' 'Metáforas de Las Mil y Una Noches,' 'Alguien,' 'Caja de música,' and 'Las causas.'

Chapter 2   The Orient as Liminal Space in Paul Bowles

1 According to Mikhail Bakhtin, an exotopic vision is situated outside the limitations of the insider's point of view (*Speech Genres* 7).
2 *An Invisible Spectator* is the title of Christopher Sawyer-Lauçanno's biography of Paul Bowles.
3 See Robert Young, *White Mythologies: Writing History and the West.*
4 In his *Arabic Glossary*, Jeffrey Miller, the editor of Paul Bowles's letters, defines 'kif' as follows: 'The fine leaves at the base of the common hemp plant, *Cannabis sativa*, chopped fine and usually mixed (in a ratio of seven to four) with tobacco grown in the same soil' (*In Touch: The Letters of Paul Bowles* 548).
5 *Paradores* in Spain are typically located in castles and historical buildings, so the word 'parador' takes on ironic connotations in this context.
6 In *Days: Tangier Journal, 1987–1989*, for example.
7 In letters to friends during the late 1940s and early 1950s, Bowles writes of his desire to build a house in Timimoun (in western Algeria): 'The Captain there is going to choose an oasis for me. It's my favorite spot.' At Taghit he writes in astonishment of the grandeur of dunes: 'five and six hundred feet

high ... , and below Kerzaz they are a thousand [feet] ... [I]t is quite the most astonishingly beautiful place I have ever seen' (Miller, *Letters* 192, 201).
8 See Monod, *Meharées: Explorations au vrai Sahara.*
9 See Lyotard, *The Postmodern Condition.*
10 See 'La Ruée vers le désert.'

Chapter 3   Hong Kong and David T.K. Wong's *Hong Kong Stories*

1 I initially came to the concept of the 'sojourner' by way of Pierre Loti and Roland Barthes, but of course it is now a popular term in discussions of the Chinese diaspora. Victor Hao Li writes:
   Virtually all started as sojourners. We left a place we wished to leave, whether for economic or political reasons. We went to a place we thought we wished to go, whether for a better livelihood or education or safety ...
   Leaving the Central Country was also an important symbolic act. In mainstream Chinese culture, a person was not defined by individual attributes as in the West, where 'I' carried my persona and my soul with me and could establish a New World wherever I went. Instead, the individual was at the nexus of a broad network of relationships that connected the person to ancestors and descendants, family, the community, and the state ... Weakening or severing these links diminished or even destroyed a person.
   Sojourners could handle these problems more readily than emigrants. Sojourners were, in theory, physically away for a time and spiritually away only in part. At the symbolic plane, they yielded almost nothing and never really left. ('From Qiao to Qiao' 213–14)
2 See also 'L'Imaginaire des langues: Entretien avec Édouard Glissant' and *Tout-Monde.*
3 The full passage reads: 'A culture of disappearance gives us identities to take away our subjectivity, emotions to take away our affectivity, a voice to take away representation. However ... such a situation can be turned against itself: the wiping out of identity may not be an entirely negative thing, *if it can be taken far enough.* Not all identities are worth preserving. This is to say that disappearance is not only a threat – it is also an opportunity ... There is one essential condition ... if the postcolonial subject is not to be reabsorbed and assimilated: it must not be another stable appearance, another stable identity. It must learn how to survive a culture of disappearance by adopting strategies of disappearance as its own, by giving disappearance itself a different inflection' (xiv–xv).

4 By 'bilingual' I mean that more than one language is spoken.
5 Concerning the notion of cultural essences and Chinese culture, David Yen-ho Wu asserts: 'Recent studies ... have shown that the existence of a superior Chinese culture is, at best, a myth. The Chinese people and Chinese culture have been constantly amalgamating, restructuring, reinventing, and reinterpreting themselves; the seemingly static Chinese culture has been in a continuous process of assigning important new meanings about being Chinese. However, the Chinese people have not been conscious of using such a cultural construction, and it has significantly affected Chinese individuals in peripheral areas because they are socially and politically situated on the border between the non-Chinese and the category of people considered Chinese' ('The Construction of Chinese and Non-Chinese Identity' 151). Hong Kong would seem a peripheral region of this sort, where the idea of radical difference, of Chinese-ness, takes shape in discourse structured by various socio-economic and political pressures and exigencies.
6 Some stories were originally published during the 1990s and late 1980s in anthologies and magazines in the United States, England, and Asia.
7 See 'Ethics without Morality' in *The Deleuze Reader* 69–77.
8 For a discussion of the relationship between modern theories of physics and astrophysics, and Buddhism, see Matthieu Ricard and Trinh Xuan Thuan, *L'Infini dans la paume de la main*.

Chapter 4   Locale and Identity in Ishiguro and Piglia

1 In the short story 'El Congreso' Jorge Luis Borges cites this passage in French.
2 I have taken the liberty, in translating the title into English, to reposition the adjective. As Roger-Pol Droit explains in his introduction, entitled 'Des aventures de tous les jours,' the focus of the book is on everyday experience and on games/experiments that can be performed or played in relation to such things as looking at oneself in the mirror, watching one's partner sleep, or (are you ready?) drinking a glass of water while you urinate. Droit recommends changing the optic through which we view ourselves and the world, which is finally what philosophy is all about; the phrase 'everyday philosophy' seems to me a bit misleading because it is not a particular kind or subgenre of philosophy that is being recommended.
3 See, among other essays, 'The Work of Art in the Age of Mechanical Reproduction,' in Benjamin, *Illuminations*.
4 For a book-length treatment of the topic of migrancy, see Chambers, *Migrancy, Culture, Identity*.

Chapter 5 Myth in Rushdie's *The Moor's Last Sigh*

1 'Cochin,' *Encyclopaedia Britannica Online*, at www.britannica.com [18 February 1998].
2 See, for example, Rush, 'Doomed in Bombay.'
3 'Kublai Khan,' *Encyclopaedia Britannica Online*, at www.britannica.com.
4 The principle of myth, Coupe states, is radical typology, wherein a 'type' (i.e., a person or event from which a narrative develops) is realized and modified by an 'anti-type,' which is not its opposite but rather its fulfilment and modification in some way (*Myth* 108).
5 Frye views all narrative as a cycle of displacement of myth through the narrative modes of romance, tragedy, comedy, and irony, with the cycle then tending to return to the mode of myth. Twentieth-century Western literature, a literature primarily in the ironic mode, contains many illustrations of this tendency of irony to move back toward myth. Conrad's *Heart of Darkness*, Joyce's *Ulysses*, and Eliot's 'The Waste Land' are a few significant examples (*Anatomy of Criticism* 33–4).
6 'Ganapatya,' *Encyclopaedia Britannica Online*, at www.britannica.com.
7 'Ganesha,' ibid.
8 'Sarasvati,' ibid.
9 We find a pre-Rushdie, postmodern version of Shahrazad in John Barth's *Chimera*.
10 Here is a brief summary of the events to which the novel refers and draws narrative parallels:

The year 1993 began amid the turmoil generated by the destruction on Dec. 6, 1992, of the medieval mosque in Ayodhya, Uttar Pradesh, by Hindu militants, who believed the building was originally an ancient Hindu temple marking the birthplace of the god Rama. The ensuing bloody clashes between Hindus and Muslims throughout the nation claimed at least 2,000 lives within a few weeks, most of them Muslims. In Bombay riots resulted in the death of more than 600 Muslims, well over 550 alone during nine days within the first two weeks of January. Hundreds of Muslims were arrested in Ayodhya as they attempted to conduct prayers at the site of the destroyed mosque. On March 12 a series of bomb explosions in Bombay linked to a Muslim criminal element killed over 200, wounded more than 1,200, and badly damaged the headquarters of the Shiv Sena, the most powerful and radical Hindu organization in the city.

Prime Minister Narasimha Rao had promised the construction of both a temple and a mosque in Ayodhya outside the disputed area. On

February 25, in defiance of a government ban, the fundamentalist Hindu Bharatiya Janata Party (BJP) attempted to hold a rally in New Delhi. Anticipating the worst, the government arrested or detained over 60,000 Hindus and sealed off New Delhi with barricades. Scuffles with the police led to the arrest of nearly 5,000, including 110 BJP members of Parliament.

See 'Hinduism,' *Encyclopaedia Britannica Online*, at www.britannica.com [8 July 2003].

Chapter 6   Identity and Citizenship in a World of Shame

1 Here we see similarities with ideas of Giles Deleuze and Félix Guattari in *Mille plateaux* (*A Thousand Plateaus: Capitalism and Schizophrenia*).
2 Elsewhere Glissant has written that a new concept of the nation is taking shape: 'The nation ... not based on exclusion; [but rather, on] ... a form of disalienated relationship with the other, who in this way becomes our fellow man' (*Caribbean Discourse: Selected Essays* 250).
3 The original reads: 'La responsabilité pour autrui est le lieu où se place le non-lieu de la subjectivité et où se perd le privilège de la question: où?'
4 See Todorov, *Mikhail Bakhtin*.
5 We can certainly agree with Todorov on this point that books expand the mind, though we should note that he himself underscores the limitations of this line of argument, as does Umberto Eco, who in a recent interview in *L'Express* notes that cultural sophistication is not necessarily a road to human understanding: administrators in the concentration camps of Auschwitz read Goethe and listened to Brahms. See Umberto Eco, 'Méconnaître les langues produit de l'intolérance.'
6 One understands Todorov's point here, although one could argue, citing Glissant's concept of creolization, that a separation between Western and non-Western civilizations has become increasingly difficult to establish, since cultures themselves exist dialogically and have been creolized.
7 Today, Todorov views himself a citizen of France – not of two countries, France and Bulgaria, nor of the world. But France, he says, is one among other countries, and like them, is not free of faults.
8 The information above was drawn from: Letter from Hong Kong Committee for UNICEF, July 2002; *South China Morning Post*, 14 May 2002: 15, 27 August 2002: 9, 29 August 2002: 10; *L'Express*, 19 April 2001: 72; Wolfensohn, 'Un Monde injuste est un monde dangereux' 28; and Attali, 'L'Année des fous' 21.

9 In Nietzsche's words, nihilism, or the doctrine that there is no objective ground of truth, constitutes a situation in which 'man rolls from the centre toward X' (quoted in Vattimo, *The End of Modernity* 19).
10 See also Michael Lind, *The Next American Nation* and Todorov, *The Morals of History*.
11 It is perhaps interesting to note that Bissoondath is the nephew of V.S. Naipaul.
12 About this phenomenon in Europe, see, for example, Jean-Sebastien Stehli with Émilie Trevert.
13 Matthieu Ricard is the son of French philosopher Jean-François Revel, with whom he collaborated in *Le Moine et le philosophe*.
14 See Vattimo, 'Hermeneutics and Anthropology,' in *The End of Modernity* 145–63.
15 'Population,' *Encyclopaedia Britannica Online*, at www.britannica.com.

Neither Subjects nor Objects: In the Middle Way

1 Here Iser notes that he is extending concepts of Gregory Bateson, *Steps to an Ecology of Mind*, and Arthur Korzybski, whose best-known book is *Science and Sanity: An Introduction to Non-Aristotelian Systems and General Semantics*.

Bibliography

Abbas, Ackbar. *Hong Kong: Culture and the Politics of Disappearance.* Minneapolis: University of Minnesota Press, 1997.
Abensour, Miguel. 'Walter Benjamin.' In Michèle Riot-Sarcey, Thomas Bouchet, and Antoine Picon, eds, *Dictionnaire des Utopies*, 22–8. Paris: Larousse, 2002.
Abrams, M.H. *A Glossary of Literary Terms.* Fort Worth, TX: Harcourt Brace, 1999.
Abu-Lughod, Janet L. *Before European Hegemony: The World System A.D. 1250–1350.* New York: Oxford University Press, 1989.
Ajami, Fouad. 'The Traveler's Luck: V.S. Naipaul's Misunderstanding of Islam.' Review of *Beyond Belief* by V.S. Naipaul. *New Republic*, 13 July 1998: 27–33.
Allen, Paula Gunn. '"Border" Studies: The Intersection of Gender and Color.' In Joseph Gibaldi, ed., *Introduction to Scholarship in Modern Languages and Literatures*, 303–19. New York: Modern Language Association of America, 1992.
Alpers, Antony. *Katherine Mansfield.* London: Jonathan Cape, 1954.
The Arabian Nights. Trans. Husain Haddawy. New York: W.W. Norton, 1990.
Ashcroft, Bill, Gareth Griffiths, and Helen Tiffin. *The Empire Writes Back: Theory and Practice in Post-Colonial Literatures.* London and New York: Routledge, 1989.
Attali, Jacques. 'L'Année des fous.' *L'Express*, 9 January 2003: 21.
– *Chemins de sagesse: Traité du labyrinthe.* Paris: Fayard, 1996.
– 'La "Coupe du monde."' *L'Express*, 30 May 2002: 17.
Bach, Caleb. 'Detective de laberintos literarios.' *Américas* 54.3 (2000): 36–43.
Bakhtin, Mikhail. *The Dialogic Imagination: Four Essays.* Ed. Michael Holquist. Trans. Caryl Emerson and Michael Holquist. Austin: University of Texas Press, 1981.
– *Problems of Dostoevsky's Poetics.* Ed. and trans. Caryl Emerson. Intro. Wayne C. Booth. Minneapolis: University of Minnesota Press, 1984.
– *Speech Genres and Other Late Essays.* Trans. Vern W. McGee, ed. Caryl Emerson and Michael Holquist. Austin: University of Texas Press, 1986.

Bakhtin, M.M., and P.N. Medvedev. *The Formal Method in Literary Scholarship: A Critical Introduction to Sociological Poetics.* Trans. Albert J. Wehrle. Intro. Wlad Godzich. Cambridge, MA: Harvard University Press, 1985.

Balzac, Honoré de. *La Comédie humaine.* 1834–7. Paris: Éditions du Seuil, 1965.

Barthes, Roland. *Alors la Chine?* Paris: Christian Bourgois Éditeur, 1975.

– *L'Empire des signes.* Paris: Albert Skira Éditeur, 1970.

– *New Critical Essays.* New York: Hill and Wang, 1980.

Bateson, Gregory. *Steps to an Ecology of Mind.* 1973: Northvale, NJ: Aronson, 1987.

Baudrillard, Jean. *Simulacres et simulations.* Trans. Sheila Faria Glasira. Ann Arbour: University of Michigan Press, 1994.

Beauvoir, Simone de. *L'Invitée.* Paris: Gallimard, 1943.

Beckford, William. *Vathek.* Ed. and intro. Roger Lonsdale. 1786. London: Oxford University Press, 1970.

Behdad, Ali. *Belated Travelers: Orientalism in the Age of Colonial Dissolution.* Durham, NC: Duke University Press, 1994.

Benjamin, Walter. *Illuminations.* Glasgow: Fontana, Collins, 1973.

– *Selections.* Ed. Marcus Bullock and Michael W. Jennings. Cambridge, MA.: Belknap Press, 1996.

Bernabé, Jean, Patrick Chamoiseau, and Raphaël Confiant. *Éloge de la Créolité.* Paris: Gallimard / Presses Universitaires Créoles, 1989.

Berque, Jacques. *Arab Rebirth: Pain and Ecstasy.* London: Al Saqi, 1983.

– *L'Islam au temps du monde.* Paris: Sinbad, 1984.

– *Mémoires des deux rives.* Paris: Éditions du Seuil, 1989.

Bhabha, Homi K. *The Location of Culture.* London and New York: Routledge, 1994.

– 'The Other Question: Difference, Discrimination and the Discourse of Colonialism.' In Francis Barker et al., eds, *Literature, Politics and Theory: Papers from the Essex Conference,* 148–72. London: Methuen, 1986.

– 'Postcolonial Criticism.' In Stephen Greenblatt and Giles Gunn, eds, *Redrawing the Boundaries: The Transformation of English and American Literary Studies,* 437–65. New York: Modern Language Association of America, 1992.

Bhabha, Homi K., ed. *Nation and Narration.* London: Routledge, 1990.

Bissoondath, Neil. *Selling Illusions: The Cult of Multiculturalism in Canada.* Toronto: Penguin, 1994.

Bloch, Ernst. *The Principle of Hope.* 1954–9. Trans. Neville Plaice, Stephen Plaice, and Paul Knight. Cambridge, MA.: MIT Press, 1986.

– *The Spirit of Utopia.* Trans. Anthony A. Nassar. Stanford, CA: Stanford University Press, 2000.

– *Utopian Function of Art and Literature: Selected Essays.* Trans. Jack Zipes and Frank Mecklenburg. Cambridge, MA: MIT Press, 1988.

Bloch, Ernst, and Theodor W. Adorno. 'Something's Missing: A Discussion between Ernst Bloch and Theodor W. Adorno on the Contradictions of Utopian Longing.' In *The Utopian Function of Art and Literature: Selected Essays*, 1–17. Trans. Jack Zipes and Frank Mecklenburg. Cambridge, MA: MIT Press, 1988.

Boothroyd, Ninette, and Muriel Détrie. *Le Voyage en Chine: Anthologie des voyageurs occidentaux du moyen age à la chute de l'empire chinois*. Paris: Robert Laffont, 1992.

Borges, Jorge Luis. *El Aleph*. 1949. Madrid: Alianza Editorial, 1994.

– *The Aleph and Other Stories, 1939–1969*. Ed. and trans. Thomas Norman de Giovanni. New York: Dutton, 1970.

– *The Book of Sand*. Trans. Norman Thomas di Giovanni. 1975. New York: Dutton, 1977.

– *Borges on Writing*. Ed. Norman Thomas di Giovanni, Daniel Halpern, and Frank MacShane. 1972. London: Allen Lane, 1974.

– 'El Congreso.' In *El libro de arena*. 1975. Madrid: Alianza Editorial, 1995: 21–38.

– *Discusión*. Buenos Aires: Emecé, 1957.

– *Doctor Brodie's Report*. Harmondsworth, UK: Penguin Books, 1972.

– *Ficciones*. 1944. Madrid: Alianza Editorial, 1995.

– *El hacedor*. 1960. Madrid: Alianza Editorial, 1994.

– *Histoire universelle de l'infamie / Histoire de l'éternité*. Ed. Roger Caillois and Laure Guillet. 1951. Paris: Union générale édition, 1994.

– *Historia de la eternidad*. 1953. Madrid: Alianza Editorial, 1994.

– *Historia de la noche*. Buenos Aires: Emecé, 1977.

– *Historia universal de la infamia*. 1935. Madrid: Alianza Editorial, 1993.

– *El informe de Brodie*. 1970. Madrid: Alianza Editorial, 1974.

– *Labyrinths: Selected Stories and Other Writings*. Ed. Donald A. Yates and James E. Irby. Preface André Maurois. New York: New Directions Books, 1964.

– *El libro de arena*. 1975. Madrid: Alianza Editorial, 1995.

– *Nueva antología personal*. 1961. Buenos Aires: Emecé, 1968.

– *Otras inquisiciones*. Buenos Aires: Emecé, 1960.

– *A Personal Anthology*. New York: Grove Press, 1967.

– *Seven Nights*. Trans. Eliot Weinberger. Intro. Alistair Reid. New York: New Directions, 1984.

– *Siete noches*. México, DF: Fondo de Cultura Económica, 1980.

– *Twenty-four Conversations with Borges*. With Roberto Alifano. Trans. Nicomedes Subarez, Willis Barnstone, and Noembi Escandell. Housatonic, MA: Lascaux Publishers, 1984

– *A Universal History of Infamy*. Trans. Norman Thomas di Giovanni. New York: E.P. Dutton & Co., 1972.

Borges, Jorge Luis, Adolfo Bioy Casares, and Silvina Ocampo. *Antología de la literatura fantástica*. Buenos Aires: Editorial Hermes, 1987.
Borges, Jorge Luis, and Alicia Jurado. *Qué es el Budismo*. 1976. Buenos Aires: Emené Editors, 1991.
Bowles, Paul. *Collected Stories, 1939–1976*. Intro. Gore Vidal. Santa Barbara, CA: Black Sparrow Press, 1980.
– *Days: Tangier Journal, 1987–1989*. New York: Ecco Press, 1991.
– *In Touch: The Letters of Paul Bowles*. Ed. Jeffrey Miller. New York: Farrar, Strauss and Giroux, 1994.
– *Let It Come Down*. Santa Rosa, CA: Black Sparrow Press, 1952.
– *Mémoirs d'un nomade*. Trans. Marc Gibot. Paris: Quai Voltaire, 1989.
– *One Hundred Camels in the Courtyard*. San Francisco: City Lights Books, 1962.
– *The Sheltering Sky*. 1949. New York: Vintage, 1990.
– *She Woke Me Up So I Killed Her*. San Francisco: Cadmus Editions, 1985.
– *Their Heads Are Green and Their Hands Are Blue: Scenes from the Non-Christian World*. 1957. Hopewell, NJ: Ecco Press, 1984.
– *Without Stopping: An Autobiography*. 1972. New York: Ecco Press, 1985.
Brady, Paul. *La Littérature chinoise moderne*. Paris: Presses Universitaires de France, 1993.
Bremond, Claude. *Logique du récit*. Paris: Éditions du Seuil, 1973.
Brown, Judith. *Modern India: The Origins of an Asian Democracy*. Delhi: Oxford University Press, 1985.
Buchanan, Daniel C. *One Hundred Famous Haiku*. Tokyo: Japan Publications, 1973.
Burke, Kenneth. '"Kubla Khan," Proto-Surrealist Poem.' In *Language as Symbolic Act: Essays on Life, Literature, and Method*, 201–22. Berkeley: University of California Press, 1966.
Burkert, Walter. *Ancient Mystery Cults*. Cambridge, MA: Harvard University Press, 1987.
Buruma, Ian. 'In the Empire of Islam.' Review of *Beyond Belief* by V.S. Naipaul. *New York Review of Books*, 16 July 1998: 8–11.
Callinicos, Alex. *Marxism and Philosophy*. Oxford: Oxford University Press, 1985.
Calvino, Italo. *Invisible Cities*. Trans. William Weaver. San Diego: Harcourt Brace Jovanovich, 1974.
– *Les Villes invisibles*. Preface Italo Calvino. Trans. Jean Thibaudeau. 1972. Paris: Éditions du Seuil, 1974.
Calvora, Robert G. 'Levinas' [*sic*]. In Michèle Riot-Sarcey, Thomas Bouchet, and Antoine Picon, eds, *Dictionnaire des Utopies*, 130–1. Paris: Larousse, 2002.
Camilleri, Carmel, and Margalit Cohen-Emerique. *Chocs de culturels: Concepts et enjeux pratiques de l'interculturel*. Paris: Éditions L'Harmattan, 1989.

Camões, Luis Vaz de. *Camões: Les Lusiades, Os Lusíadas.* Édition Bilingue Portugais-Français. Trans. Roger Bismut. Intro. Eduardo Lourenço. Paris: Robert Laffont, 1996.
– *The Lusiads.* Trans., intro., and notes Landeg White. Oxford: Oxford University Press, 1997.
Camus, Albert. *The Plague.* Trans. Stuart Gilbert. 1948. New York: Vintage International Edition, 1991.
Cavafy, C.P. *The Complete Poems of Cavafy.* Expanded ed. Trans. Rae Dalven, intro. W.H. Auden. New York: Harcourt Brace Jovanovich, 1976.
CDN Publishing Ltd. Conversation regarding dates of publication of David T.K. Wong's short stories. Hong Kong, 9 May 1997.
Césaire, Aimé. *Discours sur le colonialisme.* 5th ed. Paris: Présence Africaine, 1970.
Chambers, Iain. *Migrancy, Culture, Identity.* London: Routledge, 1994.
Changeux, Jean-Pierre, and Paul Ricoeur. *Ce qui nous fait penser: La nature et la règle.* Paris: Éditions Odile Jacob, 1998.
Charles-Roux, Edmonde. *Un Désir d'orient: Jeunesse d'Isabelle Eberhardt, 1877–1899.* Paris: Grasset, 1988.
– *Nomade j'étais: Les années africaines d'Isabelle Eberhardt, 1899–1904.* Paris: Grasset, 1995.
Cheng, Christina Miu Bing. *Macau: A Cultural Janus.* Hong Kong: Hong Kong University Press, 1999.
Chen Xiao-mei. *Occidentalism: A Theory of Counter-Discourse in Post-Mao China.* New York: Oxford University Press, 1995.
Citati, Pietro. *La Lumière de la nuit: Les grands mythes dans l'histoire du monde.* Trans. Brigitte Pérol and Tristan Macé. Paris: Gallimard, 1996.
Clifford, James. *The Predicament of Culture: Twentieth-century Ethnography, Literature, and Art.* Cambridge, MA: Harvard University Press, 1988.
– 'Traveling Cultures.' In Lawrence Grossberg, Cary Nelson, and Paula Treichler, eds, *Cultural Studies,* 96–112. New York: Routledge, 1992.
Clifford, James, and George Marcus, eds. *Writing Culture: The Poetics and Politics of Ethnography.* Berkeley: University of California Press, 1986.
Coelho, Paulo. *O alquimista.* Rio de Janeiro: Pergaminho, 1988.
– *The Alchemist.* 1988. San Francisco: HarperPerennial, 1998.
Coetzee, J.M. 'Palimpsest Regained.' Review of *The Moor's Last Sigh* by Salman Rushdie. *New York Review of Books,* 21 March 1996: 13–16.
Comte-Sponville, André, and Luc Ferry. *La Sagesse des modernes: Dix questions pour notre temps.* Paris: Robert Laffont, 1998.
Coupe, Laurence. *Myth.* London: Routledge, 1997.
Cruz, Gaspar da. Excerpts from 'Treatise in Which the Things of China Are Related at Great Length.' In C.R. Boxer, *South China in the Sixteenth Century*

(London: Hakluyt Society, 1953). Reprinted in Boothroyd and Détrie, *Le Voyage en Chine*, 114–17.

Cupitt, Don. *The World to Come*. London: SCM Press, 1982.

Dachy, Marc. 'International situationniste.' In Michèle Riot-Sarcey, Thomas Bouchet, and Anoine Picon, eds, *Dictionnaire des Utopies*, 111–15. Paris: Larousse, 2002.

Debray, Régis. *Le Feu sacré*. Paris: Fayard, 2003.

Deleuze, Gilles. *The Deleuze Reader*. Ed. and intro. Constantin V. Boundas. New York: Columbia University Press, 1993.

– 'Michel Tournier et le monde sans autrui.' In Michel Tournier, *Vendredi ou les limbes du Pacifique*, 257–83. Paris: Gallimard, 1972.

– *Le Pli*. Paris: Les Éditions de minuit, 1988.

Deleuze, Gilles, and Félix Guattari. *Kafka: Toward a Minor Literature*. Minneapolis: University of Minnesota Press, 1986.

– *A Thousand Plateaus: Capitalism and Schizophrenia*. Minneapolis: University of Minnesota Press, 1987.

Dissanayake, Wimal, ed. *Narratives of Agency: Self-Making in China, India, and Japan*. Minneapolis: University of Minnesota Press, 1996.

Dissanayake, Wimal, and Carmen Wickramagamage. *Self and Colonial Desire: Travel Writings of V.S. Naipaul*. New York: Peter Lang, 1993.

Droit, Roger-Pol. *101 Expériences de philosophie quotidienne*. Paris: Éditions Odile Jacob, 2001.

Dumont, René. *Un Monde intolérable: Le libéralisme en question*. Paris: Editions du Seuil, 1988.

Eagleton, Terry. *Marxism and Literary Criticism*. Berkeley: University of California Press, 1976.

Eberhardt, Isabelle. *Dans l'ombre chaude de l'Islam*. Paris: Charpentier et Fasqeulle, 1926.

– *The Oblivion Seekers and Other Writings*. Trans. Paul Bowles. San Francisco: City Lights, 1972.

– *Oeuvres complètes I: Écrits sur le sable*. Ed. Marie-Odile Delacour and Jean-René Huleu. Preface Edmonde Charles-Roux. Paris: Grasset, 1988.

Eco, Umberto. 'City of the Robots.' In Marjorie Ford and Jon Ford, *Dreams and Inward Journeys: A Rhetoric and Reader for Writers*, 473–480. New York: Longman, 1998.

– 'Méconnaître les langues produit de l'intolérance.' Interview. *L'Express*, 22 April 1999: 13.

– *The Role of Reader: Explorations in the Semiotics of Texts*. Bloomington: Indiana University Press, 1979.

Eliade, Mircea. *Myths, Dreams and Mysteries: The Encounter between Contemporary*

Faiths and Archaic Realities. Trans. Philip Mairet. New York: Harper & Row, 1960.
- *Yoga: Immortality and Freedom.* Trans. Willard R. Trask. New York: Pantheon Books, 1958.

Elsner, Jás, and Joan-Pau Rubiés. *Voyages and Visions: Towards a Cultural History of Travel.* London: Reaktion Books, 1999.

Fanon, Frantz. *Les Damnés de la terre.* Paris: François Maspero, 1981.
- *Peau noire, masques blancs.* Paris: Éditions du Seuil, 1952.

Fokkema, Douwe, and Elrud Ibsch. *Knowledge and Commitment: A Problem-oriented Approach to Literary Studies.* Amsterdam, Philadelphia: J. Benjamins, 2000.

Foucauld, Jean-Baptiste de. *Les 3 cultures du développement humain: Résistance, régulation, utopie.* Paris: Odile Jacob, 2002.

Foucault, Michel. *The Archaeology of Knowledge.* Trans. A.M. Sheridan Smith. New York: Pantheon, 1972.
- *Discipline and Punish: The Birth of the Prison.* Trans. Alan Sheridan. New York: Pantheon, 1977.

Foulquié, Paul. *L'Existentialisme.* Paris: Presses universitaires de France, 1968.

Fourny, Jean-François. Review of *Selling Illusions* by Neil Bissoondath. *Humanities Abstracts* 28 (1997): 142–53.

Fowler, Edward. *The Rhetoric of Confession: Shishosetsu in Early Twentieth-century Japanese Fiction.* Berkeley: University of California Press, 1988.

Friedman, Maurice, ed. *The Worlds of Existentialism: A Critical Reader.* Atlantic Highlands, NJ, and London: Humanities Press International, 1991.

Frye, Northrop. *Anatomy of Criticism: Four Essays.* Princeton: Princeton University Press, 1957.
- 'The Function of Criticism at the Present Time.' In Robert Con Davis and Ronald Schleifer, *Literary Criticism,* 4th ed., 39–49. New York: Longman, 1998.

Fuentes, Carlos. *El Espejo enterrado.* Mexico: Taurus, 1997.
- 'La Latinité, c'est un grand flueve de rencontres.' Interview. *L'Express,* 21 October 1999: 10.

Gadamer, Hans-Georg. *Truth and Method.* 2nd rev. ed. Trans. Joel Weinsheimer and Donald G. Marshall. 1960. New York: Continuum, 1994.

Gare, Arran E. 'Understanding Oriental Cultures.' *Philosophy East and West* 45 (1995): 309–28.

Gates, Henry Louis, Jr. '"Ethnic and Minority" Studies.' In Gibaldi, ed., *Introduction to Scholarship,* 288–302.

Geertz, Clifford. *The Interpretation of Cultures.* New York: Basic Books, 1973.

Gibaldi, Joseph, ed. *Introduction to Scholarship in Modern Languages and Literatures.* New York: Modern Language Association of America, 1992.

Gide, André. *L'Immoraliste.* 1902. Paris: Henri Jonqières, 1925.

Gilloch, Graeme. *Myth and Metropolis: Walter Benjamin and the City.* Cambridge, UK: Polity Press, 1996.

Girard, René. *The Girard Reader.* Ed. James G. Williams. New York: Crossroads Publishing, 1996.

– *Quand ces choses commenceront* ... Entretiens avec Michel Treguer. Paris: Arléa, 1994.

Glissant, Édouard. *Caribbean Discourse: Selected Essays.* Trans. and intro. J. Michael Dash. Charlottesville: University of Virginia Press, 1989.

– 'L'Imaginaire des langues: Entretien avec Édouard Glissant.' *Études Françaises* 28.2 (1992–3): 11–28.

– Interview with Bernard Rapp. *Jamais Sans Mon Livre.* TV5 Europe. Paris, February 1994.

– *Introduction à une poétique du divers.* Paris: Gallimard, 1996.

– *Tout-monde.* Paris: Gallimard, 1993.

Glucksmann, André. *Dostoïesvski à Manhattan.* Paris: Robert Laffont, 2002.

Goes, Benoît de. Excerpts from Matthieu Ricci and Nicolas Trigault, *Histoire de l'expédition chrétienne au royaume de la Chine* (Bellarmin: Desclée de Brouwer, 1978). In Boothroyd and Détrie, *Le Voyage en Chine,* 130–43.

Gong, Shifen. 'Katherine Mansfield in Chinese Translations.' *Journal of Commonwealth Literature* 31 (1996): 117–37.

Goodman, Nelson. *Languages of Art: An Approach to a Theory of Symbols.* Indianapolis, IN: Bobbs-Merrill, 1968.

Gordon, Ian A. *Katherine Mansfield.* London: Longmans, Green & Co., 1963.

Gouldner, Alvin W. *The Dialectic of Ideology and Technology.* New York: Oxford University Press, 1976.

Greene, Graham. *The Comedians.* New York: Viking, 1965.

Griffiths, Gareth. *A Double Exile: African and West Indian Writing between Two Cultures.* London: Marion Boyars, 1978.

Grossvogel, David. *Mystery and Its Fictions: From Oedipus to Agatha Christie.* Baltimore, MD: Johns Hopkins University Press, 1979.

Gurr, Andrew. *Writers in Exile.* Sussex, UK: Harvester Press, 1981.

Harmat, André-Marie. 'Ribni.' *Caliban* 10 (1973): 55–66.

Harris, Wilson. *The Womb of Space: The Cross-cultural Imagination.* Westport, CT: Greenwood Press, 1983.

Hayward, Jeremy W., and Francisco Varela. *Gentle Bridges: Conversations with the Dalai Lama on the Sciences of Mind.* Boston: Shambhala, 2001.

Heidegger, Martin. 'The Age of the World Picture.' In *The Question Concerning Technology, and Other Essays,* 115–54. Trans. and intro. William Lovitt. 1st ed. New York: Harper & Row, 1977.

Henderson, Harold G. *An Introduction to Haiku.* Garden City, NJ: Doubleday, 1958.

Ho, Elaine Yee Lin. 'Women in Exile: Gender and Community in Hong Kong Fiction.' *Journal of Commonwealth Literature* 31.3 (1996): 29–46.
Hobsbawm, Eric. *The Age of Extremes: A History of the World, 1914–1991*. New York: Pantheon Books, 1994.
Hussey, Edward. *The Presocratics*. London: Duckworth, 1974.
Ibañez, Paco. Interview. *Mediterraneo*. TV5 Asia. October 1999.
Ignatieff, Michael. 'In the Name of the Most Merciful.' Review of *Beyond Belief* by V.S. Naipaul. *New York Times Book Review*, 7 June 1998: 6, 8.
Inden, Ronald. *Imagining India*. Oxford: Basil Blackwell, 1990.
Ingarden, Roman. *The Cognition of the Literary Work*. Trans. Ruth Ann Crowley and Kenneth R. Olson. Evanston, IL: Northwestern University Press, 1973.
– *The Literary Work of Art*. Trans. and intro. George G. Grabowicz. Evanston, IL: Northwestern University Press, 1973.
Irving, Washington. *The Alhambra*. 1832. Ed. William T. Lenehan and Andrew B. Myers. Boston: Twayne Publishers, 1983.
Irwin, Robert. *The Arabian Nights: A Companion*. London: Allen Lane, 1994.
Iser, Wolfgang. 'Coda.' In *The Translatability of Cultures: Figurations of the Space Between*. Wolfgang Iser and Sanford Budick, eds, Stanford, CA: Stanford University Press, 1996.
– *The Fictive and the Imaginary: Charting Literary Anthropology*. Baltimore: Johns Hopkins University Press, 1993.
– *The Range of Interpretation*. Taipei, Taiwan: Institute of European and American Studies, 2000.
Ishiguro, Kazuo. *An Artist of the Floating World*. 1986. New York: Vintage International, 1989.
– *A Pale View of Hills*. 1982. New York: Vintage International, 1990.
– *The Remains of the Day*. New York: Knopf, 1989.
– *The Unconsoled*. 1995. New York: Vintage International, 1996.
– *When We Were Orphans*. London: Faber and Faber, 2000.
Iyer, Pico. 'The Butler Didn't Do It, Again.' *Times Literary Supplement*, 28 April 1995: 22.
Jameson, Fredric. 'Foreword' to Kojin Karantani, *Origins of Modern Japanese Literature*. Durham, NC: Duke University Press, 1993.
– *Marxism and Form: Twentieth-century Dialectical Theories of Literature*. Princeton, NJ: Princeton University Press, 1971.
– *The Political Unconscious: Narrative as a Socially Symbolic Act*. Ithaca, NY: Cornell University Press, 1981.
– *The Prison-House of Language: A Critical Account of Structuralism and Russian Formalism*. Princeton, NJ: Princeton University Press, 1972.

Janmohamed, Abdul R. *Manichean Asethetics: The Politics of Literature in Colonial Africa*. Amherst, MA: University of Massachusetts Press, 1983.
Jaspers, Karl. *Introduction à la philosophie*. Paris: Plon, 1951.
Jhabvala, Ruth Prawer. *An Experience of India*. 1966. London: John Murray, 1971.
Jodorowsky, Alexandro. *La Danse de la réalité*. Paris: Albin Michel, 2001.
Jones, Peter. *Imagist Poetry*. Harmondsworth, UK: Penguin Books, 1972.
Joyce, James. *Dubliners*. London: Jonathan Cape, 1954.
Kabbani, Rana. *Europe's Myths of Orient: Devise and Rule*. Basingstoke, UK: Macmillan, 1986.
Kalupahana, David J., trans. and intro. *Nagarjuna: The Philosophy of the Middle Way*. Albany: State University of New York Press, 1986.
Karatani, Kōjin. *Origins of Modern Japanese Literature*. Trans. and Ed. Brett de Bary. Foreword by Fredric Jameson. Durham: Duke University Press, 1993.
Kauffmann, Stanley. 'The Floating World.' *New Republic*, 6 November 1995: 42–5.
Kearney, Richard. *Modern Movements in European Philosophy*. 2nd ed. Manchester: Manchester University Press, 1994.
Keene, Donald. *The Pleasures of Japanese Literature*. New York: Columbia University Press, 1988.
Korzybski, Arthur. *Science and Sanity: An Introduction to Non-Aristotelian Systems and General Semantics*. Lakeville, CT: Institute of General Semantics, 1948.
Kristeva, Julia. *Étrangers à nous-mêmes*. Paris: Fayard, 1988.
Lacarrière, Jacques. Interview. 'La Grèce est le lieu où est née l'Europe.' *L'Express*, 1 July 1999: 8.
Lachaud, Martine. 'Ibañez pour l'espoir.' *L'Express*, 24 October 2002: 33.
Ladurie, Emmanuel Le Roy. 'C'est le livre qui a changé le monde.' *L'Express*, 30 January 2001; also at http://www.lexpress.fr/Express.
Lagerfeld, Karl. 'Interview.' *Double Je*. Narr. Bernard Pivot. TV5. March 2003.
Lam, Agnes. 'Writing in the Middle of the Road.' In Xu Xi and Mike Ingham, eds, *City Voices: Hong Kong Writing in English, 1945 to Present*, 339–40. Hong Kong: Hong Kong University Press, 2003.
Lapierre, Dominique. *The City of Joy*. Trans. Kathryn Spink. Boston: G.K. Hall, 1986.
Lawrence, T.E. *Seven Pillars of Wisdom: A Triumph*. Garden City, NY: Doubleday, 1966.
Le Naire, Olivier. 'Éternel Borges.' *L'Express*, 3 April 2003: 36–7.
Lenoir, Frédéric. 'Poésies du cosmos.' *L'Express*, 26 November 1998: 80.
Lévinas, Emmanuel. *Autrement qu'Être, ou au-delà de l'essence*. Dordrecht: Kluwer Academic, 2001.
– *De Dieu qui vient à l'idée*. 2nd ed., rev. and augmented. Paris: J. Vrin, 1986.
– *Totalité et infini: Essai sur l'extériorité*. Dordrecht: Kluwer Academic, 1987.

Lévi-Strauss, Claude. *Myth and Meaning.* New York: Schocken Books, 1979.
Levy, André. *La Littérature chinoise: Ancienne et classique.* Paris: Presses Universitaires de France, 1991.
Li, Victor Hao. 'From Qiao to Qiao.' In Tu Wei-ming, eds, *The Living Tree: The Changing Meaning of Being Chinese Today*, 213–220. Stanford, CA: Stanford University Press, 1994.
Lind, Michael. *The Next American Nation: The New Nationalism and the Fourth American Revolution.* New York: Free Press, 1995.
Lourenço, Eduardo. 'Une Épopée singulière.' In Camões, *Camões: Les Lusiades*, vii–xiv.
Lowe, Lisa. *Critical Terrains: French and British Orientalisms.* Ithaca, NY: Cornell University Press, 1991.
Lyotard, Jean-François. *The Postmodern Condition: A Report on Knowledge.* Minneapolis: University of Minnesota Press, 1984.
– *The Postmodern Explained.* Minneapolis: University of Minnesota Press, 1982.
Maalouf, Amin. *Les Croisades vues par les Arabes.* Paris: Jean-Claude Lattès, 1983.
– *Les Identités meurtrières.* Paris: Grasset, 1998.
– *Léon l'Africain.* Paris: J.C. Lattès, 1986.
– *Le Rocher de Tanios.* Paris: Bernard Grasset, 1993.
Macherey, Pierre. *Pour une théorie de la production littéraire.* Paris: François Maspero, 1978.
MacKenzie, John M. *Orientalism: History, Theory and the Arts.* Manchester, UK: Manchester University Press, 1995.
Magliola, Robert R. *Phenomenology and Literature.* West Lafayette, IN: Purdue University Press, 1977.
Mansfield, Katherine. *The Complete Stories of Katherine Mansfield.* Auckland, New Zealand: Golden Press, 1974.
– *The Garden Party and Other Stories.* 1922. Harmondsworth, UK: Penguin Books, 1951.
– *Katherine Mansfield: Selected Letters.* Ed. Vincent O'Sullivan. Oxford: Oxford University Press, 1989.
– *The Letters and Journals of Katherine Mansfield: A Selection.* Ed. C.K. Stead. Harmondsworth, UK: Penguin Books, 1977.
Marcel, Gabriel. *Journal métaphysique.* Paris: Gallimard, 1930.
May, Reinhard. *Heidegger's Hidden Sources: East Asian Influences on His Work.* Trans. Graham Parks. 1989. London and New York: Routledge, 1996.
McKirahan, Richard D., Jr, and Patricia Curd. *A Presocratics Reader.* Indianapolis, Cambridge: Hackett Publishing Co., 1995.
Melman, Billie. *Women's Orients: English Women and the Middle East, 1718–1918.* Ann Arbor: University of Michigan Press, 1992.

Memmi, Albert. *Portrait du colonisé et portrait du colonisateur.* Utrecht: Jean-Jacques Pauvert, 1966.
Meyer, Marvin, ed. *The Ancient Mysteries, A Sourcebook: Sacred Texts of the Mystery Religions of the Ancient Mediterranean.* San Francisco and London: Harper & Row, 1987.
Mikami, Yasuko. 'The Relationship between Katherine Mansfield and Ida Baker.' *Journal of the Faculty of Humanities* (Japan Women's University) 41 (1991): 37–52.
Mitchell, William. *City of Bits: Space, Place, and the Infobahn.* Cambridge, MA: MIT Press, 1995.
Mohanty, Chandra Talpade. 'Under Western Eyes: Feminist Scholarship and Colonial Discourses.' *Boundary 2: A Journal of Postmodern Literature and Culture* 12–13 (1984): 333–58.
Monegal, Emir Rodríquez. *Jorge Luis Borges: A Literary Biography.* New York: Dutton, 1978.
Monod, Théodore. *Mehariées: Explorations au vrai Sahara.* Arles: Actes Sud, 1994.
Mrabet, Mohammed. *The Beach Café & The Voice.* Taped and trans., from Moghrebi, Paul Bowles. Santa Barbara, CA: Black Sparrow Press, 1980.
– *The Big Mirror.* Trans. Paul Bowles. Santa Barbara, CA: Black Sparrow Press, 1977.
– *The Lemon.* Trans. Paul Bowles. 1969. San Francisco: City Lights Books, 1986.
– *Love with a Few Hairs.* Trans. Paul Bowles. 1967. San Francisco: City Lights Books, 1986.
Mukai, Kiyoshi. 'Katherine Mansfield's Observation.' *Hiroshima Studies in English Language and Literature* 18 (1972): 19–32.
Munz, Peter. *What the Golden Bough Breaks: Structuralism or Typology.* London: Routledge & Kegan Paul, 1973.
Naipaul, V.S. *Among the Believers: An Islamic Journey.* New York: Alfred A. Knopf, 1981; Vintage Books, 1982.
– *Beyond Belief: Islamic Excursions among the Converted Peoples.* London: Little, Brown and Co., 1998.
– *The Enigma of Arrival.* New York: Alfred A. Knopf, 1987.
– *India: A Million Mutinies Now.* New York: Viking, 1990; Vintage Books, 1985.
– *The Mimic Men.* 1967. New York: Vintage Books, 1985.
– 'Our Universal Civilization.' *New York Review of Books,* 31 January 1991: 22–5.
– 'Qui s'intéresse à l'Afrique?' Interview. *L'Express,* 7 July 1994: 52–5.
– 'Two Worlds.' Nobel Lecture 2001. *PMLA* 117.3 (2002): 479–86.
– *A Way in the World.* New York: Alfred A. Knopf, 1994.
Neumeier, John. *Nijinsky.* Ballet performed by the Hamburg Ballet. Hong Kong, 9 March 2003.

Ngugi wa Thiong'o. *Decolonising the Mind: The Politics of Language in African Literature.* London: James Currey, 1986.
- *Moving the Centre: The Struggle for Cultural Freedoms.* London: James Currey, 1993.
Oda, Tadashi. *Katherine Mansfield: Sozo ryoku no sekai.* Kyoto: Apolon Sha, 1979.
Pamuk, Orphan. 'Salaam Bombay!' Review of *The Moor's Last Sigh* by Salman Rushdie. *Times Literary Supplement,* 8 September 1995: 3–4.
Picon, Antoine. 'Ville idéale.' In Michèle Riot-Sarcey, Thomas Bouchet, and Antoine Picon, eds, *Dictionnaire des Utopies,* 241–6. Paris: Larousse, 2002.
Piglia, Ricardo. *The Absent City.* Trans. and intro. Sergio Waisman. Durham, NC: Duke University Press, 2000.
Pinto, Fernão Mendes. Excerpts from *La Pérégrination. La Chine et le Japon au XVIe siècle par un Portugais.* Paris: Calmann-Lévy, 1968. In Boothroyd and Détrie, *Le Voyage en Chine,* 89–109.
Polo, Marco. Excerpts from *Le Devisement du monde ou le Livre des merveilles* (Paris: La Découverte, 1980). In Boothroyd and Détrie, *Le Voyage en Chine,* 37–57.
Popper, Karl. *The World of Parmenides: Essays on the Presocratic Enlightenment.* Ed. Arne F. Petersen, with Jørgen Mejer. London: Routledge, 1998.
Porter, Dennis. *Haunted Journeys: Desire and Transgression in European Travel Writing.* Princeton, NJ: Princeton University Press, 1991.
Prakash, Gyan. 'Orientalism Now.' *History and Theory* 34.3 (1995): 199–212.
A Presocratics Reader. Ed. and intro. Patricia Curd. Trans. Richard D. McKirahan, Jr. Indianapolis, Cambridge: Hackett Publishing, 1995.
Pratt, Mary Louise. *Imperial Eyes: Travel Writing and Transculturation.* London: Routledge, 1992.
Pratt, William. *The Imagist Poem.* New York: Dutton, 1963.
Propp, Vladimir. *Morphology of the Folk Tale.* 1928. Trans. Laurence Scott, intro. Svatava Pirkova-Jacobson; 2nd ed., rev. and ed. Louis A. Wagner, new intro. Alan Dundes. Austin: University of Texas Press, 1968.
Putnam, Hilary. *The Faces of Realism.* La Salle, IL: Open Court, 1987.
Quint, David. *Empire and Epic: Politics and Generic Form from Virgil to Milton.* Princeton, NJ: Princeton University Press, 1993.
Reeves, Hubert. *Patience dans l'azur: L'Évolution cosmique.* Paris: Éditions du Seuil, 1988.
Ricard, Matthieu, with Jean-François Revel. *Le Moine et le philosophe.* Paris: Nil, 1997.
Ricard, Matthieu, and Trinh Xuan Thuan. *L'Infini dans la paume de la main: Du Big Bang à l'Éveil.* Paris: Nil éditions / Fayard, 2000.
Ricoeur, Paul. 'Between the Text and Its Readers.' In Mario J. Valdes, ed., *A*

Ricoeur Reader: Reflection and Imagination, 390–424. New York: Harvester Wheatsheaf, 1991.
- *Le Conflit des interprétations: Essais d'herméneutique.* Paris: Éditions du Seuil, 1969.
- *A l'école de la phénoménologie.* Paris: Librairie Philosophique J. Vrin, 1993.
- 'The Function of Fiction in Shaping Reality.' In Valdés, ed., *A Ricoeur Reader*, 117–134.
- *Lectures on Ideology and Utopia.* New York: Columbia University Press, 1986.
- *La Métaphore vive.* Paris: Éditions du Seuil, 1975.
- 'Myth as a Bearer of Possible Worlds.' In Valdés, ed., *A Ricoeur Reader*, 482–90.
- 'Poetry and Possibility.' In Valdés, ed., *A Ricoeur Reader*, 449–62.
- *Temps et récit.* Vols. 1 and 2. Paris: Éditions du Seuil, 1983–4.
- 'What Is a Text? Explanation and Understanding.' In Valdés, ed., *A Ricoeur Reader*, 43–64.

Rimer, J. Thomas. *A Reader's Guide to Japanese Literature: From the Eighth Century to the Present.* Tokyo: Kodansha International, 1988.

Rondeau, Daniel. 'Citati, premier rayon.' Review of *La Lumière de la nuit: Les grands mythes dans l'histoire du monde* by Pietro Citati. *L'Express*, 14 January 1999: 78.

Rubiés, Joan-Pau. *Travel and Ethnology in the Renaissance: South India through European Eyes, 1250–1625.* Cambridge: Cambridge University Press, 2000.

'La Ruée vers le désert.' *L'Express*, 4 April 2002: 72–6.

Rush, Norman. 'Doomed in Bombay.' Review of *The Moor's Last Sigh* by Salman Rushdie. *New York Times Book Review*, 14 January 1996: 7

Rushdie, Salman. *East, West.* London: Jonathan Cape, 1994.
- *Haroun and the Sea of Stories.* Harmondsworth, UK: Puffin Books, 1993.
- *Imaginary Homelands: Essays and Criticism, 1981–1991.* London: Granta Books, 1991.
- *Midnight's Children.* Intro. Anita Desai. London: Everyman, 1995.
- *The Moor's Last Sigh.* London: Vintage, 1994.
- *Satanic Verses.* London: Viking, 1988.
- *Shame.* London: Vintage Books, 1995.

Said, Edward W. *Culture and Imperialism.* New York: Alfred A. Knopf, 1993.
- *Orientalism: Western Conceptions of the Orient.* 1978. London: Penguin Books, 1995.
- *The World, the Text and the Critic.* Cambridge, MA: Harvard University Press, 1983.

Sartre, Jean-Paul. *L'Être et le néant.* Paris: Gallimard, 1943.
- *Situations.* 7 vols. Paris: Gallimard, 1947–65.

Sawyer-Lauçanno, Christopher. *An Invisible Spectator: A Biography of Paul Bowles.* New York: Weidenfield & Nicolson, 1989.

Spivak, Gayatri Chakravorty. *A Critique of Postcolonial Reason: Toward a History of the Vanishing Present.* Cambridge, MA: Harvard University Press, 1999.
- *In Other Worlds: Essays in Cultural Politics.* New York and London: Methuen, 1987.
Spurr, David. *The Rhetoric of Empire: Colonial Discourse in Journalism, Travel Writing, and Imperial Administration.* Durham, NC: Duke University Press, 1993.
Stehli, Jean-Sebastien, with Émilie Trevert. 'Rester Zen: Ce que nous apprend la sagesse asiatique.' *L'Express*, 15 August 2002: 32–8.
Steiner, George. 'Les Aventures d'une pensée.' Interview with Guillaume Chenevure. *Les Grands Entretiens.* ARTE/TV5 Asia. Gèneve. May 1998.
- 'La Culture ne rend pas plus humain.' Interview. *L'Express*, 28 December 2000: 6–9.
Tam, Kwok-kan. 'Gender Construction and Chinese Womanhood.' Paper presented at the Second International Conference on Globalism/Localism: Modernity and Cultural Production in Asia, Hong Kong, 2–5 April 1997.
Therborn, Göran. *The Ideology of Power and the Power of Ideology.* London: NLB, 1980.
Todorov, Tzvetan. *L'Homme dépaysé.* Paris: Éditions du Seuil, 1996.
- *Mikhail Bakhtin: The Dialogic Principle.* Ed. Wlad Godzich. Minneapolis: University of Minnesota Press, 1984.
- *The Morals of History.* Trans. Alyson Water. Minneapolis: University of Minnesota Press, 1995.
- *Nous et les autres: La réflexion française sur la diversité humaine.* Paris: Éditions du Seuil, 1989.
- *Théories du symbole.* Paris: Éditions du Seuil, 1977.
Tomalin, Clair. *Katherine Mansfield: A Secret Life.* London: Penguin Books, 1988.
Valdés, Mario J. *Hermeneutics of Poetic Sense: Critical Studies of Literature, Cinema, and Cultural History.* Toronto: University of Toronto Press, 1998.
Varela, Francisco J., Evan Thompson, and Eleanor Rosch. *The Embodied Mind: Cognitive Science and Human Experience.* Cambridge, MA: MIT Press, 1993.
Vattimo, Gianni. *Beyond Interpretation: The Meaning of Hermeneutics for Philosophy.* Trans. David Webb. Stanford, CA: Stanford University Press, 1997.
- *The End of Modernity: Nihilism and Hermeneutics in Postmodern Culture.* Trans. and intro. Jon R. Snyder. Baltimore, MD: Johns Hopkins University Press, 1988.
- 'Myth and the Fate of Secularization.' Trans. Jon R. Snyder. *Res* 9 (1985): 29–35.
- *The Transparent Society.* Trans. David Webb. Baltimore, MD: Johns Hopkins University Press, 1992.
Verdi, Giuseppe. *Nabucco.* Latvian National Opera, Program notes by Sze Kwanneung. Hong Kong, 11 December 2002.

Vincent, Jean-Didier. *La Vie est une fable.* Paris: Odile Jacob, 1998.
Vincent, Jean-Marie. 'Ernst Bloch.' In Michèle Riot-Sarcey, Thomas Bouchet, and Antoine Picon, eds, *Dictionnaire des Utopies,* 28–30. Paris: Larousse, 2002.
Volosinov, V.N. *Marxism and the Philosophy of Language.* Trans. Ladislav Matejka and I.R. Titunik. Cambridge, MA: Harvard University Press, 1986.
Waisman, Sergio. 'Introduction.' to *The Absent City* by Ricardo Piglia. Trans. Sergio Waisman. Durham, NC: Duke University Press, 2000.
Warner, Marina. *Managing Monsters: Six Myths of Our Time.* London: Vintage, 1994.
Weiss, Timothy. 'Naipaul's Fin de Siècle.' *ARIEL: A Review of International English Literature* 27.3 (1996): 107–26.
– *On the Margins: The Art of Exile in V.S. Naipaul.* Amherst: University of Massachusetts Press, 1992.
– 'Oriental Elements in Katherine Mansfield's *The Garden Party and Other Stories.*' In Dominique Dubois, Laurent Lepaludier, and Jacques Soher, eds, *Les Nouvelles de Katherine Mansfield.* 28–43. Angers: Presses de l'Université d'Angers, 1998.
– 'Translation in a Borderless World.' *Technical Communication Quarterly* 5.1 (1995): 401–27.
Wheeler, David L. 'The Death of Languages.' *Chronicle of Higher Education,* 20 April 1994: A8–9, 16.
Wilson, Rob, and Wimal Dissanayake, eds. *Global/Local: Cultural Production and the Transnational Imaginary.* Durham, NC: Duke University Press, 1996.
Wolfensohn, James. Interview: 'Un Monde injuste est un monde dangereux.' *L'Express,* 12 October 2000: 28–9.
Wong, David. T.K. *Hong Kong Stories.* Hong Kong: CDN, 1996.
Wood, James. 'Salaam Bombay!' Review of *The Moor's Last Sigh* by Salman Rushdie. *New Republic,* 18 March 1996: 38–41.
Wood, Michael. 'Shenanigans!' Review of *The Moor's Last Sigh* by Salman Rushdie. *London Review of Books,* 7 September 1995: 3–5.
Wu, David Yen-ho. 'The Construction of Chinese and Non-Chinese Identity.' In Tu Wei-ming, ed., *The Living Tree: The Changing Meaning of Being Chinese Today,* 148–66. Stanford, CA: Stanford University Press, 1994.
Xu Xi. Talk on *City Voices.* Department of English, Chinese University of Hong Kong, 18 March 2003.
Xu Xi and Mike Ingham, eds. *City Voices: Hong Kong Writing in English, 1945 to Present.* Hong Kong: Hong Kong University Press, 2003.
Young, Robert. *White Mythologies: Writing History and the West.* London: Routledge, 1990.
Zima, Peter V. *The Philosophy of Modern Literary Theory.* London: Athlone Press, 1999.

Index

Abbas, Ackbar, 85–90, 160
Adorno, Theodor, 210
Ajami, Fouad, 189
Algeria, x, 59, 65, 201
Allen, Paula Gunn, 177, 195
Allende, Isabel, 123
Anaxagoras, 175
Arabian Nights. See *Thousand and One Nights*
Attali, Jacques, 101, 193, 194

Bach, Caleb, 120
Bakhtin, Mikhail, 82–3, 187, 220n1
Balzac, Honoré de, 176
baroque, the, 17, 26, 30–2
Barth, John, 223n9
Barthes, Roland, 80, 221n1
Bateson, Gregory, 225n1
Baudrillard, Jean, 138
Beauvoir, Simone de, 115, 117
Beckett, Samuel, 146
Beckford, William, 36
Benjamin, Walter, 112, 148–53, 175
Bhabha, Homi, 88, 91
Bialostosky, Don, 187
Bissoondath, Neil, 177, 195, 225n11
Blake, William, 41, 118

Bloch, Ernst, 18, 148–52, 175, 177, 210, 213
Bohr, Niels, 211
Borges, Jorge Luis, 11, 17, 19–43, 46, 99, 113, 118, 120, 122, 143, 159, 164, 206–7; 'El Acercamento de Almotásin,' 38; 'La Biblioteca del Babel,' 19; 'El Budismo,' 24; 'La Cámara de las estatuas,' 26; 'Un Doble de Mahoma,' 35; 'La Enigma de Edward FitzGerald,' 39; 'El Espantoso redentor Lazarus Morrell,' 32; 'El Espejo de tinta,' 30–1; 'Historia de los dos que soñaron,' 26; 'El Inmortal,' 23; 'El Jardín de senderos que se bifurcan,' 23–4; 'La Lotería de Babilonia,' 23; 'Metáforas de Las Mil y Una Noches,' 21; 'El Otro,' 23; *Qué es el Budismo*, 22, 42; 'Las Ruinas circulares,' 23, 46; *Siete noches*, 22, 24; 'El Tintorero enmascarado, Hákim de Merv,' 25, 33–6, 39, 42; 'La Viuda Ching, pirata,' 35; 'El Zahir,' 24, 40–2, 99
Bowles, Paul, 17, 20, 43–77, 161, 206–7, 218n2; *The Collected Stories*, 47; 'A Distant Episode,' 48, 55–8; *Let It Come Down*, 47–8, 161; *Letters*, 50, 75;

The Sheltering Sky, 48; *Their Heads Are Green and Their Hands Are Blue*, 58–78; *Without Stopping*, 17, 43, 46, 58, 69
Buddha, 15, 40, 201, 212, 214
Buddhism, 7, 15–17, 20, 22–4, 37–8, 40, 42, 196, 204, 206–7, 211, 213, 218n5, 222n8; emptiness, 20, 35, 37–8, 40, 42, 57, 67, 142, 144, 197, 204, 212–13, 215; karma, 24, 30; middle way, the, 7, 9–10, 18, 203–16
Burke, Kenneth, 154
Burkert, Walter, 25
Burroughs, William, 122
Burton, Richard, 30, 39

Calvino, Italo, 18, 111, 113, 117–19; *La città invisibili*, 111, 117
Camões, Luis Vaz de, 12–13, 153, 167; *Os Lusíadas*, 12, 153, 167
Camus, Albert, 201
Casares, Aldofo Bioy, 220n13
Césaire, Aimé, 86
Chen Yi, ix
China, 12, 53, 81–2, 85, 87, 93, 95, 98, 101–2, 105, 107, 145, 154, 183
Chinatown, 112
Chirico, Giorgio de, 131
Chuang Tzu, 23
Citati, Pietro, 145, 156
citizenship, 18, 80, 176, 178, 180, 185–6, 198–9, 201
Clifford, James, 80, 88
Cochin, 223n1
Coelho, Paulo, 29–30
Coleridge, Samuel, 154–6, 171, 174
colonial, 17, 55–9, 63–6, 68, 70–1, 74, 84–6, 90, 95, 97–9, 129, 137, 157, 168

Comte-Sponville, André, 191, 199
Confucius, 201
cosmopolitan, 86, 88, 99
counter-Western discourse, 44
Coupe, Lawrence, 148–50, 194, 223n4
Cratylus, 109, 215
creolization, 83, 174, 178, 180–1, 207–8
Cupitt, Don, 148, 152
cybernetics, 211

Dalai Lama, 40, 213
Dante, 79, 122
Debord, Guy, 98
Debray, Regis, 191–2
Defoe, Daniel, 122
Deleuze, Gilles, 91, 102, 107–8, 224n1
detective story, 33, 120, 142, 161
Diderot, Denis, 109
discourse analysis, 4, 5, 7, 14, 210
displacement, 18, 80, 91, 111, 126, 156, 157
Dostoevsky, Fydor, 191
Doyle, Arthur Conan, 132, 141; Sherlock Holmes, 140–2
Droit, Roger-Pol, 110, 118–19, 142; *101 Expériences de philosophie quotidienne*, 110, 118, 222n2
dystopia, 42, 120, 206

East and West, 4, 17–18, 21, 37, 45–7, 85, 95–8, 103, 105–6, 133, 145, 150, 165–6, 170, 175, 201, 203, 207, 214
Eberhardt, Isabelle, 76
Eco, Umberto, 52, 140, 224n5
Einstein, Albert, 197, 212
embodiment, 5–7, 14, 52, 119, 153, 177, 198, 205, 208

England, 87, 94, 124, 127–9, 131, 133, 137, 183, 188
entropy, 10, 66, 205
epic, 12, 153, 156–7, 160, 163, 166–7, 169
existentialism, 45, 46, 102, 111, 113–16, 119, 142, 146, 207

Fanon, Franz, 86
fate, 21, 22, 24, 28–30, 33, 36, 41, 70, 98, 102, 140, 172; *mektoub*, 22, 27–8, 72
Ferry, Luc, 191, 199
Foucauld, Jean-Baptiste de, 18, 182, 184, 200
Foucault, Michel, 4, 7–8, 11
Foulquié, Paul, 113–16
Frye, Northrop, 156, 217n7, 223n5
fundamentalism, 12, 18, 67, 71–3, 86, 146, 148, 158, 160, 167–70, 174, 181, 189–90, 204, 209

Gadamer, Hans-Georg, 8–9, 116, 148, 200
Gama, Vasco da, 12, 147, 165–6
Gare, Arran E., 4, 8
Gates, Henry Louis, Jr, 177, 195, 196
Geertz, Clifford, 189
Girard, René, 52, 151
Glissant, Édouard, 18, 83, 120, 174, 177–81, 183, 188–9, 195, 201, 224n2; *Introduction à une poétique du divers*, 83, 177–9, 195; *tout-monde*, 83, 120, 170, 174, 179–81, 183, 201
globalization, 87, 111–12, 116, 118, 179–82, 189, 213
gnosticism, 17, 20, 26, 34–5, 38–40, 42, 206–7
Goodman, Nelson, 8
Granada, 21, 145, 155, 158, 169, 173

groundlessness, 6, 11–12, 20, 86, 194–5, 203, 205, 208, 211
Guattari, Félix, 224n1

Hawthorne, Nathaniel, 35
Hayward, Jeremy, 22, 40, 214
Heidegger, Martin, 30, 114–15, 177, 179; *dasein*, 114
Heraclitus, 109–11, 113, 143, 156, 211, 215
hermeneutics, 8–9, 30, 130
Hinduism, 21, 24, 147, 150, 158, 160, 168, 170, 172, 190
Ho, Elaine, 105
Hong Kong, ix–x, 12, 17, 49, 61, 79, 80–3, 85–6, 88–96, 98, 100–4, 106–7, 110, 129, 139–40, 201, 206–7, 214–15; anthology of the city, 17, 90–1; *City Voices: Hong Kong Writing in English 1945 to Present*, 90, 215
hybridity, 74, 88, 95, 97–8, 103, 147, 157, 162, 164, 173–4, 178, 186

Ibañez, Paco, 177, 183, 184
identity, 17–18, 71, 81, 109, 119, 127, 131, 140, 142, 169, 176–8, 181, 183–4, 188–9, 198, 207–8, 211
ideology, 3, 5, 16, 60, 93, 153, 169, 171, 188, 204–5, 208
India, 12, 23, 59, 145, 147, 150, 153, 165–6, 168–9, 172, 173, 188, 190, 201, 223–4n10
Ingarden, Roman, 7
interdependence, 7, 11, 17, 22, 104, 196, 208, 212
Internet, 79, 118
intertextuality, 8, 21, 25, 38, 40, 151, 206, 207
Irving, Washington, 173; *The Alhambra*, 173

Iser, Wolfgang, 8–12, 55, 89, 90, 122, 205–6, 209
Ishiguro, Kazua, 17, 109, 111, 126–44, 207; *An Artist of the Floating World*, 127, 136, 143–4; *A Pale View of Hills*, 127, 144; *The Remains of the Day*, 127, 129, 144; *The Unconsoled*, 127, 128, 129, 138, 141, 142, 144; *When We Were Orphans*, 17, 109, 120, 126–44, 206–7
Iyer, Pico, 142

James, Henry, 125
Jameson, Fredric, 47–8
Japan, 20, 42, 87, 100–1, 127, 133, 183, 192
Jaspers, Karl, 116, 142
Jhabvala, Ruth Prawer, 201
Jodorowsky, Alexandro, 19
journey, 19, 27, 29–30, 46, 56, 60–1, 63, 65, 93, 109, 126, 138, 186, 189
Joyce, James, 111, 122, 127, 156, 180
Jurado, Alicia, 22

Kafka, Franz, 121–2
Kalupahana, David, 203
Karatani, Kōjin, 97, 135–6
Kearney, Richard, 7
Kubla Khan, 111, 154, 156, 171, 174, 223n3

labyrinth, 6, 66, 80, 89–91, 101–3, 107, 119, 123, 126, 138, 144, 154, 164, 206–7
Lagerfeld, Karl, 177, 186
Lam, Agnes, 214–15
landscape, 12, 21, 42, 47, 57, 60–1, 73, 105, 114, 126, 130–1, 135, 136, 179, 206
Lao-tseu, 212

Lawrence, T.E., 70, 186
Le Naire, Olivier, 20, 42
legend, 18, 22, 34, 36, 39, 40, 148, 152, 155, 157–9, 162, 164–5, 167, 169, 173–5, 206–7
Lévinas, Emmanuel, 18, 148–9, 152, 177, 185, 197, 202, 211; *au-delà*, 202, 211
Lévi-Strauss, Claude, 59
Li, Victor Hao, 221n1
locale, 52, 79, 82–3, 86, 109, 120, 135, 138, 143–4, 180, 187, 211
London, 17, 82, 95, 129, 141, 144, 166, 191
Loti, Pierre, 80–1, 221n1
Lowe, Lisa, 44
Lyotard, Jean-François, 45, 75

Maalouf, Amin, 18, 144, 170, 177, 180–3, 186, 188–91, 199, 202–3; *Les identités meurtrières*, 144, 177, 180, 191
Macau, 12, 129, 139
MacKenzie, John M., 43, 44–5, 210
Malraux, André, 174, 186
Manguel, Alberto, 20
Mansfield, Katherine, 12, 15–16, 218n10; 'The Daughters of the Late Colonel,' 12, 15–16
mapping, 40, 80, 83, 89, 133, 181, 206, 209
Marcel, Gabriel, 114
Marrakesh, 65
May, Reinhard, 177
Médecins Sans Frontières, 193
Melman, Billie, 44
Memmi, Albert, 86
memory, 65, 73, 84, 100, 117, 125, 127, 132–3, 140, 151, 162, 180, 188, 214

Miller, Jeffrey, 220n4
mimesis, 51, 53–4, 58–9, 206–7
mock epic, 166, 167
modernity, 46, 48, 73, 84, 93–4, 96, 103, 106, 112, 181, 184, 189, 201
Monegal, Emir Rodríquez, 20
Monod, Théodore, 74
Monti, Vittorio, ix
Moore, Thomas, 25
multicultural, 13, 48, 88, 147, 157, 173, 195–6, 208
Munz, Peter, 148–50
music, ix, 14, 31, 43, 49–50, 59–64, 66, 69, 99, 124, 127, 134, 161, 188, 214
mutual implication of subject and object, 7, 75
mystery, 11, 17, 20, 25–38, 41, 66, 68, 121, 129, 165, 188, 207, 214, 218n6–7
myth, 11, 18, 124, 137, 145–75, 195, 206–7
mythmaking, 146, 148, 152, 159, 162, 174

Naipaul, V.S., x, 18, 59, 114, 177, 188–91, 225n11; *Beyond Belief: Islamic Excursions among the Converted Peoples*, 177, 188–90; *The Mimic Men*, 114; 'Two Worlds,' 188; 'The Universal Civilization,' 188
Nāgārjuna, 203
network of stories, 125
Neumeier, John, 214; *Nijinsky*, 214
Ngugi wa Thiong'o, 86
Nietzsche, Friedrich, 86, 97, 203, 225n9
nirvana, 42
nomad, 45, 49, 75
North Africa, 16, 17, 27, 43, 45–6, 49, 51, 56, 62, 68

North and South, 203

Ocampo, Silvina, 220n13
Odyssey, The, 167
Oliveira, Manoel de, 19
Orient, 3, 5, 13, 15, 17, 19, 20–1, 24–5, 38, 40, 42–5, 47, 56, 69, 73, 75, 77, 117, 147, 153, 160, 171, 206–7, 209–10
Orientalism, 4–6, 10, 13–16, 43–4, 76, 170, 210

phenomenology, 7, 75
Picon, Antoine, 79
Piglia, Ricardo, 17, 109, 111–13, 120–7, 142, 203, 206–9; *La ciudad ausente*, 17, 109, 111, 112, 113, 120–7, 147, 203, 206–7; *Nombre falso*, 120; *Plata quemada*, 120; *Respiración artificial*, 120
Poe, Edgar Allan, 122
Polo, Marco, 12, 53, 111–12, 117–19
Popper, Karl, 109
Porter, Dennis, 44
post-colonial, 4, 10, 58, 79, 81–3, 85–6, 88, 91, 97, 113, 118, 125, 142–4, 147, 153, 156, 163, 165–6, 168, 196, 207–8, 213
Pratt, Mary Louise, 44
Presocratics, 109, 111, 113, 143, 156, 175, 199, 211
Putnam, Hilary, 203
Pynchon, Thomas, 121–2, 124

Raabe, Wilhelm, 210
Ravel, Maurice, ix
Reconquista, 158, 168, 170
Reeves, Hubert, 212
reorientations, 18, 122, 147, 207, 211
representation, 11, 12, 15, 17, 50–1,

60, 62–5, 67–8, 71, 75, 77, 190, 204, 209–10, 214
Revel, Jean-François, 225n13
rhizome, 107, 158–9
Ricard, Matthieu, 7, 18, 177, 196, 225n13
Ricci, Father Matteo, 53–4
Ricoeur, Paul, 7–9, 16–18, 29–30, 148–9, 153, 165, 173, 175, 177, 184, 205, 217n5
Rimsky-Korsakov, Nikolai, 3, 214
Rushdie, Salman, 18, 73, 145–75, 206–7; *The Moor's Last Sigh*, 18, 145–75, 206–7; —, Boabdil, 145, 155, 158, 169, 173; —, Bombay, 157, 159, 161–2, 166, 168–9, 170–3; —, Hindu mythology, 160

Said, Edward, x, 4–7, 10–11, 13, 15, 43–5, 76, 88, 210, 217nn1, 2, 6
Sartre, Jean-Paul, 114–16; *l'en-soi*, 114–16, 130; *le pour-soi*, 114–15, 130
Sawyer-Lauçanno, Christopher, 48, 220n2
Senghor, Léopold, 86
Shanghai, 129, 131–41
Sheherazade, 3, 121, 125, 214
Singapore, 88, 103
Socrates, 201
Spain, 27, 64, 146, 155, 157, 158, 164, 167–9, 173, 202
Spurr, David, 70
Steiner, George, 18, 127, 174, 177, 183, 186
Stevenson, Robert Louis, 122
Stravinsky, Igor, ix
sublime, 45, 47, 75
Swift, Jonathan, 122
symbol, 13, 30, 31, 35, 130, 153

Tam, Kwok-kan, x, 104
Thousand and One Nights, the, 3, 21, 22, 24, 26–9, 33–4, 42, 122–3
Todorov, Tzvetan, 18, 177, 185–8, 191
Tomalin, Claire, 15
tradition, 26, 73–6, 84, 87, 91, 93–4, 103–4, 113, 120, 150, 177–8, 180, 196
transcultural, 17, 38, 53, 84, 99, 101, 104, 106–7, 186, 191
translation, 3, 6, 9, 11–13, 17, 18, 25, 30, 37, 39–40, 42, 45–6, 49–51, 54, 60–2, 65–7, 73, 75–6, 81, 83–4, 90, 95–7, 104, 106, 108, 120–2, 124, 147, 151, 156–7, 198, 200, 204–9, 214–15; circularity, 130, 209, 210–11; cognition, 12, 15, 214; emergent reality, 12, 15–17, 20, 33, 206, 208–9, 213; feedback, 9, 55, 62–3, 66–7, 198, 210, 214; four modes of, 10; heuristic, 3, 8, 12, 16–17, 81, 205, 208–9; identity formation, 204, 211; interpretation as translation, 4, 7, 9, 206; liminal space, 9–10, 12–13, 16–17, 20, 42, 46, 56, 69, 73, 89, 97, 122, 205–9; metonymy, 209–11; phenomenological-hermeneutic approach, 6, 36; possibility seeking, 154, 204–5, 209, 211; recursion, 3, 6, 9, 10–11, 37, 50–1, 54–5, 62–3, 65–7, 71, 77, 81, 89, 177, 188, 198, 200, 204, 207, 209–10, 214; register, 3, 6, 9, 11–12, 20, 25, 30, 37, 40–2, 59–62, 68, 73, 84, 91, 95–6, 121–2, 124, 183, 205–6, 210, 213, 215; resistance, 204; sidewise movement, 81–4, 200, 209, 211
travel, 3, 17, 42–5, 50–1, 53–6, 59, 61–8, 71, 73–7, 112, 119–20, 145, 156, 192, 206–7; travel as performance,

206; travel writing, 17, 51, 55, 59, 61, 67, 78
Trinh Xuan Thuan, 18, 177, 196, 211

universal, 17, 25–7, 29, 31, 33, 35, 37–9, 41, 138–9, 152, 168, 175–6, 179–80, 182, 187, 191, 197–201, 206–7
utopia, 3, 16, 94, 113, 146, 148, 150, 152–3, 202, 205, 208

Valdés, Mario, 8–9, 91
Varela, Francisco, 22, 90, 203, 205, 214, 217n3, 218n9
Vattimo, Gianni, 18, 177, 194–5, 225n14; *Beyond Interpretation*, 194–5; *The End of Modernity*, 194
Verdi, Giuseppe, 12, 14–15; *Nabucco*, 12, 14–15
Vidal, Gore, 47–8
Vincent, Jean-Didier, 215
virtuality, 110, 113, 127, 143, 171, 207–8

Waisman, Sergio, 111, 120–1
Warner, Marina, 152
Wiener, Norman, 211
Wong, David T.K., 17, 79–108, 206, 207; *Hong Kong Stories*, 17, 79–108, 206, 207
Wordsworth, William, 119, 155
World Soccer Cup, 192–3
World Summit on Sustainable Development, 192
Wu, David Yenho, 222n5

Xanadu, 154, 158, 170–1
Xu Xi, 215

Yang Yong, ix
Yeats, W.B., 124, 132, 155

Zen Buddhism, 22
Zeno, 109
Zima, Peter, 45